Direct Democracy
in Switzerland

D0145041

with a foreword by *Alfred R. Berkeley III*
and a preface by *Richard Holbrooke*

Gregory A. Fossedal

Direct Democracy in Switzerland

Transaction Publishers
New Brunswick (U.S.A.) and London (U.K.)

Second paperback printing 2006

Copyright © 2002 by Transaction Publishers, New Brunswick, New Jersey.

This book is printed on acid-free paper that meets the American National Standard for Permanence of Paper for Printed Library Materials.

Library of Congress Catalog Number: 2001027202
ISBN: 0-7658-0078-0 (cloth); 1-4128-0505-8 (paper)
Printed in the United States of America

Library of Congress Cataloging-in-Publication Data

Fossedal, Gregory A.
    Direct democracy in Switzerland / Gregory A. Fossedal ; with a foreword by Alfred R. Berkeley III and a preface by Richard Holbrooke.
        p. cm.
    Includes bibliographical references and index.
    ISBN 0-7658-0078-0 (cloth : alk. paper)
    1. Federal government—Switzerland.   2. Democracy—Switzerland.   3. Political participation—Switzerland.   4. Switzerland—Politics and government.   I. Title.

JN8788 .F67   2001
320.4494—dc21   2001027202

Si le théâtre est petit, le spectacle a donc de la grandeur.
—Alexis de Tocqueville

Contents

Foreword

Important books must either impart vital information or expose an important new idea. Interesting books must tell a good, human story. In *Direct Democracy in Switzerland,* Gregory Fossedal has done something rare—he's done a bit of all three.

The result is a highly readable narrative, a tale of William Tell defying arrogant lords, and brave mountain men and women fighting off gangs to establish independent towns and villages. Some of these have enjoyed a substantial element of local autonomy or democratic practices, going back more than five centuries.[1]

At the same time, Fossedal tells how one of the world's countries least blessed with physical resources has come to be, arguably, the most successful economy in the world, and how a nation with pervasive religious and linguistic divisions enjoys profound social tranquillity—information that is surely important to people around the world.

Finally, *Direct Democracy in Switzerland* raises important issues for the future of democracy itself. In this it resembles Alexis de Tocqueville's *Democracy in America,* which suggested the need for political freedom to a Europe straining under the dead hand of aristocrats and top-down, elitist politics. For, as Fossedal notes, the Swiss democracy is very different from any other system in the world. Switzerland's direct democracy—in which the people, by initiative and referendum, wind up voting directly on a large number of policies that affect their lives—is sufficiently different that it might be called, as the former foreign editor of *The Economist*, Brian Beedham, once suggested, a "different system" altogether.

Certainly, democracy in Switzerland is very different in some important features than democracy in America, Asia, or the rest of Europe today. Switzerland thus may function as a kind of laboratory. It has a purity in applying the democratic idea, and it has a long history as a functioning cluster of democracies. That history is more than three times as long as the next-longest-running democracy, the United States.

These attributes are precious because, as Morton Kondracke once observed, in political affairs it is impossible to set up scientific experiments and petri-dish control groups. Switzerland's long experience with its unique type of democracy, not always under the most favorable material circumstances, enables other countries with Swisslike diversity to make analogies to some of its experiences. "Like policies," as Abraham Lincoln wrote, "imply like results."

It is possible, Fossedal notes wryly, that even Americans might learn something from the Swiss experience.

In most Western democracies, the people make only a small number of decisions about economic or social policy for themselves. Instead, we hire experts and elect representatives to make many of these decisions for us. Every now and then—every two, four, or six years—we hold another election to review the last 10,000 or so decisions by those leaders, and, vote for one of two alternatives who will handle the next cluster of thousands of decisions.

Switzerland uses some of these devices too, but to a much greater extent than other democracies the voters make dozens and even hundreds of the particular decisions themselves. The Swiss have a highly devolved system of federalism in which many decisions that would be made by the federal government or "state" governments in other countries are made by cantons (some fewer than 100,000 in population) or communities (of which the average is about 3,000 persons). Where the Swiss do employ professional politicians, both their pay and their power pale against the clout and compensation of a typical state legislator or even city council member in much of the U.S. The federal parliament meets about twelve weeks a year, its members earn perhaps $40,000 in compensation, and they have virtually no full-time staff—not even offices. The Swiss president is the chairman of a seven-member committee that alternates once a year. The supreme court is comprised of some four-dozen judges, many of them without a law degree, who have no authority to discard federal laws, even if they deem them unconstitutional.

At the core is the Swiss constitution, which, as Fossedal notes, is literally written by the people. More than half its provisions, as of the late twentieth century, were derived from popular ballot initiatives or referenda voted on directly by the people.

On the other hand, every male from age twenty to fifty, with a very few exceptions, is a member of the Swiss army. Although it is difficult to measure, the typical Swiss adult probably spends several more hours per week or month in volunteer service to the cantonal, or community government, than does his or her counterpart in Germany, Japan, Britain, or the U.S.

Does all this matter? Or does Swiss democracy differ from U.S. and European representative democracies only in trivial ways?

As Fossedal narrates the story, one comes to the conclusion that Swiss democracy does differ importantly. We tend to think of "democracies" in Europe and the Americas as more or less the same. There is, however, a different animating spirit to the Swiss democracy, and that different spirit produces different results.

By analogy, Fossedal reports, the representative democracies are closer in operation and spirit to the highly managed, traditional equities markets. Swiss democracy—direct democracy—is a kind of Nasdaq exchange, something familiar to me after many years as president of that market. In both markets, the investor is ultimately sovereign. But in the one he exercises sovereignty himself, while in the other his control is far more subtle and indirect, a sovereignty filtered through a large number of intermediary elites and institutions.

Nasdaq, then, provides an economic analogy to Swiss politics. To many people, markets are indistinguishable in the way they work. Yet, as Nasdaq shows, seemingly small structural differences can have profound implications.

Like Swiss democracy, Nasdaq is an open, inclusive system. Nasdaq permits investors to control pricing and trade executions directly. Traditional markets do not. Nasdaq insists on competition for every trade; no monopolies are awarded or permitted. Anyone can subscribe to the information on what is available to buy or sell, and can receive that information in real time. The investor is at no disadvantage to the professional.

While these differences among markets may seem trivial, the implications for the country, compounded over time, are significant. Nasdaq has become a key element in economic growth, a key element in the great American dream machine.

Nasdaq provides investors a way to participate directly in companies of all sizes and all industries. Nasdaq's managers make no judgments as to the investment merit of any company. Nasdaq provides a fair market; investors decide on the risks they are willing to take. The goal is to have the merit of an investment decided directly by investors, not by market managers.

Direct Democracy in Switzerland starts from this assumption that the differences matter—and proceeds to narrate how and why they do. Switzerland might be called the Nasdaq of democracies. With its highly decentralized system, its easy access for new entrants, and its relentless focus on the citizen "investor," Switzerland functions as a highly efficient political market. It brings ideas to people faster—and with fewer means of choking them off in transit—than perhaps any other political system in the world. If only on material grounds—even if we care nothing about treating investors equally as a goal in and of itself—Switzerland has given ample reason why this very special direct participation bears close study.

Fossedal is a more than capable observer to tell this story—the story of a people and a political economy. His book is part docudrama, part financial reporting; a mix of think tank statistics and affable vignettes.

The author's affection for his object is not hidden and is, in fact, a necessary part of telling the story of a country. Were there no respect, and even warmth here, such a book could easily become arid and antiseptic, a kind of literary social studies film.

At the same time, Fossedal is an acute and objective observer. He sees Swiss flaws and reports them. To be sure, he does so with a sympathetic eye that keeps such flaws in perspective. His chapter on Switzerland and the Holocaust—on the Swiss resistance to Nazi aggression and its well-meaning but ill-conceived (and at times stubborn) oversights on dormant accounts after the war—is well-reported and cogent. One might even call it moving, as he gets at the drama and emotion of an issue that cannot be discussed only in footnotes to 1940s bank balance sheets.

Above all, perhaps, Fossedal has an attribute all too rare among the modern journalists and authors: a self-critical faculty that enables him to suspect when his own observations are biased. Quick to observe and illuminate, he has a Tocquevillian caution about pronouncing final judgments, especially ideological ones. Throughout the book, one has the feeling that Fossedal's first interest and passion is actually democracy itself, the notion of how debates are settled politically, rather than any socialist or libertarian or any sort of agenda.

In much Western discussion today, a love of "democracy," as Tocqueville observed, is basically "a tactic" for advancing the interests of a group or the economic program of a party. It is a means, not an end. Fossedal, it seems, cares about democracy itself; political equality and popular sovereignty as an end, not a means. His interest is not any of the specific companies, so much as the science of how a market is best conducted so all ideas (or companies), and all investors, benefit as much as possible.

We may yet find, in our materialist age, that this focus on first things, on making decisions in a fair way, and in disciplining the caprices of the rulers to the wisdom of the people, winds up being the key to material prosperity itself. In any case, there is a certain refreshing quality about a book that talks about politics as something that matters, something vital—even something healthy and positive. Is democracy, like a capital market, capable of evolution and perfection? The implicit answer of *Direct Democracy in Switzerland* is yes, it is.

Indeed, if we consider the advances made in information flow, in the rise of consumer and investor sovereignty through the growth of stock markets and Internet technologies, what is more remarkable is the extent to which our political market has remained unchanged. It may be that those very forces that have revolutionized the world economy will soon lead to demands for a comparable increase in the responsiveness of our institutions of government.

This evolution, as Fossedal notes, may or may not be towards the kind of highly populist, highly decentralized political market sketched by *Direct Democracy in Switzerland*. It may, furthermore, be highly desirable for other democracies to be more like that of the Swiss, or it might be highly inappropriate and undesirable.

In this extensive report on the world's most distinctive democracy, he provides a valuable service. He has taken apart that most delicate and complex of organisms, a political regime, and shown us what makes it tick.

No sooner has democracy triumphed on the world stage, as *The Economist* noted in 1991, than a great new debate has begun—the debate over what democracy is, and what it should be; over what is a higher stage of democracy, and what is a regression. No sooner do nearly all men and women agree that the people should rule, than we confront the seemingly prior question of what this means, and how it can best be accomplished.

Direct Democracy in Switzerland does not settle that debate. The debate is only just beginning. It will never be finally settled because, as Fossedal writes, "there is no end of history." But it is a worthy start to the discussion, an acute and insightful report on a subject that is, as an economist might put it, "on the margin."

It is, as well, a compelling drama, a good story by a writer who combines high ideals with a human touch. A great nation deserves a great work that defines, explores, and elaborates its truths and myths. In *Direct Democracy in Switzerland,* a great nation has received the telling in history and the placement in history it deserves. It should be widely read in America and Europe, and will, hopefully, have a significant influence on man's understanding and practice of democracy itself.

Alfred R. Berkeley III

Note

1. Modern Switzerland, with its present borders and basic constitutional provisions, was founded in 1848 following the *Sonderbundkrieg*, or Swiss Civil War, of 1847. The Swiss confederation extends back through 1647 (when the first unified military command structure was formed) to the year 1291 with the signing of the *Bundesbrief,* or "federal charter," by the three "forest cantons" of Uri, Schwyz, and Unterwalden. This charter was written in Latin, pointing south for the immediate origin of its political ideas in Renaissance Italy and, through it, in Roman Republican thought. In Roman times what is now Switzerland was inhabited by Celtic tribes of which the most important, the *Helvetii*, has given the country its Latin name: *confederationus Helvetica*. Julius Caesar found the Helvetii stalwart adversaries with a tendency to do away with overbearing nobles. However we date it, Swiss democracy—a regime in what we now call Switzerland, as distinct from the specific national state now in place—goes, in places, back at least 800 years. Its roots lead straight back to antiquity.

Preface

As a child, I spent several summers in Switzerland, in what I suspect was a vain hope by my half-Swiss mother and my Swiss grandmother that I would acquire some European manners and sophistication. Not much came of this effort, but I did absorb a sense of the remarkable mountain nation that Gregory Fossedal describes so well and sympathetically in this book.

Stories from those summers have become part of our family legend, gentled and amusing in retrospect. But at the time, I definitely did not enjoy the camp in Zug where we helped clean out septic tanks and endured a quality of toilet paper (read: old newspaper) to which a delicate American was not accustomed. Nor did I welcome, as a seven-year-old, the lecture to which my mother was subjected one day by a typical Swiss citizen, who, upon seeing me drop a candy wrapper on the street, strode over to denounce her as a bad parent. Nor the time that my beloved uncle Erni and I were told by a waitress in a Zürich restaurant that we had eaten too much and could not order another portion of fondue.

Today I share these memories, softened by time, with Swiss friends who tell me that they, too, endured such things as time in a septic tank. And I have many other warmer remembrances that stay with me still: the bonfires that arose on every hilltop on August 1 to celebrate Switzerland's National Day; the perfect blend of people and mountains; the family outings; the boat trips on Lac Leman; sneaking on the trains between Rougemont and Gstaad (and getting caught, of course); and, from my great-grandmother, the sturdy lessons and values of Switzerland.

My great grandmother was in her early nineties by then, and the part of the summer I spent with her in Sils Maria in the Engadine was always especially memorable. She had stayed in the same hotel (The Waldhaus, of course) for decades, and one day, when a slightly less elderly woman sat after dinner in an easy chair that my great grandmother usually occupied at that time of day, my great grandmother berated the other woman for usurping her place earned by years of seniority. Realizing, in true Swiss fashion, the superior strength of my great grandmother's claim (and perhaps looking towards the future) the other woman quickly yielded in the face of such an obvious *grand dame*.

During the day I often hiked into the snow mountains with members of the hotel staff, once almost falling while attempting an incline beyond my ability. My love of the mountains surely dates from those days, and other days spent climbing in other parts of Switzerland.

My great grandmother's doctors had warned her that simply driving over the high Julier Pass from Zürich to Sils-Maria could endanger her life, but she was not willing to give up her beloved annual vacation. However, she would not leave the revered soil of Switzerland, fearing that she might die outside Switzerland's sacred soil. So each year, we would go by car to the Maloja Pass near the border and she would point into Italy—but we never set foot in it.

She and my grandmother often related to me the Swiss view of history. The mined tunnels that would have been blown up if Hitler had invaded. The standing army ready for mobilization at a moment's notice. The reasons why neutrality fit Switzerland's situation perfectly, even to the point of not joining the U.N. The legend of William Tell. Why women could not vote.

All of this I absorbed without question. Switzerland was not taught in the European history courses that I took in college, or given much attention by the Foreign Service, which I entered immediately after graduating from college.

My career took me elsewhere, to Asia first and then to North Africa, but eventually I returned to the Europe I had once thought of as a second home. Bosnia was aflame, and, curiously, something called "the Swiss model" was being discussed as a possible solution to the dilemma of another multiethnic country. But few people understood what this actually meant. As I got pulled into the Balkan mess, I returned to Switzerland for the first time as a government official, and found enlightened and surprisingly engaged Swiss officials ready to play key roles in international affairs. These men and women (for the vote had finally been granted in 1971) included the Swiss foreign minister Flavio Cotti, who, by rotation, assumed the Chairmanship of the Organization of Security and Cooperation in Europe during a critical year for the Balkans, and Carla del Ponte, the tough and able chief prosecutor for the International Criminal Tribunals for the former Yugoslavia and Rwanda.

Talking with them, and then later serving as American Ambassador to the U.N., I came to hope that the Swiss people would become even more actively involved in world affairs, and, at the earliest possible opportunity, vote in favor of joining the United Nations as a full member. Switzerland has much to contribute to a troubled world, and, as Fossedal points out, the world can learn much from Switzerland.

In a remarkable coincidence, for three years between State Department assignments, I worked as a private citizen for the First Boston, the New York-based investment banking arm of Credit Suisse First Boston. It felt strange to be back in my grandmother's hometown as a government official or, even stranger, as my uncle joked, as a "Swiss banker"; he said that my grandparents would have been proud.

All this may seem a long way from Gregory Fossedal's book. But reading it, I learned for the first time why those bonfires were lit each August 1; how the "Swiss model" might be valuable to other situations where different ethnic groups must live together or else suffer endless strife; what the banking system is really about, and why; and, in general, why Switzerland evolved the way it has. Too little has been written about this amazing country, which is treated by the rest of the world as unique; therefore, as conventional wisdom goes, one cannot learn from it. Furthermore, for the most part the Swiss like it that way. As my grandmother told me years ago, the Swiss do not like outside scrutiny—and not just in their fabled banking system.

Fossedal effectively disputes this conventional wisdom, and offers many thoughtful suggestions on what the rest of the world can learn from Switzerland. He is especially interesting in his discussion of that most-disputed of all events in Swiss history: its role and activities during World War II. His chapter is essential reading for anyone confused over whether the Swiss "behaved correctly" or not. Whether or not one agrees with his conclusions, the chapter is essential reading. For me, it carried special meaning: I learned for the first time that Jews had not only been allowed to be a part of Swiss life for many years, but, in fact, were positively welcomed in from France by a treaty signed in 1864.[11] This was the very decade in which my great grandmother, who was Jewish, had been born. I had never been able to reconcile her (and my grandmother's) great pride in being Swiss with the seeming indifference of the Swiss to the tragedy going on around them during the war. Fossedal shows how one could be both Swiss *and* Jewish and take pride (as my family did) in both.

I hope the reader will forgive me for having linked my deep respect and admiration for this book so closely to my own background. You do not have to be part Swiss to appreciate what Fossedal has done, and everyone who reads this book will learn a great deal of wider relevance from it.

Richard Holbrooke
New York
July 2001

Note

1. The treaty had to pass a popular referendum to become official, and did so in 1866. Most countries in Europe, which saw rising anti-Semitism over the next 100 years, did not pass similar provisions encouraging Jewish immigration until after World War II, and many, of course, positively closed their doors. Further information is in chapters 3 and 9 of this book.

Part 1

Conception

1

Pilgrimage

Most visitors to Schwyz ride down from Zürich on the train. The approach is pleasant, as is practically all of Switzerland. For Switzerland, however, it is an ordinary beauty—a picture postcard on the rack, but not the one of the four or five you would buy. The small-town buildings are tired, a bit faded; not the crisp whites and criss-crossing browns that you expect, and usually find. There are no spectacular castles or mountain passes, or if there are, they have eluded me on more than one trip as grey mist slumps around the train.

About halfway through the one-hour trip it hits you that just because a place is historic doesn't mean it's going to be inspiring. Maybe it is better to keep expectations low.

But to anyone making a pilgrimage to the Schwyz archives, there's also a sense of anticipation. Each stop brings you closer to a piece of history. The geography reinforces this, the train winding along a river surrounded by mountains. One cannot see far horizontally; the view is mainly upward. So you never know; on rounding the next curve, you might arrive at your stop.

When we do arrive at the Schwyz station, though, the scene, despite the gloomy weather, is anything but *Death in Venice*. The first thing to catch my eye is a medium-sized news stand. Medium-sized for O'Hare airport or Penn Station, that is: For a small rural town, this one, like many in the country, is huge. (An article in the paper several days later boasted, accurately by my experience, that the Swiss consume more newspapers per capita than the people of any other country—twice the European average.)

My thoughts are broken by the hiss of bus brakes. Like taxi cabs at La Guardia airport, they have rushed up to meet the train. There is added hurry; the drivers seem to know (and it concerns them) that they are about ninety seconds late. Swiss punctuality may be a stereotype, but it is an accurate one.

Climbing onto the bus are five or six others: A pair of teenagers; a woman of about forty-five years, her hair dyed an extreme brassy red-orange color of the type normally seen only on teenagers in America, but which is surprisingly popular among older women in Switzerland; and a man with muddy boots and blue jeans and a red plaid shirt. The man is talking with his son in a dialect that's hard to make out, but he uses the German word for "fertilizer." The bus pulls back, bumping and hissing me into the real, tangible world.

A short ride, mostly uphill, brings me to my destination: The Schwyz information center, near the post office. Actually, the information center has closed. Luckily, a travel agency next to where the old center was helps me out with directions to the archives. The young woman there, who is fluent in English and Japanese, has obviously given these directions before, and has a map of the town to point out the simple turns one needs to make. But there is no fanfare about it—no official transfer of duties, and, one senses, no great hue or cry in the town or among the occasional tourists about the loss of the center. With characteristic low-key efficiency, the travel agency appears to have stepped in, seamlessly, for the old center.

The archives are closed until 2 p.m. anyway, and something urges me to soak in a little bit of the town. It is more inspiring than either the train ride or the literature about Schwyz have led me to believe. A tour book describes a somewhat dingy village "cowering under the peaks of the Mythen." In fact, the buildings—though none is more than a few stories tall—seem to tower above the mountains. This is only an illusion resulting from the structure of the town, but it feels no less real. Though the streets are newly paved, they are narrow, some dating to Medieval times. This makes it difficult to stand back and get a perspective accurately contrasting the buildings with the mountain's far greater height.

Whatever the cause of this effect, an unpretentious nobility whispers from the old white homes and inns, the granite town hall at the end of the street, and even the old wooden storehouse and stone tower that both predate the Bundesbrief itself. And far from cowering, they seem—partly due to the lay-out of the streets, partly due to a natural romanticization—to gently rival the mountain and the sky. There is a quiet greatness.

August 1, 1291—that is the date that brings me to a small mountain town in central Switzerland.

The year isn't as famous as 1776. And the document that was signed—now called the *Bundesbrief,* or what might be translated as a "letter/contract/charter of allegiance/confederation/bond"—isn't as well known as the Magna Carta. On that date, though, human freedom made an important advance. It is the oldest written record of a confederation that gradually became Switzerland. It led directly to extended charters of freedom for the tiny states near here, for a period of two decades and, ultimately, to an historic military victory that confirmed their freedom in 1315: the battle of Morgarten.

What happened, in the words of one historian, not only explains the birth of Switzerland, it "*is* the birth of Switzerland." As well, like America's own declaration of independence, this is a story of more or less "people's diplomacy," in this case between the rugged communities of the central Alps.

There is probably no exact historical enactment of the signing of a social contract. As Rousseau suggested, the "social contract" is more an abstraction from events than an event itself. But the Swiss Bundesbrief has some of its characteristics. It comes close.

Does any of this matter? That is to say, Why study Switzerland?

One obvious reason is Switzerland's material and, one might say, cultural or social greatness. It is perhaps the richest country in the world in terms of per capita income, which is about $40,000 per year. The Swiss economy is one of those—Taiwan, Japan—that seem blessed by a poverty of physical resources. The country mines neither precious metals nor fossil fuels, and is even, despite its dairy industry, significantly dependent on imports of certain foods. Yet by thrift and invention, the Swiss people have made pioneering advances in manufacturing, pharmaceuticals, and other industries. When the country's jobless rate nosed above 1 percent late in the twentieth century, Swiss politicians, straight-faced, talked about the nation's "employment crisis."

Culturally, the Swiss have managed to accommodate language, religious, and ethnic diversity with unusual harmony. The country has three official languages in wide use and a variety of ethnic groups. Switzerland has been a nation of immigrants and refugees in Europe for centuries, and continues today: close to 20 percent of the resident population is foreign. Yet crime and social tension are low, cohesion high. Even prosperous countries with a degree of Switzerland's language "divisions," as they are called in other countries, seem nagged by the complexity: Canada and Belgium, to name just two. Poor countries in these conditions are simply overwhelmed. Yet the Swiss navigate between French, German, and Italian in their market places, their civic institutions, and in everyday life, with an easy grace. Many university presidents and mayors in the United States, and heads of state in Asia or Central and Eastern Europe, have cause to envy and perhaps emulate Switzerland.

An interesting statistic is that when asked an open-ended question as to what makes them proud about their country, more than 60 percent of Swiss give as their first answer something having to do with their political system. In many countries, rich and poor, neither politics nor the system is so esteemed.

These very achievements, however, have generated a certain bias in recent thought about Switzerland. The country is regarded as somewhat narrow and calculating by some, merely fortunate by others; at best, as a kind of bucolic land of women with puffy white sleeves and yodeling—a lovely cheese and chocolate store, but no more. The notion is that Switzerland has enjoyed centuries of what one American writer called "uninterrupted peace and prosperity."

These notions of Switzerland, however, are a myth. What is worse—for myths can do great good—they are a debilitating myth. They make it hard to think seriously about Switzerland—and therefore, hard to take advantage of the lessons it may have to offer.

In fact, parts of Switzerland were occupied by French troops for a generation (1792–1813). The Swiss fought a civil war at about the time America and Europe fought theirs (1847), and were surrounded and land-locked by Nazi Germany (1940–1944). The country suffered bitter religious divisions for centuries, and in recent years (1970s) had to combat—albeit successfully—a "secession" movement that featured domestic terrorism, in what is now the independent canton of Jura. Despite the liberal attitudes of the Swiss, women were not empowered to vote until 1971. And some Roman Catholic orders were outlawed until very recently. In short, Switzerland has not been immune to the plagues of history, and if it is healthier now, it is because its people seem to have found cures for at least some of the more fatal diseases.

Therefore, in an age when many countries have not yet been able to surmount some of these difficulties, there is much to be learned from the Swiss. One might say there is a certain urgency. It is doubtful whether the solutions of a country like Switzerland can be directly transplanted to Bosnia, Poland, Vietnam, Korea, or South Africa. It is also doubtful, however, that these countries will be able to solve their religious and ethnic divisions, natural partitions, or the tensions of federalism without applying measures based upon certain general principles. As the Swiss have worked on many of these successfully, it is only by a perverse insularity, or a stubborn ignorance, that one would want to ignore the Swiss experience.

Europeans, meanwhile, are now engaged in a great process of economic integration. They are learning that this implies a degree of political and even spiritual integration as well—quite a task given the state of the polyglot that is Europe. What nation has more to teach on these matters than Switzerland? In the narrow sense, Swiss education and cultural systems have achieved a remarkable degree of integration of three great European cultures. In a broader sense, as the Swiss parliamentarian Andreas Gross has observed, it may just be that to deal with the politics of European Union as a kind of unpleasant afterthought may be a backward approach. It is possible, if the Swiss are any guide, that Europe can gain much by considering such matters as a truly federal assembly, and a right of approval of laws by referendum, first rather than last. Indeed the Swiss, in a sense, have already accomplished on a small scale what Europe hopes to do on a larger scale. The measurements are different, but not necessarily the operating forces. Thus there may be lessons for Europe in the experience of what might be called the first European nation.

Some Swiss wonder whether they should join the European Union. But there is another question: Should Europe, in some ways, join Switzerland? For America (yes, even for America), it is possible to learn as well. This is especially true given the concerns about the state of our politics, our institutions, and our mores.

In recent years, one hears words such as "responsibility" and "citizenship" more and more often—surely a healthy sign. But the mere fact that these are raised in the manner of a plea, or as a proposed counter-culture, suggests how far out of practice we have fallen. Switzerland, since the time of Machiavelli, has been characterized by a tenacious and somewhat mystical patriotism and civic dynamism. In Switzerland, even today, one feels somewhat transplanted into the American democracy observed by Alexis de Tocqueville: a regime characterized by bustling activity, a "constant generation" of community activities, private initiatives, and civic improvements and associations.

In his classic, *Modern Democracies*, James Bryce outlines some of the reasons why students of history and politics should take a special interest in Switzerland.[1] One justification, of course, is its longevity. "It contains communities in which popular government dates farther back than anywhere else in the world." There are practical reasons as well. The Swiss reliance on, and affection for, local government has generated "a greater variety of institutions based on democratic principles than any other country, greater even than the Federations of America and Australia can show."

Most important, however, is the extent to which Switzerland has placed a unique degree of faith in the people. Through its use of initiative and referendum at the national level, its citizen-based legislature, and similar devices, the Swiss have established a very different kind of democracy than is seen anywhere else. As Bryce writes:

> Among the modern democracies, Switzerland has the highest claim to be studied.... Switzerland has pushed democratic doctrines farther, and worked them out more consistently, than any other European state.

In short, it is an important laboratory not just for a collection of ideas, plural, but for an idea, singular, that unifies these innovations: the most populist (in the objective sense of the term) democracy in the world.

Switzerland answers the potential question of the political scientist or citizen: What happens if we place so much faith in the people that we make them lawmakers? The much earlier experiences with this far-reaching democracy, as in the city-states of Greece, took place without the benefit of the advances in communication that make it possible to have popular government without having government by physical assembly.

Switzerland has taken democracy down a path not taken by others. Does this path, like the "road less traveled by," to paraphrase Robert Frost,[2] differ only sentimentally from the other? Or is the Swiss path meaningfully different, perhaps even advantageous?

The great dynasties of Europe and Asia, in other words, have much experience. But the Swiss have much experience with democracy. America is great in space; a majestic continent of vast powers. But Switzerland is great in time; a bold experiment sweeping back almost a millennium.

To understand democracy in Switzerland, then, we must survey not merely the country's topographical features, or even its present institutions, but its origins. We must travel not merely to Schwyz, but to 1291 and earlier—to the Bundesbrief, and the still more ancient heritage of democratic practices implied by history and the language of the Bundesbrief and the earlier Freibriefe themselves. The roots of democracy in Switzerland are deep indeed.

Notes

1.   James Bryce, *Modern Democracies*, MacMillan Company, 1921, Volume I of II.
2.   From *Collected Works of Robert Frost*, New York, Viking, 1977.

Part 2

History

2

1291

"Switzerland is a product of both creation, in its constitution of 1848, and evolution, in hundreds of years of people in sovereign states, learning to get along. You must understand both elements to understand Switzerland today." —*Edgar Brunner*

If you look at a relief map—which is almost essential to understand Switzerland—you can see the logic of Switzerland's development in a series of quasi-independent villages, towns, and cities. If you were to place a group of marbles at the center of the map, among some of the highest peaks of the Alps, they would eventually meander to the long, Norway-shaped plain of the northwest, and the lakes of Como and Maggiore to the southeast. But the route the marbles would travel would bounce down around the Lake of Luzern, and of course the Saint Bernard and Gotthard Passes routes.

This imaginary route of the marbles more or less defines the outer border of the three original cantons of Uri, Schwyz, and Unterwalden, as well as those that soon became part of the Swiss confederation: Luzern, Zürich, Bern, Zug, Appenzell, and the lands of what was later Aargau. The main grooves, some six or seven, are chopped up into dozens of smaller rivulets. They form semi-isolated units suitable for similarly independent human communities. A town planner setting up Switzerland from scratch today would probably follow this design, toward which the country was evolving naturally from the twelfth to the fourteenth centuries.

To extend on our analogy above, if you were to sprinkle small ball bearings on our relief map, they would bump and nudge their way down to settle into these nooks and crannies very much where the actual towns are today. Even the "great plain" of Switzerland, stretching from Geneva in the southwest across Lausanne, Bern, Basel, and Zürich up to the Bodensee in the northeast, is diced into a hundred or more natural towns—of which there are more than 3,000 in Switzerland today, for an average population per unit of only some 2,000 people, and a median of perhaps 1,500 or less.

11

These relatively low-lying areas have the climate to support high-altitude farming, and the river transport to export its products. By the late thirteenth century, they had even developed some reputation for producing quality woven textiles and other products that could benefit from their access to large and wealthy markets all around the region, including France, Germany, Italy, and Austria.

As the calendar pushed on toward the year 1300, outside forces began to attack the independence of these communities. This happened for several reasons. First, the nations around Switzerland—the kingdoms of Lombardy, Burgundy, and Savoy; the emerging empires of France, Germany, and Austria—were expanding. By tradition, most of the cantons that formed the original Swiss confederation, located in what is now central-northern and eastern Switzerland, were possessions or protectorates of Austria or of the Hapsburg family, which later ruled Austria, but originated in the present-day Swiss canton of Aargau. The Habsburgs, however, were never popular in their own place of origin, and grew less popular as some of the Habsburg nobles became more arrogant over the years 1200 to 1350. The Swiss, for their part, complained of high tax rates and arbitrary judgments from the local courts run by Habsburg nobles.

With Austrian and Habsburg influence waning, and popular affiliation with Austria weak at best, France, Burgundy, Germany, and the lords of Lombardy looked to fill the void. Switzerland, situated in the middle of these competing states, became a battleground as the borders of these emerging empires crept toward one another.

A second factor, stronger in the centuries that followed but present even in 1291, was the mild rebuke to top-down rule posed by the very existence of Swiss communities with their mixed democratic practices and traditions. We cannot document the exact shape of the politics of those local villages, which in any case varied widely, because most of what we know about them either comes from less reliable oral history or must be inferred from the small number of documents. But it is generally accepted that even in the thirteenth century, the Swiss—particularly in such fiercely independent cantons as Uri and Schwyz—made use of local, popular assemblies to decide many broader and nearly all local questions of policy. These certainly were more democratic than any of the nearby empires. Naturally, not everyone "voted," but in some communities, landowners and even burgers probably did.

The Swiss, even in the midst of the Middle Ages, also offered something of a demographic haven. Uri, one of the three original cantons, had its origins, as historian J. Murray Luck has written, as "a kind of Siberia" to which mountain farmers, too rough for the tribes of Germany and Alsace, were banished. If there were few or no formal individual rights, there was an ethos of independence and political equality, and the right to speak your piece. "From even these early times," as former Senator Franz Muheim impressed on me during long discussions of Switzerland's animating principles, "there has been a code of, 'I mind my own business, you mind yours.' It is easiest to understand if you start by trying to assume that someone wanted to go against this principle, such as the Habsburgs. Then you look at a map, and you see all these valleys, lakes, rivers, and steep hills and mountains, breaking the country up into a tapestry of thousands of natural villages. If you wanted to impose your will even on your neighbor, how would you do it? It would take a large army just to conquer a few such communities. How would you then take over dozens or hundreds of them?"

This haven naturally had an impact on the surrounding aristocracies. It put ideas into the heads of peasants and laborers bound to service in the more feudal communities around Switzerland. In Uri and Schwyz, the grant of rights had been made directly from the emperor to the people at large, making the Swiss example especially dangerous for the neighboring aristocracies.

Finally, as is common when we find human competition and conflict, there were economic elements. Sometime shortly before or after the year 1200, the freemen of canton Uri opened a small bridge across the river Reuss. The bridge wobbled several hundred feet above the torrent during low periods, precariously close to it when the river rose, and connected two sides of a deep gulch not far from the Gotthard Pass.

It was called *Teufelsbrücke*, or devil's bridge. Some attributed this to a large bulge of rock above that appeared suspended by occult forces. Others note the bridge itself stood somewhat athwart nature and normalcy. Man seemed to issue to the rocks, like Satan to God, his own defiant *non serviam*.

Crossing was no exercise for the meek. Even riding over today's modern, concrete bridge, not far from the original, in a four-door sedan, the winds are enough to bounce your car around a little, and the occult shadows thrown off by the high and jutting cliffs menace. The combination of height, galloping waters, howling air currents, and sharp rocks stabbing out from tall cliffs all around creates a feeling of great precariousness.

Nevertheless, the bridge became a transportation jugular, and a catalyst for a rapid increase in economic exchange for all the surrounding countries. Before, there had been no economical way to transport cattle and other products from the dairy farms of Uri and its neighbors to the wealthy regions surrounding Milan to the south. Now these products could make it through, and more developed products from north and south could be exchanged more efficiently, spurring trade between Germany, Italy, and France.

No one kept elaborate output or trade statistics in those days, but we can infer the impact of the *Teufelsbrücke* from related measures. For example, as Swiss historian Werner Meyer has noted in his fine history (*1291: L'Histoire*), there was one major chateau in the central Swiss region in the year 1000: Rotzberg in Nidwald. This grew to four by the year 1100, and stood at five at the turn of the century in 1200, roughly the completion of the bridge. By the year 1250, however, this number tripled, to sixteen, with nine of the eleven new structures in Uri, Schwyz, and Unterwalden. These figures suggest a rapid expansion of economic activity during the period.

The population of many existing towns in Uri, Schwyz, Luzern, Unterwalden, and the region around Zürich more than doubled between 1200 and 1300—a time of relatively slow rises in life expectancy, and many conflicts in Switzerland. This was much faster than the surrounding towns, many of which saw flat population growth.

As one direct measure of the economic impact of the bridge, in 1359, Uri paid approximately 100,000 francs for lands in its district held by the Fraumünster cloister of Zürich. This was only a fraction of Uri's collection of tolls from the bridge, since the canton made similar purchases from the Habsburgs, individual lords, and other abbeys during the same decade.

On May 26, 1231, Emperor Friedrich II sent a *Freibrief*, or freedom charter, to "the people of the Uri valley," recognizing and formalizing in law the independence from the Habsburgs that they had gradually won in fact. It is worth noting that this letter was addressed to "the people," not a particular official, institution, or lord. The Swiss cantons asserted, and the emperor recognized, not merely a set of terms for a set of nobles and their king to agree on privileges, but of rights enjoyed in common by the inhabitants of the Uri valley.

Friedrich was succeeded by several emperors of lesser note and by an "interregnum" (1256–1273) between emperors. In 1273, the nobles selected no populist to head the empire, but one of their own in spirit: Rudolf I.

Rudolf was a Habsburg, the first in a long line to serve as emperor for much of the next 500 years. Rudolf was interested in recovering his family's holdings and influence in Switzerland, now all but crumbled, as a long-term guarantee of Habsburg rule. In this, he may have been shrewd, but his methods made enemies both in the Waldstätte and the empire at large. He attempted to raise taxes and to exploit many feudal obligations. For example, he called upon his subjects to send troops for sham or at best uncertain battles, then negotiated with them to waive his rights in return for cash payment. Rudolf appointed family members and foreigners as judges and other officials to the Swiss cantons.

The simple Swiss villagers resented these bureaucrats not only as economic dead weight, but as arrogant overlords. Several of the Habsburgs apparently used their position to seduce or compel women in their districts to convey sexual favors and join them in what the Bundesbrief itself alludes to as "unnatural" perversions. [2]

By the end of his life, the excesses of Rudolf and his family had alienated most of Switzerland. Close to the end he tried to recoup popular support by offering to reconfirm the essence of the freedoms of the Waldstätte in a slightly repackaged form. Rudolf promised to appoint judges only from among the

Swiss. But this was only a promise not to assert his right to appoint other judges, not a limitation of his own power per se. And his description of who would be covered by these rights was ambiguous—clearly including the nobility, not so clearly the general population. Gone was the clear-cut *universis hominibus* of Friedrich, to be replaced by an elitist and unprincipled game of divide and conquer.

Rudolf's death on July 15, 1291, was preceded by two years of obviously declining health. Even so, the Swiss rebels moved with surprising speed, considering the state of communications in those days—suggesting that such moves had been orchestrated in anticipation of his death. Within two weeks—August 1, 1291—they had sealed a pact for "everlasting cooperation," the Bundesbrief.

We have no recorded debates or newspaper accounts of the actual event. In this sense, almost anything said about the drafting and approval of the Bundesbrief is speculative. But there is intelligent speculation based on evidence. From this, without making too many leaps, we can ascribe a number of features to the event.

The text of the agreement refers to a renewal of the "ancient" cooperation between the cantons, suggesting that no dramatic departures were needed and the requirement for popular oversight was light. On the other hand, this was a dramatic time, and the declaration of a perpetual alliance at a time of possible war. The very fact that something was being put on paper suggests a heightened solemnity.

The Bundesbrief describes itself as a pact between "the people of Uri, the community of Schwyz, and representatives of the people of Underwalden." Read literally, this sounds like a meeting, probably in Schwyz, at which the "communitas" (community) of Schwyz was largely in attendance, a large popular assembly of Uri, and a group from Unterwalden more in the character of a chosen assembly or group of representatives. We need not read it so literally, of course, but we have no strong reason to prefer a different interpretation, especially given the broader context. Whatever combination of leaders and common farmers joined together, they met, in all likelihood, in some village along the Lake of Luzern or of one of the rivers nearby. Such a choice would have made for a central location, and would have made broader participation possible by allowing for use of the rivers, lakes, and nearby roads that were much of the transportation network. The author Schiller, among others, placed the events on the banks of Rütli, certainly one possible location. Another is the town of Schwyz itself, where the Bundesbrief is now kept.

The composite scene that emerges is not necessarily far from the legendary paintings, tapestries, and operatic versions—an indication that either the artists did their historical homework, or that the Muse that moved them did so in emulation of the fact. The men stood out along one of the gentle hills that have formed a backdrop to so many popular deliberative assemblies over the last 1,000 years and, looking forward as well as back, sealed a solemn "and perpetual" oath. Even in this setting, at Rütli or nearby, Switzerland seems almost designed to be a democracy. The slopes make for a natural stadium or amphitheater, allowing a large number of citizens to participate in a discussion and then vote.

That there was some kind of democratic assent is implied not merely by the political system of the villages in the cantons, but by the document itself. The Bundesbrief notes, for example, that there was near unanimity, but not total unanimity, of the participants—suggesting some sort of measurement or discussion or both. It refers several times to the document as an "oath," renewing, solidifying, and perfecting an "ancient alliance." This suggests, particularly in the Middle Ages when oaths were taken seriously, an actual oath of some sort. Yet the Bundesbrief is also self-consciously a document, referring to the statutes and promises "above," and those "now written." Hence it was not merely a *pro-forma* repetition of whatever old oath of alliance may have existed.

Here again, Schiller and the artists may be saluted for either happily or artfully conforming their representations to the likely facts. And Tschudi, Gagliardi, and other historians sometimes taken to task for their credulity may turn out to have greater skeptical acumen—refusing to judge a thing wrong just because it is deemed true by the oral tradition—than some revisionists who are merely contrarian. Aspects of the Bundesbrief's content are worth noting. The document contains no "signatures," unlike the Declaration of Independence or Magna Carta. In this sense, it is highly populist, almost corporatist. At the bottom are the community seals of Uri and Unterwalden, and on the left, a mark where the corporate seal of Schwyz once was.

In some ways, this anonymous character is appropriately Swiss, the product of a politics of consensus by a group of equal citizens.

The new agreement did not set up a mechanism of government; it did not proclaim itself a new republic or even promise one. In this sense, the Bundesbrief is indeed a limited document. It is, however, a social contract as well, albeit a focused one. And because the participating communities were already significantly democratic in form and practice and assumption, it set up a very important experiment, and proclaimed the legitimacy of doctrines implicitly contrary to monarchy and feudalism.

For the most part, the empire was much too absorbed in wider and more immediate problems to deal with the Swiss. It took nearly a year for the bitterly divided electors of the Holy Roman Empire to select a successor to Rudolf, whose own holdings had to be divided among his sons. Adolf of Nassau (1292–1298) was killed in battle trying to keep his empire stitched together. Albrecht I (1298–1308), the son of Rudolf I, tried to create trouble by encouraging the Habsburg nobles in Austria and Aargau to re-assert their ancient rights, but the lords, as noted above, were expelled rudely. Not until

Friedrich the Beautiful (1314–1326) was the empire sufficiently stable for the Habsburgs to mount a serious effort to overturn the upstart confederation.

The Swiss founders, by luck or shrewd design, took advantage of this confusion to consolidate their own internal relations and to add allies. The powerful surrounding cities of Bern, Zürich, and Luzern were natural allies, and longed to free themselves from the Habsburg influence. But they would be more inclined to take part in an alliance that seemed solid than to gamble their prosperity on a mere chance coalition of farming communes. The Bundesbrief served not only an internal function, but an external one, projecting a picture of solidarity to potential friends and enemies. This was a touchy game to play: Too brazen a rebuke of the nobles might have focused the counter-revolution in Switzerland. Instead, the royals fell out among themselves—the German princes versus France versus Burgundy; Saxony against Austria for influence in Bern, Fribourg, and Aargau; and others.

If this account does not overcredit, then the founders of the Rütli emerge as not only effective nation-builders, but shrewd strategists. The Bundesbrief, in combination with economic boom and a citizen's army of growing effectiveness, helped shelter the Swiss from foreign intervention for a generation—roughly from 1291 until the Battle of Morgarten in 1315.

Morgarten added the seal of military history to the Bundesbrief. Some 15,000 Habsburg troops from Austria—noble, well-armed, mounted, and skilled—marched toward the central cantons. Through a clever series of roadblocks, the outnumbered Swiss farmers and village craftsmen drew the attackers into a narrow passage between the Aegerisee and Mount Morgarten. With perhaps only 100 troops, and certainly no more than 250, the farmers fell upon the Austrians in the narrow pass, suffering little disadvantage from numbers under the cramped quarters, and surpassing the Habsburg contingent with their courage and resourcefulness. Many Austrians were slaughtered in the "bloody rocks" just west of what is now a nearby town; the Swiss rolled boulders, logs, and (in some accounts) wild animals onto them. Other Austrians were driven into the water and reportedly drowned. About 2,000 Austrian and twelve Swiss troops died.

"Morgarten," as one military historian put it, "shocked the world," much as the success of the American Revolution over the British Empire. The Swiss had proven, in their first great test, that a popular, citizen army could hold its own against elite forces from one of the great European powers.

Indeed, "Switzerland," though not yet existing, was an attractive political economy and an attractive idea even early in the fourteenth century. Before and after Morgarten, the Swiss managed to form important agreements with Glarus, Arth, Milan, and Luzern. Even the ill-fated first alliance with Zürich, which ended when besieging Habsburg troops crushed the town in 1292, rebounded in favor of the Swiss. After the sacking, the resentment of the people of Zürich for the Habsburg dominance was, like the Bundesbrief, "in perpetuity."

It was only a matter of time—and a few more victories like Morgarten—before the forest cantons convinced Zürich, Bern, and other great cities of the region decided that this was a confederation worth joining. Morgarten was the material manifestation of a long policy of intelligent statecraft by the central Swiss, a combination of internal political justice and equality with prudent external alliances.

Notes

1. The diffusion of wealth and breakdown of feudal privileges seen in Uri and in Switzerland generally went against the trend of the times. Danish peasants and private farmers, for example, owned more than half of the land in the year 1250; by 1650, this figure had declined to just more than 10 percent. For most of Europe, the transition enjoyed by Switzerland came only in the 16th Century, and in some cases, later still.
2. See for example Jürg Stüssi-Lauterburg, and R.Gysler-Schöni, *Helvetias Töchter*, Huber, Zürich, 1999.

3

Willensnation

Victory at Morgarten established the upstart confederation as a viable emerging confederation. It also set off the dynamic of growth by attraction—the voluntary association of neighboring principalities, cities, and individuals—that makes Switzerland a nation created by acts of the free will.

The Swiss call this concept, and the political entity based on it, *Willensnation*, and use the term with pride. It is a nation of people who have come to Switzerland (even today, nearly 20 percent are foreigners) or whose ancestors did, or whose ancestors belonged to towns or small principalities that freely joined the confederation. The common point is some attraction to the idea of Switzerland with its freedom and cultural diversity under a banner of strong national ideals.

In this way, as in many others, Switzerland bears some resemblance to the United States.

The term *Willensnation* is apt in a second sense—one used by few or no Swiss today, and certainly not intended at the start, but nevertheless appropriate. For Switzerland was also "willed" in the sense that the country's independence, neutrality, prosperity, and special political and social culture resulted in part from a long series of deliberate policies. Switzerland's position and its geography sometimes aided these developments, sometimes frustrated them. They were not, however, sheer accidents of climate and other facts of nature, contrary to much commentary from Sully to Montesquieu to Jean-Jacques Rousseau, and down to the present.

These tendencies, once established, reinforced one another. As Switzerland became known as a haven for the industrious, the freedom-loving, the independent, it tended to attract more such people. Many emigrated to escape ruinous taxes, or the feudal duties that acted like taxes. As this turbulent frontier attracted such pioneers, the traits of independence and fortitude were reinforced, and so on. All these dynamics, however, required a point of crystallization, some core, at the start—much as the "Norwegian section" or "little Vietnam" of Chicago, after reaching some critical mass, became a self-generating phenomenon.

Without this core, we might have seen simply a long history of bloody rebellions along the borders of the three great empires—France and Burgundy; the German-Austrian Hapsburg Reich; and Italy and (to some extent) Lombard and the Papacy to the South. Instead, the confederation of independence-minded states at the crossroads of Europe became an example and a magnet. Suddenly, and ever since, the idea of liberty had enough soil for something living to grow on.

If we examine Switzerland's history from 1291 up through the twentieth century, its political economy and culture can be seen as represented in Figure 3.1. The figure is not exactly a map, though it roughly positions the main actors geographically. It is more of an historical flow chart that represents a number of Switzerland's roles in Europe and, indeed, the West.

For 800 years, Switzerland has served as a natural crossroads for the exchange of goods between Germany, France, and Italy. By the early eighteenth century, more than 10,000 persons passed over the Devil's Bridge annually—often accompanied, of course, by more than one cart or horse of products per traveler. There were other ways to travel between France, Germany, and Italy, of course, but—especially for transporting livestock or large caravans of goods—the most efficient way was to cut through the Alps, especially as this became more and more efficient with improvements to the bridge and the surrounding roads and towns.

Figure 3.1

**The flow of goods, people, and ideas in Western Europe—
roughly 1200 to the present. The core: Switzerland.**

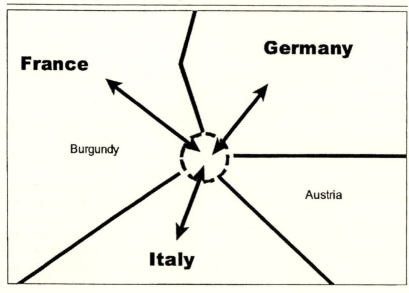

To attract a growing volume of traffic, even this strategically situated crossroads had to be adept, or at least competent, at many tasks. Merchants needed a safe road to travel on, with inns and churches and other essentials of life along the way. They would prefer traveling through areas where the legal system was fair, prompt, and relatively simple to deal with. Money—preferably a single, reliable currency; certainly a multitude of them if not one—was essential. When Plato sets about establishing the ideal state in his *Republic*, he starts with the need for a market for exchange and for a market to carry out that exchange—money is needed. Naturally it would be helpful to find people along the way who could converse in your native tongue, particularly in the larger cities where contracts and exchanges might have to be worked out.

Switzerland has benefited from the earliest times in that it had a strong incentive to develop this kind of efficient, stable political economy. All nations have an interest in this, of course, but for the people that inhabit what is now Switzerland, the potential gains were even larger—and the potential for division and violence, arguably, greater too. Much was riding on the successful maintenance of this position, both for the original cantons of Uri, Schwyz, and Unterwalden, and for the surrounding cities—Zürich, Baden, Luzern, Bern—that prospered in part thanks to the success of the confederation.

The geographical additions to the confederation began almost immediately. Zürich joined in a separate alliance weeks after the Bundesbrief. It proved ill-fated when the Hapsburg Austrians destroyed much of the city in revenge two years later, and was tested again throughout the fourteenth century, but eventually proved solid. Luzern, likewise, sometimes leaned Hapsburg, sometimes toward the Alpine *Bund*. These two rich cities had the largest stake of any in a free, prosperous transit across the Alps.

In a sense, the early Swiss were in a competition with the Hapsburgs—with the support of the merchant cities likely to swing toward the group they thought could provide the most effective economic and political regime. Who could run the trans-Alpine marketplace best? Inexorably, both Luzern and Zürich took advantage of every opportunity to side with the confederation, and generally tacked back toward the Hapsburgs only under duress. There were divisions within their own populations as well, of course, but these were evidently few. Note, for example, how eagerly the Zürich elite sided with the unproved alliance within ten weeks of the sealing of the Bundesbrief in 1291.

By 1393, the original confederation of three cantons had grown to eight: Uri, Schwyz, and Unterwalden were joined by Luzern, Zürich, Glarus, Zug, and Bern as confederates. This central core was working cooperatively with communities on the next periphery to solidify the new *de facto* state still further. Bern reached out toward the now-French-speaking cities of Fribourg and Lausanne, Uri and Luzern looked south toward what is now the Italian portion of Switzerland, and Zürich and Schwyz aimed at popular diplomacy with the independence-minded farmers and merchants of Aargau to the West and St. Gallen to the East to provide a buffer zone from the Hapsburgs—and, of course, potential ground for the federation's own growth. This process is represented in Figure 3.2. Note that Switzerland was not yet a "country" as such, and would not be for many years. Some would place the date as late as 1648 and the treaty of Westphalia—or even 1848 and the constitution following Switzerland's final major religious war. On the other hand, attributes of sovereignty were forming out of this *Willens-confederation* as early as 1291, as we have observed. This makes assigning an exact date both difficult and, in a sense, arbitrary and unnecessary.

The white core in the center represents the three original cantons of Uri, Schwyz, and Unterwalden (Obwalden and Niwalden) roughly as they were in 1291. The four gray regions that seem to move out from that core represent the confederation's expansion to include Luzern (1332), Glarus (1352), and Zug (1352), and the cities of Zürich (1351) and Bern (1353). Some of the territories not marked as part of the confederation were already, in the mid-1300s, "subject territories" of Bern, Zürich, or of the confederation. For example, Fribourg (associated with the confederation in 1481). The broadest

Figure 3.2

The Growth of Willensnation
(snapshots from 1291, 1353, and 1999)

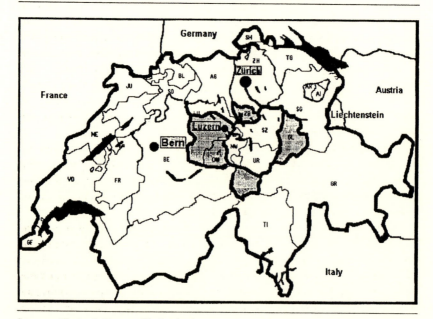

Source: Alexis de Tocqueville Institution.

dark line around the outside is the border of modern-day Switzerland with France, Germany, Italy, Liecthenstein, and Austria.

An illustrative addition to the confederation during this period was Zug, a city (and now canton) on a still lake south of Zürich. The Hapsburgs strove to retain control there as they did in Bern and Zürich—anything to avoid being completely cut out of the picture in a region evolving as a crossroads. Parts of the town sympathized with the earlier confederation, and probably fought as individuals at Morgarten. Some of the ruling aristocracy were Hapsburg and pro-Hapsburg; others not. After securing the support of Zürich and Luzern in 1351, the central cantons moved against Zug in June 1352. It fell in a matter of weeks. From a Hapsburg point of view, one might say that the Swiss confederation seized the town by mere physical force. This, though, is only part of the story. There was in fact a vigorous faction within the city that supported incorporation within the confederation. Families within the township of Zug and in the surrounding countryside organized themselves and were fighting for the confederation within the city. Few details of the battle remain and there were apparently few casualties, all suggestive of a short battle in which the conqueror was welcomed as a liberator.

It was at the end of the century, however, that the real cement was applied to the confederation. In that year, Emperor Friedrich III died, succeeded by his son Maximilian I. To a treasury already strained by rivalry with the French, Maximilian added an untimely taste for luxury and even display. He established a tax, the *Pfennig* tax of one penny, throughout the kingdom. Maximilian also strove to centralize the judicial system, introducing an Imperial Chamber of Justice and allowing appeals of purely local cases. Here were two matters, taxes and centralized justice, on which nearly all Swiss, peasant and landowner, worker and merchant, could agree. After winning an alliance that brought money but no troops from France, the Swiss confronted the Austrians, the kaiser's initial proxy, in a series of campaigns running from the Jura in the Northwest through Basel and Baden in central Switzerland and Graubünden and St. Gallen in the East.

The decisive battle took place on July 22, 1499, near the Solothurn fortress of Dornach. The Austrian troops assumed the Swiss were far away and were bathing lazily in the Birs to escape the heat. The Swiss fell on the Austrians and killed many of their 16,000 men, including the Austrian commander. The kaiser relented and agreed to a peace treaty at Basel on September 22, 1499.

Within two years, Basel itself joined the confederation, which grew to thirteen cantons with its entry in 1501. Basel illustrates the attraction of the confederation's free democratic model in a highly positive way. Even the city's ruling class had reason to admire the tenacious fighting spirit that the mountain democracy of the forest cantons seemed to breed. Swiss troops had heroically defended the city in 1444 in what might be called the Pyrrhic defeat of St. Jakob's. Marching with the intention of absorbing Basel and nearby areas into France, the French troops slaughtered their opponents. But they were chastened by the courage with which some 1,500 Swiss held off 40,000 trained and well-armed troops, inflicted great casualties, and fought to the death. The French decided there were better places to expand than this region where they would be resisted with such ferocity. The people of Basel realized they had been rescued by this act of self-sacrifice, and relations between the city and the confederation grew closer in the coming decades.

The cities joining the federation took the lesson of Willensnation to heart, adapting some of the principles of democracy at work in the rural cantons to their own use. Bern, one of the most aristocratic entrants into the confederation, adopted democratic political reforms after resentment of the city's ruling elite resulted in riots in 1470. Zürich's ruling families ceded increasing powers to an elected council and acquiesced in the rise of the guilds, whose power transformed the city. These reforms did not put the more elitist cities on a democratic par with the rural *Landsgemeinde*, or community meetings, but they were a significant step.

Thus, even Switzerland's conquests represent persuasion and example as much as sheer muscle. It was at popular diplomacy that the Swiss excelled. Such cities as Bern, Fribourg, and others followed the pattern of Zürich in many ways. They could surely have resisted the mountain men of the Alps, had it not been for the fact that many of their people sympathized more with, and longed for the freedom of, the *Waldstätte*. They evidently felt an alliance with these rugged folk was more reliable than those based on the caprice of the dukes and princes and clergy that dominated the rest of Europe. "The Swiss are not easy to win as allies," as the Duke of Milan said during one of Switzerland's less creditable hours as the Duke and France engaged in a bidding war for the use of Swiss mercenaries. "But they are highly sought because, as allies, they are extremely valuable." Machiavelli, who observed the Swiss in battle and traveled extensively in Switzerland, regarded the Swiss as perhaps the toughest fighters in Europe, comparing them—the highest compliment possible from Machiavelli—to the soldiers of the Roman Republic. This reputation as fierce fighters stayed with the Swiss down through the centuries, leading to comparisons to the Vietnamese in the 1960s and 1970s and the Afghanistan rebels of the 1980s.

Like the Romans, Machiavelli observed, the Swiss fought well in part because they had something to fight for. Their free lives and republican virtues not only gave them better weapons and better leaders to fight with, but animated great individual courage among this "army of citizens."

By the time Machiavelli saw the Swiss defeated by French forces at the battle of Marignano (1515), Switzerland's growth by absorption of territory was almost at an end. Thirteen of the present twenty-three cantons belonged to the confederation, stretching from the Bernese territories in the west across Basel, Zürich, and down through the forest cantons and into Appenzell and

Glarus in the East. The full inclusion of many of the French-speaking cantons in the West in a multilingual Switzerland was not complete until the nineteenth century. But already there was great affinity and extensive trade, monetary, and other links with Geneva and Lausanne, as well as with some of the towns of what is now the Italian-speaking Ticino in the South. This affinity became formal defense treaties with Lausanne in 1525 and Geneva in 1526. The Duke of Savoy made a final attempt to assert his rights over Geneva and was crushed by a confederate force composed largely of troops from Bern and Solothurn.

It would be wrong, however, to think that Switzerland ceased to be a political magnet after 1500. From the sixteenth century onward, Switzerland didn't absorb bordering cities and territories at the same rate, and it began to follow a policy of neutrality in foreign affairs that has survived to the present. It did, though, continue to attract large numbers of people. Some were religious, political, or ethnic refugees. Others were risk takers, entrepreneurs. Still others were the rebellious and the contrary who didn't like the taxes, the feudal dues, or the social elitism of European society. Almost all took part willingly in the culture of freedom, tolerance, and democracy.

In short, before about the year 1530, Willensnation moved borders. Afterward, to a large extent, it moved people.

In 1685, Louis XIV revoked the Edict of Nantes, setting forth a great exodus of Huguenots and other Protestants from France. In the coming years, an estimated 120,000 poured into the Swiss confederation. Many of these resettled into Germany, America, and other countries, but many chose to remain. In percentage terms, those figures compare with the great Irish migration to the United States. A deliberate policy to control the population growth played a role in how the immigrants were assimilated (or not) into Swiss society. In the 1670s and 1680s, Bern, Luzern, Solothurn, and Geneva established fees before one could become a burgher. Smaller towns followed suit and the fees generally grew throughout the century until they were prohibitively high. The result was that skilled laborers, who valued their ability to export readily into the French market, had the wherewithal to remain in Switzerland: approximately 3,000 in Geneva, 1,500 in Lausanne and Bern, and a significant number in the smaller towns of Vaud and Fribourg. Of these, a disproportionate number consisted of highly skilled artisans, employers, and financial elites.

"Much of Swiss industry (watches and textiles, to name just two) owes its origins, not to economic causes, but to religious oppression in neighboring countries," writes J. Murray Luck in his *History of Switzerland*. "The refugees from France and Italy brought with them invaluable skills and know-how."

Data from Geneva and Zürich for the year 1700 indicate the population of both cities consisted of 28 percent or more of immigrants. If we add in the number of persons who came from other parts of the federation—such as

Italian-speaking and German-speaking Protestants from the forest cantons and the Ticino—the proportion of refugees and immigrants would surely have approached or exceeded 40 percent.

In 1864, the confederation concluded a treaty with France that provided for the establishment of Jews in Switzerland. The treaty obliged the Swiss to allow French Jews to settle freely in Swiss territory. This was followed by a popular vote, in 1866, that codified the right of Jews to settle anywhere they wanted in the country. If it seems a grudging measure by today's standards, it came some eighty years before similar protections were provided in the rest of Europe. Coming at a time when anti-Semitism was on the rise again in Europe, as the industrial age advanced and paranoia about "Jewish capitalists" resurfaced, this was an important gesture by the newly reconstituted nation. In Geneva (about 6 percent) and Lausanne (close to 10 percent), the percentage of Jews in the population was higher. A number of Jews, of course, emigrated to Switzerland only to relocate in a few years to such destinations as Poland and the United States. Those who remained made disproportionate contributions to scientific, financial, and other core economic activities, and helped generate the kind of critical mass in intellectual brilliance that would attract other leading researchers and entrepreneurs, making Switzerland the greatest contributor to increased productivity of the nineteenth and twentieth centuries. (Switzerland has won more than five times the Nobel Prizes for science of any other nation on a per capita basis.)

If generous, then, the policy was also wise. Jewish immigrants from France and (later) Germany formed the basis of a great expansion of the Swiss banking, construction, and manufacturing industries. The contribution from immigrants was by no means limited to Jews. Arab traders and financiers fled from Spain and helped make Basel a center of science and trading in the fifteenth and sixteenth centuries, and their descendants remain today. Protestant refugees from France, fleeing to the Western cantons, and later Catholic refugees from Holland, England, and Scotland flocked to the central cantons—Switzerland, at times, was a magnet for both confessions. It was the willingness to accept people power of many different races, faiths, and ideologies that helped Switzerland thrive. Diversity, it turns out, is competitive.

For example, two engineers who left France in the 1860s played a key role in the construction of a railroad through the St. Gotthard pass, completed in 1882. The initiative, financed privately by the leadership of investment magnate Alfred Escher, spawned a number of spin-off innovations in engineering by immigrants in Geneva, Lausanne, and Bern. This intelligent but much-disputed decision by government and industry (debated from the late 1840s onward) acted somewhat like the U.S. space industry or the Internet, catapulting Swiss firms to the lead in a number of technological fields. The direct impact resembled that of the *Teufelsbrücke*: the new trans-Gotthard route reduced transit time from a period of several days to less than ten hours.

The list of Swiss immigrants (Jewish and non-Jewish) from the mid-nineteenth to the mid-twentieth centuries reads like an international Who's-Who of overachievers, job generators, and breakthrough scientists. In 1858, Henri Nestlé left Germany to work in the pharmacy of another Swiss immigrant; during his apprenticeship he first began to toy with improved infant food formulas that were not only to form the basis of one of the world's largest conglomerates, but would save countless lives. He was spurred on by the work of two American brothers, Charles and Henry Page, who in 1866 had founded a condensed milk factory in the small Swiss town of Cham. The development illustrates the important "critical mass" feature seen in places such as America's Silicon Valley, where the presence of so many bright minds, finance capital, and new ideas becomes a synergistic, self-generating boom.

In the same period, Brown Boveri of Baden was founded by a Scottish engineer and a German financier. Today, Asea-Brown-Boveri, or ABB, employs several hundred thousand workers in Switzerland and around the world. French immigrants had already brought the manufacture of muslin to Zürich in the 1690s; in the early nineteenth century the textile industry attracted more immigrants as Escher Wyss and other spinning establishments, not allowed to import equipment, brought spinning experts from Britain and the United States to develop their own. In the nineteenth and twentieth centuries, Switzerland proved an attractive haven for such diverse intellectuals as Victor Hugo, Madame de Stael, Gibbon, and Albert Einstein.

In flipping through five or six centuries in as many pages, we run the risk of missing some important intervening developments, rather like a time-lapse photographer snapping a shot only once a generation. For the purpose of understanding Switzerland, however, it is enough to describe the *dynamic* that was at work over those many years—and to provide some examples and anecdotes that illustrate the basic historical movement.

One danger is that we make the development of democracy in Switzerland seem easier than it really was. There were, after all, jealous and powerful princes who would have loved to seize control of the chokepoint in the Alps. For all the advantages geography gave to the Swiss in defending their mountain redoubt, geography also placed most of the country's arable land and natural living space in a valley wide open to French and German attack, and naturally drawn toward those lands by many habits of language and culture. Swiss toleration for religious differences seems simple looking back, but then, so does most history when we can look back on it. For four centuries, the Swiss were as divided between competing religious ideas as the rest of Europe, and, indeed, gave birth to two of the more searching critics of Catholicism, Zwingli and Calvin, the West has seen.

Before we begin to survey the operation of Swiss institutions in the present and recent past, it is important to examine some of the difficulties they had to overcome to arrive at their present state.

4

Geodeterminism

"Switzerland," avers Alfred Defago, "was made for federalism and democracy." Defago is the Swiss ambassador to the United States and the former head of one of Switzerland's broadcasting services, a sophisticated communicator and politician.

He leans back in a slim, comfortable chair—ostentation, no; functionality, yes; he is Swiss—and continues. "I doubt our institutions could simply be copied and replicated elsewhere with the same results. We are a small democracy with certain geographic features, cultural pluralism, and political consensus-building. Others would not enjoy these traditions and this landscape."

This is vintage Swiss: Keep it small. It works for us, but we make no large claims. But before my opportunity to object—"Mr. Ambassador, without copying the Swiss system wholesale, surely other countries can adapt your institutions, and profit from your experience"—Defago seems to recollect himself. He is speaking to an American—and one interested in the historical overlaps and parallels of "the Sister Republics," as the United States and Switzerland have been called.[1] Defago rocks forward.

"Then again, I guess what we did is more or less copy the U.S. constitution." He is right: The Swiss constitution of 1848 was largely based on the U.S. constitution of 1789. (The U.S. constitution in turn drew on the Swiss experience, while avoiding some of the perceived pitfalls by setting up a more coherent central government than the Swiss enjoyed at that time.)

"Then, Mr. Ambassador, perhaps the system can be exported—provided it is copied from the U.S. and not Switzerland."

Defago relaxes into the smile of both an intellectual patriot, who appreciates his own country being understood, and a satisfied politician, who likes to see a problem solved with a turn of phrase.

The Swiss have benefited of a number of accidents of nature that make them seem, at times, a kind of geographically chosen people. Mountains and ridges offer a defensive redoubt. The Alpine passes make it a natural transportation node, and therefore, a cultural and economic one as well. It would be wrong to infer, however, that Switzerland has enjoyed an "uninterrupted... peace and happiness," as a *Baltimore Gazette* correspondent gushed in 1788.

This is a common mistake, repeated by visitors in each of the last seven centuries. "The entire people," as an English merchant put it during the Thirty Years War (1618–1648), "seem blessed" with a "felicity ordained from the mountains themselves." This geodeterminism is seductive because it has some truth. Nowhere else in the world, perhaps, is one so aware of the role the land must have played in human activities as in Switzerland. And Switzerland, while by no means always affluent, has traditionally enjoyed a balanced development in which extremes of rich and poor are rare. These facts are abetted by the Swiss, with their self-minimizing temperament: They would rather point to nature or fate as explanations for the country's achievements, than their own skill or that of their ancestors.

The result can be to sell short what has been achieved by statesmanship, leading us to overestimate the forces of nature, and underestimate the potential for human action.

The constitution of 1848 is one example. Its basic arrangements survive today, a tribute to the political acumen of the framers, who had to deal with religious, social, and economic conflicts against a backdrop of foreign meddling in Swiss affairs and a general European revolution. It was not, however, written by rivers or mountains, but by men. If we think in terms of geographic predestination, then we may miss valuable lessons.

The view of Switzerland as a merely fortunate accident of geography, a sort of historical boutique, is simply inaccurate.

One obvious barrier for Switzerland is geography itself—something that cuts in different directions. To whatever extent the Swiss landscape tends to impose a certain natural federalism, it also frustrates Swiss nationhood. Imagine trying to unite these different communities of aggressively independent farmers and merchants, especially when ties of religion, language, and power were often tempting them to turn outside.

For purposes of review, we can group these entropic forces into several broad categories: economic factors, using the term broadly to cover matters of domestic policy and politics; military-strategic elements; and religious divisions, including those between Christian sects since the Reformation, but also those within the Catholic Church both before and after it.

If we look at some defining moments of Swiss development, we nearly always find one of these factors present—usually two or three. It then becomes clear that Switzerland came about because human ingenuity was able, at critical times, to surmount large difficulties

Economics are at the heart of Swiss political development, and not always a positive factor. The potential for passage through the Gotthard and other passes was only economically relevant with the effort of the people of Uri to build the Devil's Bridge. Even this act of community entrepreneurship, however, was only necessary, not sufficient, for significant commercial traffic. Someone would have to supply money, security, lodging, and other services critical to a marketplace and a highway. And provision of these, while in the interest of Uri and indeed all the cantons, was rendered difficult by the very federalism, independence, and do-it-my-way spirit of the Swiss.

As the historian Arthur Mojonnier noted, even after the Napoleonic occupation ended in 1815, the route to and through the Devil's Bridge was a tangled thicket of regulations, special charges, and other expensive complexities.[2] Linen manufacturers of St. Gallen often sent their wares all the way through Strassburg to reach the Western parts of Switzerland, rather than across their own country. Foreign companies in the 1820s and 1830s sometimes bypassed the country entirely, at a cost of many added days, rather than pass through a number of its competing twenty-two cantons. A piece of cloth, cheese, or other item passing through the Gotthard was liable to some 400 taxes on the transport of goods. The Ticino alone, one Swiss canton, managed to apply thirteen taxes and tolls. At each stop, merchants had to take their goods, unload them, and allow customs bureaucrats to weigh them. The cantons grew vexed at one another, each one wishing its neighbors would leave the revenue collection to it and stop clogging the road with competing taxes; trade and tax wars were set off as each one tried to dream up new charges.

Taxes weren't the only problem. "Money," as one historian put it, "was a mess." Before 1848 each canton, many cities, and even some ecclesiastical lords had the right to issue currency. There were more than fifty such authorities in Switzerland, producing an estimated 700 different pieces of gold, silver, and other types of coinage. The only saving grace for the Swiss was that their own little currencies were of such limited use that most cantons by statute, and the entire country as a matter of practice, tended to accept the French franc and écu as legal tender. From time to time, the currencies of Bavaria and Württemberg were also accepted. Still, acceptance of the franc, along with associated free trade and other privileges extended to France, created other problems, making the Swiss economy more vulnerable to the swings in value of the French economy and monetary authorities.

Money and taxes were only two of the most visible downsides of radical federalism. Legal codes were distinct from canton to canton and even town to town. Some descriptions make the cantons sound like an accumulation of speed traps and rigged courts. Cloth was measured according to more than five dozen units of length; liquid volume stated in some eighty-one different measures. There were, of course, four languages, and many different subdialects of the most common, German.

France's invasion of Switzerland in 1798 suggests weaknesses in the Swiss position of a military and strategic nature. Perhaps just as impressive, the French occupied the country until 1815. These facts illustrate the fact that not all geography works in favor of Swiss independence.

The French made substantial preparations, illustrating some of Switzerland's vulnerabilities as a multicultural hub. For months prior to the invasion, the Directorate flooded Western Switzerland with pamphlets, news-papers, and speaker-agitators, urging its comrades to take arms against the aristocrats, particularly in the frankly oligarchic cities of Lausanne, Bern, and Fribourg. These arguments played to an already strong and fast-growing com-munity of expatriate dissidents and Swiss fellow travelers—a subsidized Fifth Column—present since the run-up to the 1789 revolution. "The Swiss loved these fugitives," a French nobleman living in England remarked as the jug-gernaut pointed East. "Now they will be reunited."

The campaign began on an inauspicious note when several regiments from the city of Geneva, assigned by the Swiss Diet or cantonal congress to aid in the defense of Bern, declined to take an oath of allegiance to the confedera-tion. There were few or no outward demonstrations against *l'ancien regime de Suisse*, but many of the people were lukewarm in their support. French troops marched down off the heights West of Switzerland and into Vaud, proclaim-ing liberation. History books barely even speak of the battles in this war. Some Swiss troops tried to make a stand and were out-maneuvered; many dissolved as units and returned home; a small number, perhaps two or three percent, joined the French. The canton of Vaud fell without a shot being fired, and on January 28, the French occupied the important city of Lausanne with-out resistance. In late February, French forces occupied most of Fribourg and the canton of Bern; General Schauenburg entered Solothurn on March 5. On March 14, after being issued an ultimatum by Brune without a fight, the Great Council of Bern abdicated. Zürich and Basel did not fight, and though proud Schwyz and later Nidwalden made a stand, it was not a memorable one. On March 28, Lecarlier, commander-in-chief of the occupation forces, could in-form the French government that he had assumed "the full powers of govern-ment over the whole of Helvetia." By May, he was generally in control.

Where were the country's unassailable mountains, not to mention the fight-ing spirit of its militia, as the French strolled across Switzerland?

One answer is that while most of the country in terms of square miles consists of mountains and is highly defensible, the bulk of the population and economic output are located in the crescent-shaped valley that runs across the Northwest, from Geneva across to Zürich. One need only seize control of perhaps 20 percent of Swiss territory to have control of most of its population and economy.

Another answer can be found in the cultural affinity between Switzerland and France. This is particularly evident in the French-speaking region in the West, but extends East by tradition and psychology. For hundreds of years Swiss mercenaries, largely from the poorer German-speaking cantons in the center and East, earned a small fortune from the kings of France by offering their services on the country's behalf. That the communities could be tempted into this sort of arrangement is another illustration of Switzerland's some-times precarious position; the country is always vulnerable not only to the cultural pull of the great nations around it, but to economic and military manipulation.

Switzerland was also somewhat divided by political and economic class. In fits and starts but for centuries, the cities of Bern, Zürich, and Geneva had undertaken gradual political reforms to enfranchise the burghers and the guildmen. In the early and middle eighteenth century, however, this progress in voting rights, due process, and other democratic reforms had been halted and, in many cases, reversed. When Russian and Austrian troops marched in from the East and South, they were treated as forces of freedom. There was, however, a substantial minority, the disenfranchised and the radical, who welcomed the French invasion. And the majority, while certainly patriotic, was lukewarm.

Switzerland was not sharply divided, but it was not unified to the extent required for tiny countries to resist large-scale invasions. The Swiss lacked the fighting spirit they showed when the mountain men resisted the Austrians in the fourteenth century and booted them across the Rhine in the fifteenth century; the people did not fear and loathe the French leadership as they would Bismarck in 1870 and Hitler in 1935. The Diet barely began military preparations even though it had debated defense improvements at almost every session from 1793 on.

Geographically, Switzerland was and is divided and small. Three distinct language and economic zones are separated by mountains as if they were a television dinner tray. "The natural conditions," as James Bryce writes, "might seem most unfavorable to the creation of a State or even of a nation. The Swiss people ¼ dwell on different sides of a gigantic mountain mass ¼ separated from one another by craggy heights and widespread snow-fields. [Given the easy crossing at many points of the Rhein,] no natural boundary marks them off from the Germans to the north and east, from the French to the west, and from the Italians to the south."

By virtue of its historic tolerance, and its relatively recent social consen-sus, Switzerland is often wrongly perceived as having missed the religious quarrels of the rest of Europe. "The cantons of Switzerland," as the Reverend John Witherspoon wrote during the American Constitutional Convention, "have never broken among themselves, though there are some of them Protes-tants, and some of the Papists, by public establishment."

In fact, Switzerland has suffered its share of religious divisions. From the intra-Catholic disputes of the Middle Ages through the strife of the Reforma-tion, Switzerland sometimes escaped the fury of the times—it came nearly unscathed through the Thirty Years War—but more often did not. Figure 4.1 lists just some of the large-scale religious conflicts experienced by Switzer-land.

Table 4.1

Swiss Religious Wars

1525 Repression of the Anabaptists	Religious leader Huldrych Zwingli declares the Anabaptists, who favor "full acceptance" of the Sermon on the Mount, are "heretics," and the city of Zürich begins a repression. Anabaptists are expelled, drowned, hung, and burned.
1531 Battle of Kappel	Catholic cantons, with outside backing from Austria, defeat a force of Protestant forces from Zürich. In this battle the Swiss religious leader Zwingli—a pacifist—fought for the Zürich forces and was killed along with 500 compatriots. (October 11, 1531).
1586–89 Civil War Plans; Savoy hits Geneva	Central cantons form an alliance with Spain. Catholic Savoy attempts to take over Protestant (Calvin) Geneva. (Catholic cantons opposed.) "Civil war was probably averted," the Catholic historian Hillaire Belloc argues, "only by the defeat of the Spanish Armada" in 1588.
1618–1649 Wars over Graubünden	Reformed Synod of Bergün condemns local pacts with Spain, Austria, aimed at preserving Catholic predominance. Prominent Catholics are driven from their homes; some killed. In July 1620, Catholic bands retaliate, murdering 500 persons. Spain, Austria, France, and Venice intervene, with major engagements in 1621, 1622, 1624, 1633, 1635, and 1637. A "permanent peace" was signed in 1649.
1633–1634 Swedish intrusions	Zürich (according to Catholic cantons) allows Swedish troops, on their way to battle the forces of the Kaiser, safe passage through Thurgau. Catholic cantons demand resistance. Reformed cantons make plans for a war, the Catholic cantons allege, at Zürich in January 1634. The Swiss Diet (May 21, 1634) approves a plan for internal peace and neutrality vis-à-vis Sweden. This statecraft, according to Gagliardi, "saved the country," and leads to conclusion of the *Defensionale* of Wyl (1647).
1655–1656 First Villmergen War	Schwyz confiscates properties by citizens converting to Protestant faith, beheads others, and demands return of subjects who fled to Zürich. Zürich (aided by Bern) mobilizes 25,000-man army against 6,000 Catholics, but the confrontation dissolves. Erupting again, the two forces meet at Villmergen on January 24, 1656. The forces of the mountain Cantons crush the Bernese forces (backed by Zürich), and craft an agreement confirming cantonal sovereignty for confessional matters (Baden, March 7).

1667–1681 French Comté	Louis grabs the French Comté without strong resistance. Switzerland's newly federalized war council tries to organize a response, but too late. The cantons renew the *Defensionale* in 1668 and briefly win the return of the region to Spain. But France re-enters in 1674. As the War Council contemplates retaliation (1675–76), Schwyz, then other cantons, withdraw (1679) from the *Defensionale*.
1701–1735 Expulsion of the Anabaptists	Bern, Zürich, and other cities engage in large-scale expulsion of Anabaptists. Some Anabaptists are compensated, but others suffer property confiscation and harassment. Bern hires Ritter & Company to assist the effort, paying a fee for every *Taüfer* Ritter could dispatch to America or Canada; there was a bonus for paupers.
1712 Baden and the Freiämter	Zürich and Bern combine against five of the central cantons to fight over administrative control of Baden and the so-called *Freiämter*. "The Swiss lack only one thing," the Swiss historian Abraham Ruchat comments. "They are not united ... and the cause of their division is religion."
1732–1768 Geneva: Burning Rousseau	Geneva, Swiss historian Johannes von Müller commented, was "nearly always" troubled in this period. Peasant demands focused on economics but had a sectarian edge given the Calvinism of the ruling aristocracy. In 1738 the city gave in to many of their demands. The ruling class attempted a reversal in 1760, and held a celebrated burning of the books of Jean-Jacques Rousseau in front of the Geneva Council House. The burghers again revolted, and though Bern and Zürich sent aid to their fellow Protestant elites, the oligarchs retreated in 1768.
1798–1815 French Occupation	Only partly religious, but there were confessional and clerical issues at stake. These strengthen after Napoleon declares the Protectorate Constitution in 1803. (See text.)
1802 Federalist Revolution	Due to the treaty system of Lunéville and Amiens, French troops had to evacuate Switzerland in 1802. Immediatly afterward a federalist popular revolt swept away the centralist government left by the French and installed a government at Schwyz. Napoleon Bonaparte sent his troops a second time and had them stay until 1804 to stabilize his clever adaptation of the newly federalist Swiss system, the so-called Mediation of 1803.
1847 Sonderbund War (Swiss Civil War)	Civil war between Catholic cantons, which formed their own "defense league" against alleged intrusions against cantonal rights to allow Jesuit instruction in the schools, and Protestant cantons opposed to what they term *de facto* secession. (See text.)

A recurring theme of these conflicts is the presence of, indeed manipulation by, foreign interests. Switzerland's geopolitical position at once excites the interest of these powerful states, and, at the same time, exerts a certain cultural pull on the people toward them.

This is not to say that Switzerland was overcome by these difficulties; this would be geodeterminism merely redirected. The Swiss were able to conquer their challenges, for the most part. The point is, they did, in fact, have to conquer them.

The *Defensionale* of 1647—which helped cement Switzerland's independence and growing prosperity from 1600 to 1800—was written and concluded not by rivers but by men, and approved by a referendum-like popular assembly in the *Landsgemeinde* cantons. Likewise the declaration of neutrality in Baden on May 3, 1764, despite its flaws, was a helpful instrument and guide to the future in helping the Swiss avoid some of the entanglements of European affairs. But it was a man-made instrument.

All of these factors—economic, political, and religious fissures, abetted by foreign meddling—came together in 1847 in Switzerland's civil war, the Sonderbund War.

The war was rooted not only in Swiss internal factors, but in the effort of European statesmen to build stability after the ravages of the Revolution and Napoleon. European maneuvering to control, influence, or simply divvy up Switzerland began as early as the first grand coalition. In 1813, as the troops of Austria and Russia swept across Switzerland, all the powers had ideas about the proper shape of a new regime. Friedrich Wilhelm of Prussia disliked Swiss liberal tendencies, but was concerned about French influence of any sort. Even with Napoleon gone, maps, institutions, and sympathies had been rewritten in the generation since 1789, and he feared a strong France. Tsar Alexander I of Russia felt neither great sympathy nor enmity toward the Swiss, but as a practical matter, favored a buffer state against the French dominated by him and his fellow royalists. Britain felt a certain natural sympathy for the Swiss as a democratic republic and a victim of continental meddling. Robert Peel was serving as Ambassador to Bern for Palmerston's government and developed a deep respect for the Swiss. The British also viewed a strong Switzerland—armed and neutral—as a bulwark against aggression in any of several directions. More than most of the other diplomats, Peel and Palmerston understood that Switzerland's high ideals and democratic institutions were helpful, if not essential, to the country's ability to play this role.

Animating and shaping the approach of the great powers for the first half of the nineteenth century, however, was Metternich of Austria. Though seen as a dispassionate diplomat of the chessboard school, Metternich was anything but cool and analytical regarding the Swiss. His memoirs, private correspondence, and accounts of his conversations with the British suggest a contempt bordering on fury. He loathed the way this "Germanic people" showed historic sympathy to the French. He disdained the "former strength" of Swiss arms in the divided nation and was vexed that the Swiss were not more grateful for their liberation from Napoleon by the Austrians. Perhaps, too, like a suitor somewhat scorned, Metternich knew that Switzerland's ancient mistrust of the Hapsburg Empire to the East had never really disappeared.

Above all, though, and simply put, Metternich seethed at the Swiss democracy. He loathed its toleration of intellectuals and dissidents—loathed it, and feared it. He blamed Switzerland, in part, for harboring some of the revolutionists that had brought chaos to Europe for thirty years. He seems to have been determined, even passionate, to bring this mysterious and uppity renegade—"perhaps the greatest threat to peace in Europe" —to heel.

Insisting that others abstain from involvement in Austria's internal affairs, Metternich meddled liberally in Swiss domestic politics. In 1830, the Swiss made efforts to revise their constitution in a manner that would have strengthened the central government but, naturally, reduced somewhat the autonomy of the original Waldstätte. Metternich growled that respect for Swiss neutrality was dependent upon the constitutional state of affairs as of 1815, strongly suggesting armed intervention. He encouraged the Catholic cantons of *Innerschweiz* to toy with the usual special leagues in 1830 and again in 1845. When the Swiss declined a French demand that they extradite Prince Louis Napoleon, Austria and Russia encouraged the French to mobilize 25,000 troops. The Swiss prepared for battle. War was avoided only when Louis Napoleon voluntarily left Switzerland in 1838.

By 1845, developments within Switzerland had the country on a path to civil war. In the canton of Aargau, newly molded after the French occupation and precariously balanced between Protestant and Catholic, Reformed forces gained the upper hand and began demanding taxation, regulation, and expulsion of the monasteries. Nearby, Luzern and other cantons wanted to accept the offer of the Jesuits to provide teaching in the schools, based on both sectarian grounds and economic: the Jesuits cost far less to maintain than regular public school teachers. Under the constitution and the practices of many years, both efforts were probably within the legal competence of the cantons in question, but they were resented by opponents. Both sides began to get jumpy. In 1844 and again in 1845, radicals from the Reformed cantons formed a small private militia and attempted an assault on Luzern. The threat was marginal but the fears and suspicion aroused were not.

As fears mounted, the cantonal governments began to take preemptive action, while the relatively weak federal government was paralyzed, in effect divided within. The Protestant cantons formed an economic league that had no formal religious purposes but had strong anti-Catholic overtones. Uri, Schwyz, Luzern, and other central Catholic cantons formed a mutual defense league, the Sonderbund. The Bund aimed narrowly at protecting their distinctive religious preferences. More broadly, the agreement was viewed as a secessionist arrangement by the other cantons that violated the spirit of the confederation. In effect, the Sonderbund was a Catholic version of the Protestant alliances already aligned against it. Elements of the old rural peasants versus urban elites were involved, along with economic issues (such as taxes) and regional disputes (very roughly, Austria and France with the Catholics, versus Britain and Germany with the Protestants).

While all this was going on, the political and economic power of Switzerland was gradually shifting back to the cities, thanks largely to the appearance of steam engines and other advances. Center-left coalitions favoring a stronger federal union won elections in both Zürich and Bern. Politicians in the Diet realized there would soon be enough votes to pass a measure discussed in 1846 and early 1847, mandating the dissolution of the Sonderbund. The vote took place in July 1847, with Swiss military leaders on both sides already making plans for armed conflict. The confederation chose Henri Dufour to head its army and, on November 4, passed a resolution instructing him to bring the rebel cantons into compliance by force of arms.

The war itself, viewed in retrospect, was anticlimactic. The cities were larger, better armed, and better prepared. The forest cantons wanted their independence, but the invaders were not foreign enemies; in this war, they were marching not against French or Austrian troops, but against other Swiss. The federal forces under Dufour won a pair of relatively minor skirmishes and a truce was called before the end of the year. The business lasted twenty-six days and produced 435 wounded and 128 killed in battle. If estimates of participation by different immigrant groups are accurate, there were probably more Swiss killed in the American Civil War than in their own. Dufour won the appreciation of the rebellious cantons, and the respect of his own side, by insisting that there be no reprisals, lootings, or other such acts. "The men we are fighting," Dufour reminded his troops, "are Swiss."

The war did not end without a final spasm of interventionism. Twice in December the continental powers—France, Austria, Prussia, and Russia— wrote to the Diet expressing their concern and threatening to intervene. Metternich reasserted Austria's view that the peace of 1815 gave them the right to do so. The Swiss politely informed the powers, to the bemusement of Peel and the British, that they would need no assistance putting their affairs in order as the civil war had been ended. In less than a year, Metternich himself was ousted in a civil coup and became a refugee, as the revolutions of 1848 swept Europe. The Swiss, meanwhile, had drafted a new constitution, strengthening the federal government but wisely conciliating the defeated forest cantons.

Swiss today are mildly proud of their civil war. For although it followed upon and was sparked by abuses and errors, it also removed those abuses. In fact, the Swiss civil war of 1847 was the catalyst for the new constitution, a constitution that finally reconciled the Swiss love of cantonal and community autonomy with a coherent (but limited) central government. The basic framework survives today, a tribute to those who were able to construct it under the press of domestic religious quarrels, economic and cultural debates, and the interference of foreign states.

It is fruitless to debate whether men govern forces, or forces govern men. Obviously, the two act and react upon one another; history in some sense is merely this reciprocal action. Geography did not write the Bundesbrief or unite the forest cantons with Zürich and Bern; it never wrote a single constitution. Yet it played a role in the development of Switzerland.

Perhaps the highest tribute one can give to statesmen is to say that they conformed their actions intelligently to these factors—accepting the material they are given, but shaping it too. If the design works, we may learn from it.

Notes

1.   The phrase was probably coined by Johann Rodolph Valltravers, councilor of Bienne, in a letter to Benjamin Franklin dated 14 April 1778. An excellent book on this subject is published by the Library of Congress: See James H. Hutson, *The Sister Republics: Switzerland and the United States from 1776 to the Present.*
2.   In E. T. Rimli (ed.), *Histoire de la Confédération*, Stauffacher, 1967.

Part 3

Institutions

5

Constitution

Albert Blaustein, the great scholar of world constitutions, once devised a simple and intriguing method for assessing them at a glance. According to Blaustein's rule of thumb, the shorter a constitution, the better it probably is. Corrupted polities tend to cram such documents full of sham "rights," complex rules, and pompous pronouncements. The constitutions of such countries, like the tombs of the self-important Egyptian kings, often run to 50,000 words. By contrast, the constitutions of the United States, Germany, and other successful republics tend to be shorter and more limited. Powers are distributed and denied. Popular liberties are stated or implied, and then followed. Naturally there are caveats and exceptions, but this is a very fast way to form a general impression of a country's fundamental law and government.

The Swiss constitution of the late twentieth century didn't perform terribly on this "Blaustein test," but at some 15,000 words, or about sixty-five pages of normal-sized type, it didn't achieve the economy we normally attribute to the Swiss.[1] Unlike a recent Asian constitution, it contains no elaborate listing of the rights of tenants in high-rise buildings. Nor, as distinct from the constitution of Cuba, are the people guaranteed progressive and inspired leadership; and the civil liberties of left-handed persons, generously shielded in Nigeria, are not pledged protection. The Swiss constitution in place until January 2000, however, did "encourage the growing of table-fruit," and provide for a tax of "1.9 percent on radio and television activities of a non-commercial character." It also compelled the civil authorities to "make sure that every deceased person can have a decent burial," and, importantly, established "the total tax rate for beer" at "the level of 31 December 1970."

The picture suggested of a highly encumbered document, though, is misleading. The constitution's core sections, such as those outlining the powers of and limits on the different branches and providing for election to the various federal offices, occupied little more than 10 percent of the document. This portion of the old Swiss constitution, in about forty brief articles, comprised perhaps 2,000 words and was comparable in brevity and clarity to the

American Constitution—on which it is partly modeled. The articles referenced above, on everything from the prohibition of absinthe to federal authority to regulate "the slaughter at abbatoirs and other methods of killing animals," came under the headings "general provisions" and "transitional provisions." These made up some ninety or one-hundred longer articles and took up more than 85 percent of the document.

Such provisions were enacted not as part of the basic governing structure when the constitution was written in 1848 and revised (but with many key provisions left unchanged) in 1874 and 1999. Rather, they became part of Switzerland's fundamental law by public referendum over the last 125 years. Under a quirk in the system, citizens are allowed to "initiate" a constitutional change by collecting 100,000 signatures, leading to a vote of the people by referendum. (To take effect, the referendum must achieve a double majority of the popular vote as a whole, and within the individual twenty-three cantons.) By contrast, the right to pass on regular laws is limited to challenging certain laws already passed by parliament in a referendum—mere laws can only be *initiated* by the parliament, but can be challenged with as few as 50,000 signatures. The Swiss also enjoy a right to petition, and to have their petition answered by officials. The result is that matters of policy that would normally be mere statutes are often the object to constitutional amendment. It is sometimes easier to change the constitution by this manner, despite the large majorities required, than it would be to persuade a bare majority of legislators to enact the same change. That this is the case—and probably would be in many other democracies—may itself be instructive about the state of our politics.

The length of the constitution, and its forays into seeming arcana, is also an indication of the extent to which the Swiss people have been able to shape the fundamental law of their own land. The accretion, while troublesome (the Swiss have discussed making initiative possible for federal laws, and likely will in the coming years) is also suggestive of the openness of the system to the action of citizens as individuals and groups. The working of the initiative and referendum process is of sufficient importance to merit its own examination later in the book. It must, however, be discussed in considering the working of the whole as well, given its importance to the whole operating spirit of the regime and its institutions.

Naturally, the amendment process is only one of many important revisions in the constitution. It was not even a major controversy when the basic ideology of the current constitution took shape in 1848, following the civil war; initiative and referendum at the national level came about late in the nineteenth century, during and following the rewriting of the constitution in 1874.

As if to improve their performance under the Blaustein Test, or perhaps simply out of a desire to consolidate and perfect, the country drafted a revision of its constitution in the late 1990s, which took effect early in the year 2000. The new constitution, in the assessment of its framers and advocates, made no significant changes over the old. Certainly, on a structural level, this appeared to be so. The new constitution, at about forty-five pages of single-spaced type, achieved the same ends as the older, longer version. It retained some of the penchant for unusually specific provisions seen often in the old, such as a passage providing the Confederation may "encourage the variety and quality of cinematographic works offered" (article 71) or a clause "on avoiding abusive notices of termination" (article 109). For the most part, however, these provisions were moved into a final section of "transitory provisions" that will drop off the basic document as soon as they are enacted in the form of laws per se (Title 6, Chapter 2—article 191). "These provisions," as former President Dr. Kurt Furgler noted in an interview, "are more properly matters of regular legislation. The Swiss had always recognized this, and, being Swiss, have a desire to revise their fundamental law so as to put things in their proper place."

More controversial was a statement of "Social Goals" contained in article 41. Among the notable provisions, "every person shall benefit from necessary health care." As well, "every person looking for housing shall find... appropriate housing at reasonable conditions." On the other hand, "every person capable of working shall sustain himself or herself through working under fair and adequate conditions." Although this section of the constitution makes clear that this listing of goals implies no "direct subjective right" to receive them from the state, the wary Swiss, particularly in some of the central cantons, wondered whether the elaboration of social goals, albeit brief, might lead to subtle changes in their political fabric.

Indeed, the debate over the new constitution, in the words of Bernhard Ehrenzeller, "focused largely not on any of the positive provisions, but on the document's preamble and purpose sections." Ehrenzeller, a professor at the University of St. Gallen and adviser to former President Raoul Kohler, was part of a team of scholars that worked with Kohler to craft the new constitution and win support for it. One offending section of the preamble called for "solidarity and openness towards the world." This might seem an unobjectionable phrase, particularly since it follows a commitment to "liberty, democracy, [and] independence." To some Swiss, however, it seemed an erosion of Switzerland's tradition of neutrality, and its reticence toward involvement in international organizations that might compromise neutrality. Did the new phrase imply Switzerland's eventual entry into the United Nations, or even the European Union? "We certainly didn't intend to insert such a meaning," Ehrenzeller said, "and I don't think it's the right reading of the constitution. But, it became a controversy." Regardless of this original intent of the founders, a lively opposition formed in the weeks leading up to the vote on the new constitution. Swiss in nine cantons voted against the new design. Nevertheless, in April of 1999, the Swiss voted by a 59-41 percent margin to approve the work of the new framers.

The most striking aspect of the Swiss design, of course, is its use of direct democracy. Almost equally different, however, compared to other constitutions of the world, is the new constitution's federalism—the extent to which rights and prerogatives are delegated to the cantons and communities. Indeed, to the Swiss, such matters are not merely "delegated," but "reserved," having been retained by the local units of government all along.

Federalism was central to the framers during the constitutional sessions of 1848. The issue was how to create a stronger federal core without driving the independent-minded cantons to another civil war. Their first remedy was to follow the American Constitution, with its blend of states' rights and new federal powers. The opening paragraphs mention each of the "sovereign cantons." These are sovereign wherever there is no explicit federal power to make laws. Yet the constitution also speaks in the name of "the people" of each of the cantons. It proclaims citizens of one canton citizens of Switzerland—and declares that citizens of Switzerland have those rights in any of the cantons. This incorporative language was retained and strengthened over the years. The federal constitution also contains limits on what the cantons may do even within their own constitutions. For instance, confederation's guarantee of cantonal constitutions is conditioned on the assumption that "they have been accepted by the people and can be amended whenever the majority of citizens so demand."

The confederation wisely did not place a large number of such limits on the cantons, but this one is significant and, indeed, unusually sweeping among Western democracies. The United States, for example, proclaims the federal Constitution the supreme law of the land. It does not, however, specify that state constitutions must be amendable—still less, that they must be amendable by the people. Many U.S. states, particularly in the South and the East, have no such provision, and indeed, some have no referendum or initiative process altogether. That this is one of the more stringent impositions on the cantons reveals something of the Swiss faith in popular government. Like the U.S. Constitution's Tenth Amendment, the Swiss constitution reserves all powers not specifically delegated to the confederation for its states or cantons. The Swiss have followed this tenet more strictly than the Americans. The cantons remain the largest unit of government to this day, whether measured by revenues or employees.

The Swiss cantons enjoy rights not common among the local levels of government in many Western countries. They can establish religious institutions and support them with tax money, and provide religious teaching in the public schools. There is freedom of choice for the individual worshipper, protected by the constitution. There is, however, no "wall of separation" between church and state of the kind so often spoken of in other Western democracies. The remedy for a Roman Catholic living in Bern, or a Protestant or Jew living in Schwyz, is to attend his local independent church, or move to another canton. In practice, since all the major faiths are now recognized, and the school instruction and religious content is not aggressive, this is not a major issue. It is, however, a measure of the power of the cantons that they still enjoy such autonomy. The cantons also maintain control of roads and bridges, except for a few federal roads. And, unusually, each canton establishes its own system of criminal and civil court procedure. Court decisions and police actions taken in one canton are binding upon another. The cantonal courts enjoy significant discretion and exhibit a wide variety of methods.

Most powers reserved to the cantons were, in fact, merely reserved—not "given" to them in the federal constitution, because they had been enjoyed all along. As long as these were not, in fact, reserved to the federal government, they remain the province of the sovereign cantons. Among these are many nonenumerated powers over the police, public works, and education and the schools. It is difficult for many modern Americans and Europeans to grasp the idea of dual sovereignty inherent in this. Although we have traditions and rhetoric of federalism, the practice of federalism was significantly eroded over the nineteenth and twentieth centuries. In the United States, as well, the use of "states' rights" arguments by the Southern states before the Civil War, and again in the 1950s and 1960s, to oppose some civil rights measures, has somewhat discredited the very idea of federalism. This is not to say that state government has disappeared in the United States; still less so in Germany. Few take seriously, however, the idea that these units of government are truly sovereign. In Switzerland, this concept is still held and felt strongly, particularly by Swiss over the age of fifty.

The constitution gives the federal government oversight of the army. "The army is the province of federal legislation." The cantons may continue to administer elements of their own armed forces, but they do so "under the supervision" of the confederation. No canton may maintain a standing army of more than 300 persons—nor may the confederation itself. The army is another of those Swiss institutions that requires a separate examination. We cannot understand the working of the constitution, or the balance of its design, without at least referencing it here, for it is the most national and perhaps the most nationalizing institution the Swiss have devised.

In a very general way, the operations of Swiss federalism may be summarized as follows: The framers, in 1848 and 1874, did not provide the federal government with a large number of powers. (These have been added to over the years, however, through the referendum process.) The federal government at the center has only a few powers in number—but of those, several are highly compelling and strategic. Among these are its power to decide disputes between the cantons, its power over the currency, the unitary power over the military and over decisions of war and peace, and the sole power to negotiate treaties and nearly undivided power to approve or reject them. Many more powers, in number, were retained by the cantons, and are today.

Alexis de Tocqueville anticipated this when he advised his colleagues in the French Parliament what to watch for in the unfolding constitutional debates. The Swiss federal government, Tocqueville argued, did not need to provide most or all of the goods, services, and functions of government in order to be effective. But it needed to provide some of them. In particular, it needed to provide some of them itself, in a direct intercourse with the people—instead of always acting through, and therefore somewhat at the discretion of, the cantons. The Swiss federal constitution set up several such arrangements in 1848, to which more have been added. The creation of the Swiss franc, and abolition of cantonal currencies, was certainly one. Money is a "bottom line" in so many economic and even social transactions, and sound money provides a real service to the people and the economy. The frequent elections set up by the federal constitution and its requirement of amendability for the cantonal constitutions provides another unifying source, a sociological one.

The need to prevent a too-powerful federal government was also met through indirect means. The Swiss, like the Americans, divided the powers of the federal government between branches and then, for good measure, divided the branches somewhat within themselves. Thus the executive branch in effect has not one president, but seven council members, each of whom serves a term of one year as president in rotation. Legislation must pass both houses of parliament to become law, but it needs no further signature from the executive. This check, the "veto," was thought to be unnecessary: it is carried out by the people through initiative and referendum. Similarly, while judges are certainly respected in Switzerland—perhaps more so than in the United States and Britain—they are not appointed for life. The judiciary's independence is guaranteed, first by the good faith of the legislature, and second—this factor must always be kept in mind—by the ability of the people to overturn capricious or vindictive legislation directed at the judiciary, were such legislation to pass.

Here again we see a distinctive element in the Swiss system. No less than other democracies, the Swiss have checks and balances. A larger share of them, however, tend to involve popular checks—restraints imposed by the people on political elites, rather than by one group of elites on another. The difference in spirit can be seen if we compare various provisions in the Swiss constitution with those of other democracies, as in Table 5.1 on the next page.

The Swiss regard their constitution somewhat differently than the people in other Western democracies. Some of these differences appear to be advantageous, others not so.

On the one hand, in political and even everyday discussions, it is treated with a little less reverence than in the United States. If the constitution is a holy oracle or fixed tablet in the United States, France, or Germany, in Switzerland it is more of a home medical guide. The Swiss are more used to taking the thing off the shelf and using it—possibly doing damage, sometimes do-

Table 5.1

Constitutions at a Glance: Provisions for Selected Countries

	Switzerland	Germany	France	Mexico	U.S.
Federalism					
Federal is largest government unit ($)	no	yes	yes	yes	yes
Citizenship voted at local level	yes	no	no	no	no
Legislature					
Proportional representation	yes	yes	yes	no	no
Two chambers	yes	yes	yes	yes	yes
Term limits	no	no	no	yes	no
Executive					
Direct election	no	yes	yes	yes	yes #
Veto power	no	yes	yes	yes	yes
Single executive	no	yes	yes	yes	yes
Judiciary					
Executive appoints	no	yes	yes	yes	yes
Life appointment	no	yes	yes	yes	yes
Popular Access					
Initiative @	yes	no	no	no	no @
Referendum @	yes	yes %	yes %	no	no @
Have government *answer* a petition	yes	yes	no	no	no
Primary system *	no	no	no	no &	yes

Source: "Constitutions at a Glance," research memorandum, Alexis de Tocqueville Institution, 1999. Copyright © AdTI, all rights reserved.

Notes: #—U.S. termed a direct election system for practical purposes since (1) electors have little discretion, (2) results of unit-rule at state level seldom vary from national popular vote, and (3) executive is not normally chosen by members of the legislature. @—at the federal level. %—infrequent and not mandatory for certain laws. *—not a constitutional provision unless indicated. &—Some parties in Mexico, including ruling party (PRI), plan primary system for its elections in 2000.

ing good, and in any case, having it out for use. It is treated less like an icon, and more like a tool.

On the other hand, there is a certain friendly familiarity that results from such experience. This is particularly so given the somewhat greater ease of changing the constitution in Switzerland and, more importantly, the fact that the way one changes it involves the common people to a greater extent, both at the front end and the back. In the United States, since the passage of the initial ten amendments in the Bill of Rights, the Constitution has been altered some one dozen times over two centuries and only once since World War II. The typical Swiss voter of age fifty has seen about twenty to twenty-five constitutional changes in his lifetime, and as an adult has voted on an average of more than one per year. Perhaps he even volunteered time to help support the passage of one or the defeat of another. In any case, if he is a typical Swiss, he was reading regular newspaper articles about the merits of this change or that change. In this process, implicitly, he was engaged in a kind of rolling review of his country's fundamental law. This process makes the constitution alive and the people its owners, in a more tangible way than in nearly any other country. To say this is not to comment on the wisdom or lack of wisdom of the measures themselves. It is an observation about the process and its impact upon the sociology, if you will, of the Swiss constitution as against others.

The Swiss constitution, for all its flaws, is less an object for handling only by an opaque priesthood of attorneys and officials, and somewhat more of a living document and a family member. If familiarity breeds a certain rough contempt, the overall impact appears to be a healthy, balanced respect and a greater sense of pride and participation.

Note

1.   During the work on this book, Switzerland passed a new constitution, consolidating the language of the old into a more terse document, but kept the same structure. We can expect this new document to be subject to *some* of the same accretions and alternations through the process of initiative and referendum. Hence, references to length and complexity refer to the constitution in place for most of the twentieth century, though observations about substantive provisions apply equally to the new constitution that came into force in 1999. The fact that Switzerland's whole framework of government can be so smoothly altered every few years, and even consolidated into a whole new draft, is evidence of the kind of flexibility and populism that are the Swiss constitution's defining characteristics. The fact that many of its provisions, popularly enacted, were for a time not "written" through this process does not substantially alter the character of the document.

6

Executives Branch

Unusual though they are, most Swiss political institutions can be readily categorized. Many laws are made using a device employed elsewhere only occasionally: direct democracy. The army, with few exceptions, has universal male service. The courts are businesslike; the society, if we may use a much-abused term, multicultural; the press, low-key; and the businesses are even more businesslike than the courts.

The Swiss executive is equally distinctive, but harder to characterize. It is corporate in nature. Most executive decisions are rendered by an executive council of seven members. There is a president, who chairs the meetings of the council and acts on its behalf in certain cases where a single authority may be needed. Yet a visiting king or queen is normally met at a reception by all seven members of the council. The president serves only a one-year term, elected by the others but normally in an informal (but not mandatory) rotation with the others. Even as such, he or she takes practically no actions, at least of a policy nature, as president. Rather, the seven-member board acts as one body. The votes are confidential and each member, regardless of his vote, is expected to stand by and indeed energetically defend the decision of the group.

At any meeting of the council, then—about once a week in modern times—the president is looking at a group of former and future presidents, and they look at him as a former and future energy minister, secretary of state, or other officer in one of "their" administrations. Conveniently, there are precisely seven ministries, each one filled by one member of the council: The president and vice-president continue to run one of the ministries during their term. When asked recently what would happen if the Swiss decided they needed eight cabinet agencies or, say, ten council members, a Swiss diplomat smiled at me and said, "Right now, we have seven councilors and seven ministries, so it works rather well." Thus, the cabinet reshufflings are among the most frequent in the modern world, rivaling Italy or Russia. But they take place on a schedule, every December, and with many of the changes preordained. The Swiss executive branch is a little bit chaos, a little bit minuet.

One might say that "the Swiss have no chief executive," as political scientist Oswald Sigg has written. At the least, one is reminded of the scene in Monty Python's "Holy Grail" in which the peasant Dennis attempts to explain the workings of his "anarcho-syndicalist commune," with its quaint aroma of nineteenth-century socialism. King Arthur, befuddled and increasingly impatient, keeps asking, "But where is your lord?"

Members of the executive council are not chosen directly by the people—here the Swiss system departs from its usual populism—but by the two houses of parliament meeting in joint session. The parliament may choose anyone it likes under the constitution for the executive council and thus, as a future president. In practice, though, the matter is more complicated. Under an unwritten arrangement going back many decades, the "magic formula," a series of guidelines for selection that work somewhat like a quota—and somewhat not like a quota. For instance, it is thought desirable to have at least one person on the seven-member council to represent one of the three national languages: Italian, French, and Swiss. As well, each of the three largest cantons—Zürich, Berne, and Vaud—normally receives a representative. On the other hand, no canton is to enjoy two residents on the Federal Council—again by practice and tradition, but not by legal requirement.

Furthermore, each of the four largest parties customarily has an assigned number of seats: two seats for the Radical Democrats (which is actually a centrist or center-left party), two for the Christian Democrats, two for the Social Democrats, and one for Swiss People's Party. None of this is a matter of constitutional or even legal formula, though. Most of this web of understandings is not even written down, except in the sense that it has been discussed much since evolving—parts of the agreement, such as the need for a balance of languages, going back to 1848.

The formula for the parties has inhered since 1959, despite the ebb and flow of certain parties since. At the start, it probably underrepresented the Christian Democrats and Radical Democrats; it may now overrepresent them.

During the replacement of two federal councilors in 1999, which it was my privilege to attend by invitation of the parliament, there was much speculation in the galleries about the possibility that the Radicals (the equivalent of the Christian Democrats in Europe, the Tories in England, or the Republicans in the U.S.) might lose one of their traditional seats. Ultimately the party held onto its seats, in part by the device of nominating two young women to fill the two posts. The Swiss are no less eager than others to advance qualified women to such posts, given their desire to be and to appear to be fair on questions of gender. The Swiss, indeed, may be more keen to do so, as women were only given the vote in national elections in 1971. In any case, the magic formula was clearly under stress, but this time, it held.

It is a measure of the discipline of the Swiss voters and their politicians that such an arrangement could long endure even were it a binding, legal contract. Here, we are talking only about a handshake, a verbal promise, that has been honored by dozens of politicians over four decades.

Not only the composition of the Federal Council, but also its workings, are remarkable. The members meet in a "respectful, even collegial manner," according to Kurt Furgler, a distinguished former Federal Council member and the former president of Switzerland. "I cannot tell you we did not disagree, or that the disagreements were not, on rare occasions, highly unpleasant. But they were no worse, and probably better, than the other political bodies and meetings I have been a part of." We must remember that this particular arrangement would seem to be a highly combustible one. This "cabinet" does not consist of members of a single party nor does it have such a party or even unified philosophy at the core. The cabinet members were not appointed by the president; there is no person or even unified office to whom they owe their loyalty. Instead we find members of four competing parties, covering a wide portion of the ideological spectrum—with linguistic, religious, and other differences thrown in for good measure. It would seem, on the surface, to be as much a very exclusive senate, or council of lords, as an executive.

After reaching its decisions and voting (in private) on the results, the members of the Federal Council join in supporting and explaining the policy to the public as one body. They do not take sides against one another regarding a decision thus made. Naturally nuances of difference may emerge when discussing ongoing issues and problems, but even these are rare and are carried on in a constructive, not a bitterly partisan, tone. There would be little to gain from this, since the next election will not cause a revolution in the composition of the executive, and there is little need for it, since policies that are not in line with the popular will are inevitably overturned or adjusted anyway.

Only a few times have the voting results from a national council meeting leaked out in the press—generally close decisions on a 4–3 vote, on highly sensitive issues such as genetic research, abortion, and welfare reform. The editors of the major Swiss papers who met with me said that they have never spiked a story with such information out of sheer patriotism, but neither do they press their reporters to come up with such stories.

"We respect the government's right to have a confidential conversation," as Konrad Stamm, the editor of *Der Bund*, one of the oldest and most distinguished papers, put it, "as they respect our right to have a confidential conversation here. And it is after all our government, the government of Switzerland."

This spirit on the part of the Swiss press—which is more vigorous than the press in America or Britain with respect to discussing policy issues, but far less interested in reporting on political conflict and personal scandal—is one of many special factors that make the executive-by-committee system workable for Switzerland, but arguably not for the United States, at least under present conditions. It is hard to imagine such a convention being respected in the U.S. media, particularly for the executive branch, though something like it is extended to other institutions, such as the Supreme Court.

One obvious danger comes in time of crisis. Without a unified executive, who is to rally the country? The proverbial horse designed in committee is known for its unworkability; but it might be added that such a horse may also take forever to be produced. This was the Swiss experience during the French Revolution, when the hapless *Vorort*[1] proved unable to mount even a serious resistance to the French invasion. The weakness of such structures is also historically evident from the experience of the United States during its Revolutionary War and the Articles of Confederation.

A review of the system in times of need provides only ambiguous evidence regarding the institution's functionality, since many factors other than the executive itself are at work at such times. From this review, however, we can derive some general principles regarding the dangers and advantages of this "non-chief executive."

Switzerland has had few domestic crises since the Sonderbund War, itself suggestive, perhaps, that public order and democracy at least can be reconciled without a powerful, unitary chief of state. Even so, some episodes of national turmoil suggest themselves for review. Among the notable domestic crises are the national strike (Switzerland's last) of 1918, the coming of the Great Depression in 1929, the Jura uprisings of 1960–1978, and the cantonal and city fiscal crisis (Geneva, Zürich, Lausanne) of the 1990s. Episodes of a foreign or military nature include the dispute with Prussia over Neuchatel in 1856–1857, World War II, and the government's handling of accusations that Swiss banks or political institutions are tainted by an association with the Nazi Holocaust.

Switzerland's national strike involved elements of both a domestic crisis and a foreign intervention. Domestic factors were foremost. Though not a combatant, Switzerland suffered economically during the war like most countries, and by 1918, shortages were becoming acute. Also like the combatants, Switzerland had been forced to adopt a "war economy." Switzerland was neutral, but an occupation by Germany or even the Allies was possible. Hence the Swiss had to maintain states of readiness and training, diverting resources to the prevention of war even as others were doing to fight it. The end of war, however, did not bring a return to "normalcy," as U.S. presidential candidate Warren G. Harding complained in 1920. Wartime tax rates remained in place, and partial rationing schemes were in effect.

At the same time the strike was not a matter of spontaneous combustion. It was supported and encouraged by Communist Russia. Having just left Switzerland in April of 1917 and taken power in the November revolution, Lenin was interested in weakening the position of capitalist countries abroad, if for no other reason than to give him a respite to consolidate his new regime in Russia. Despite the falling out between Lenin and some of the leading Swiss Communists, whom Lenin deemed too *bourgeois*, the Russian Comintern did its best to encourage the movement in Switzerland, as in Germany and other European countries after the war.

This could have been, arguably was, a crisis *d'etat*. As in Kerensky's Russia, Switzerland's institutions seemed hapless and decentralized. There was—in a sense, never is—a strong national political leader. It is hard to see, given the absence of a president with the powers usually accorded one, who could persuade radicals to temper their demands, and elites to grant some—let alone have the clout to make such a solution stick with both sides grumbling.

What the council did was to work with the natural forces of decentralization and consensus building within the labor movement and a country as a whole. Another way of saying this was, it divided and conquered.

On the first day of the strike—November 11, 1918—members of the federal council met with several of the leading labor representatives to listen to their demands. This meeting included the radicals, but was aimed more at the moderates, some of whom—such as the Action Committee in Olten—had already issued a proclamation stating their demands. Most were unexceptionable, and none of the demands by the moderates involved circumventing the democratic process. Among the chief demands of the moderates was establishment of a forty-eight-hour work week; the retirement of the national debt by a tax on capital; introduction of labor conscription; passage of a public works program; and the reformulation of the National Council by a proportional system. At the same time, some forces in the labor movement—Fritz Brupbacker, co-editor of the *Revoluzzer*—were more frankly extreme and insisted that only a takeover of the government by dictatorship of the proletariat would suffice.

Having shown that it would listen to all sides and collaborate with the nonextremists, the council, on the afternoon of November 11th, also called out the police and the militia. The council members issued a stern statement indicating that no violence would be tolerated. Members of the Soviet legation in Bern, which had been collaborating with the most extreme pockets of discontent, were escorted out of the country under heavy guard. Leading members of the parliament commenting in the press indicated a willingness to legislate many of the demands in the nine-point statement issued by the moderates, but not while under the implicit threat of mass disorder and even violence.

On the morning of November 12th, some labor leaders began to split off from the more radical elements. The radicals, nervously sensing the defections, pushed for more aggressive action in the street. But by now the partial military mobilization was complete; in Bern and Zürich, the streets filled with uniforms. Small incidents took place but the perpetrators were detained immediately.

Meanwhile, the Federal Council had convened an extraordinary session of the parliament, with both chambers convened as one body. Parliament stood firmly behind the Federal Council, repeating its willingness in a near-unanimous resolution to enact much of the labor agenda, but only once had the strike been called off. That evening, the leaders of the radical wing of the strike organizers, including the executive secretariat of the Social Democratic Party, surrendered themselves at the Federal Council. The next day they capitulated to the council's demand that they call off the strike. In a sense, their action was irrelevant; the strike was dissolving anyway as the rank-and-file workers and peasants read in their newspapers that many of their demands would be met, and that more extreme leaders were under arrest. By the afternoon of November 13, parliament was debating some of the action items. As E. Bonjour, H.S. Offler, and G.R. Potter wrote in *A Short History of Switzerland,*

> the most serious constitutional crisis of the war had been overcome. Work was resumed immediately almost everywhere. Proceedings against the strike leaders led to sentences of imprisonment varying from four weeks to six months. But reforms were carried out which the Socialist minority had demanded in vain both before and during the war.

Naturally the crisis had its particular heroes and antagonists. The most active member of the National Council during the national strike was Felix Calonder, who, appropriately enough, was serving his (only) term as president in 1918. Calonder was a popular, no-nonsense politician from Graubünden—hearty, Alpine country. He was an advocate of some of the things the socialists and the unions were demanding, having for many years advocated expansion of highway and railway systems for the southeast. He was also a thoughtful student of politics who wrote a university thesis on Swiss neutrality and the challenges to it. Among those he saw, ironically, were troubles arising out of Switzerland's status as a refugee haven—a practice that brought angry intervention from Metternich and the right in the nineteenth century. An army major, he had no qualms about crushing the strike, if need be.

It was Calonder who devised the somewhat curious order for the strikers to disband. The terse ultimatum carried little by way of legal justification nor, really, any explanation of what would happen if the order was disobeyed. It was, however, effective, especially coming from and in the name of the Bundesrat. Troops marched through the streets of Bern and Zürich in horseback and on foot with mobile artillery in tow. All the while parliament was in session, glancing approvingly at the government's carrot and stick. Fortunately for Switzerland, the strategy worked, and so Calonder can go the way of the other great Swiss presidents—remembered with a few pages in specialty biographies.

Calonder also made the wise tactical decision, in his opening speech to the special session of parliament, to separate the methods of the strikers from the economic policies they sought. Many of the latter could be discussed, he suggested; a sentiment in line with the members. But the "Swiss democracy" was not negotiable and it was not going to overturn itself. After the strike had wound down, Calonder went back to parliament, informing his colleagues and the country that the "free and proud" Swiss could now come together because "their democracy" stood tall.

It is tempting to dramatize Calonder's role, to present him as the man who rose to the occasion and dominated events. To do this, however, would be to misunderstand what he did and what the office allowed him to do—the nature of the Swiss presidency. Calonder took advantage of the opportunities available, yes, and in that sense deserves much credit. But he could have done little or none of this without the backing of his fellow executives and most of parliament, including some who simply wanted the strike crushed and others whose sympathies were more leftist. It was the fact of a rough consensus by those groups that made his actions so powerful.

Was the Swiss presidency responsible for producing this consensus? One could hardly say it was the sole or primary cause. At the very least, though, the corporate executive did not prevent such a consensus from forming. Calonder had enough tools to spur the system, particularly because he wisely mobilized the other arms of the government—parliament and the council. The seven-member council is one of a number of republican features that cause a broad array of politicians, private institutions, and citizens to instinctively rally at such times of crisis.

Today this phenomenon is called a "culture of political consensus." It results, in a positive sense, from the referendum process, from decentralized decision-making, and other such practices. But in a negative way, the capacity is nourished by the lack of men or women of great charisma and sweeping powers. When the people rally behind such a government at such times, it is all the more powerful, for there is less manipulation and Caeserism than with other democracies, and more of spontaneous and broad-based popular initiative.

Switzerland recovered faster, and more solidly, from the war—without the Versailles hangover that was to vex Germany and weaken France and Britain over the next generation. In Southern Germany, for example, the post-war strikes were one of a number of grievances against the economic dislocations aided and in some cases caused by Versailles. Thousands of young men, returning from the war to find the jobs all taken and their sacrifices in vain, took to political and paramilitary agitation as the logical solution—burning with hatred for the conspiracy of Bolshevists, intellectuals, and Jews. One of the young men was a corporal and former Austrian living in Munich: Adolph Hitler.

In Switzerland, no such passions developed because the labor movement was confronted in an orderly, reasonable fashion—and parts of its economic program adopted. As in 1848, the revolution seemed to come early to Switzerland, but was also dealt with more swiftly and more effectively.

In the long term, the council's handling of the national strike was the basis for a kind of concordat between labor and capital and management that has brought more than eighty years of harmony. Although there were signal advances in this harmony in 1947 and again in 1959, the national strike of 1918 and the reform legislation that followed were the starting point.

From 1918 through 1998, Switzerland suffered a total of less than 800 strikes with a total of 1.2 million man hours lost. On a per capita basis, this is less than one-fifth the average of the United States or Germany, and still smaller compared to Italy and Great Britain. Yet industrial wages—whether in spite of or because of this labor harmony—are the highest in the developed world.

The Depression speaks less clearly to the ability of Switzerland's executives to handle a crisis, but it is by no means entirely unfavorable. Every government in the world did something to try to combat the joblessness and lowered volume of production that seemed to afflict, at least in part, every developed economy in the world. Switzerland was no exception, with public works programs and a program of expanded training for workers in the trades. The Swiss effort was small potatoes—the total of special public works and increases in transfer payments was less than one percent of gross national product—compared to the ambitious New Deal in America, the socialist program in France, and the aggressive industrial subsidies in Italy and Nazi Germany. Officials also devalued the franc to put prices for Switzerland's key exports back on a par with international competitors. Thanks to a combination of labor discipline and skill in calculating the initial magnitude of the devaluation, the device seemed to work: Inflation blipped up by a few percentage points, but was acceptable, and employment remained strong.

At the height of the Depression, while Franklin Roosevelt was speaking of a nation "one third" in economic distress, the Swiss suffered a maximum unemployment rate of 4.2 percent. This compares favorably to rates of 20 percent and more common in the industrial countries. Swiss output was flat for four years, but this compared to plunges of 10 percent per year or more in England, Germany, and the United States.

"Switzerland," as one economist observed, "never had the New Deal." If we remember that the New Deal was advanced as a practical stopgap measure, a way to "do something" rather than merely mouthing platitudes about supply and demand, then the relative Swiss torpidity can be seen as excusable, as the crisis never reached the dimensions it did elsewhere. Free-market economists would argue that the decision not to launch vast spending programs actually aided the country's economic recovery. At the worst, one can say that during economic crises in both 1918 and 1929–1933, Switzerland's diffused executive in no way hampered the government from taking steps that produced one of the most dynamic economies in the world during the pre-war 1930s.

"The first thought of a Swiss," as President Furgler commented, "is not, 'let us go to the federal government for this,' but rather, 'let's bring it up at the town council.' And even when you are at the national level, it is not, 'what can the president do about it?' but rather, 'what do we need to do about it?' The 'we' includes the president, but does not orbit about him in the way it does in the U.S. system." This is certainly visible in the domestic-economic crises that the institution has had to deal with.

Crises of a foreign or military nature offer perhaps more of an acid test of the executive's ability. In the case for the U.S. Constitution made in *The Federalist*, much effort goes into defending the power of the federal government and of the presidency in particular. Most of the arguments over the president's authority have to do with the necessity of having a unified command for dealing with foreign antagonists swiftly and, at times, secretly. Switzerland lacks America's size and its oceanic buffer from the European powers. Hence its need for such a president would appear even more acute.

Switzerland has not had its neutrality tested by full-scale war on its soil since the French occupation. At least several times, however, it faced imminent and substantial danger of an assault from the German army. These took place during the Franco-Prussian War, World War I, and World War II. In addition, Switzerland faced challenges to its territory or opportunities to regain territories that were taken from it wrongfully. These disputes centered on Neuchatel, the Valtellina, and the Savoy. Switzerland's record of achieving what might be called its objective in these crises, as Table 6.1 (on the next page) suggests, is mixed.

Switzerland's inability to regain territory it long held, and valued defensively, in Valtellina—on the southern approaches to the Gotthard—is not a light failing. Had the Swiss simply sent in a few troops, as they might have in 1813 as well, there would have been little European resistance. Switzerland had never ceded the justice of the area's seizure after the war against Napoleon; it had only prudently declined to start a war over the matter. The people of the district wished overwhelmingly to be reaffiliated with Switzerland.

Imagine that a critical piece of Ohio or New York—say, the Hudson River approach to New York City or the railroads East of Chicago—had been seized by a foreign power or proclaimed itself an independent kingdom. If after some years events forced the interloper to abandon his ridiculous claim and withdraw his forces, the U.S. would be expected to gather itself and reclaim what had always been rightfully its own. If it could not it would stand indicted for at least a certain lack of alertness. This may sound petty or even jingoistic, but we should consider that the U.S. Civil War was begun by just

Table 6.1

Military Crises and the Swiss Executive

Crisis	Outcome and Assessment
Neuchatel 1856–57	Neuchatel canton declares itself independent of its ancient ties to Prussia. The German states mobilize an estimated 125,000 troops and prepare for war. The Swiss Federal Council remains unyielding toward Prussia despite the daunting military force arrayed against them. Neuchatel remains an independent Swiss canton as Prussia backs down. *Assessment:* It is unlikely a U.S.-style presidency could have handled the affair better.
Franco-Prussian War 1870–71	Bismarck's Germany crushes the French army; Napoleon III abdicates; 100,000 French troops flee to Switzerland. Swiss mobilize promptly against both the threat of a French escape in force and a German attack against the French troops. The Swiss allow the French sanctuary as internees but only after they completely disarm. They also spurn German pressure to turn the French armies over to them as prisoners. *Assessment:* Probably no advantage or disadvantage to Switzerland's executive structure.
World War I 1914–18	*Assessment:* Executive structure weakened Swiss war-fighting capability marginally. Note though, that a stronger executive might have led Switzerland to enter the war on behalf of Germany in 1914, or of France thereafter. The stubborn slowness of executive by committee works against prompt change and foreign intrigue for both good and ill.
World War II 1939–45	Virtually alone among the countries of Europe, Switzerland stands free and democratic against the Fascist domination of Europe. *Assessment:* Executive structure works marginally to Switzerland's advantage in rallying the country for a long resistance to the Nazis (see discussions in Chaps. 17 and 18).

such a dispute, and over a smaller piece of property than the Valtellina: Fort Sumter. On the other hand, this is the extent of the flaw: That in this case the diffuse executive branch of the Swiss government was unable to move promptly in response to a legitimate opportunity. In the behavior of nations and their institutions, there are worse possible tendencies.

Prussia's threats over Neuchatel (1856–1857) and Bismarck's demand for the surrender of French troops (1870) are interesting because they predated a constitutional change in which the federal government consolidated more control over the Swiss military. One of the arguments in the constitutional debate of 1874 in favor of slightly increasing the power of the central government, and greatly consolidating the military, was the need to counteract the growing German threat to the North. Yet even before these fixes, the Swiss were able to resist German pressure. Swiss institutions may have played a role.

It may help to note that the Swiss have a time-honored method of preparing for war, one used more in anticipation of German aggression than for any other country: the election of a general-in-chief to command the armed forces. This is done for the simple practical reason that once war threatens there is a need to organize the Swiss military, consisting normally of some 200 to 300 officers, for a different sort of activity, and to rally the country behind a strong commander. Military efficiency too requires someone to make the decisions. The Swiss, always suspicious of concentrations of power, prefer not to have such a commanding figure during peacetime. Hence there is no general-in-chief, indeed normally no Swiss general, except in time of war, and one must be chosen to meet the crisis. Naturally, the Swiss method of appointing such a person is to hold an election; in this case, before parliament.

The point is not that this method necessarily produces the best military mind, or fails to. The important thing to notice is the drama of the event—a kind of public sacrament in which the state, this most democratic of states, prepares for the ultimate act of statehood: the defense of the homeland. This ceremony, and the political act it represents, has an important impact on the ability of the Swiss to prepare for war with a ferocity that goes against some conceptions of neutrality.

In the Franco-Prussian War, the man chosen was Johannes Herzog of Aarau, the capital city of the canton of Aargau. Herzog was a participant in the Sonderbund War and a trusted associate of the victorious General Dufour, who would later head the Red Cross. It was Herzog, of course, who had to prepare the army to repulse first a French incursion (or simply a disorganized retreat) while being ready, possibly within a few hours, to deal with the pursuing Germans. Herzog set the tough terms that probably helped save the French from the tender mercies of Bismarck. No one who saw the thorough disarmament of the French could claim that Switzerland had violated its neutrality. And the British, not to mention the French and the Russians, were watching with concern to make sure the rising power of unified Germany did not get out of hand.

"The head of the Swiss army in wartime is a very powerful man," a former Swiss official who engaged in economic planning during the 1940s comments. Henri Guisan, the Swiss commander-in-chief during World War II, "had only to ask for materials and he had them." This was not because Guisan could legally compel compliance. Rather, the emergency itself provided the man in such a position with the authority he needs.

In effect, in time of war the Swiss elect a commander-in-chief, something closer to the American or European conception of a head of state, though still subordinate of course to the civil authorities. The man holding this position enjoys a tremendous prestige and, by virtue not of enumerated functions but of moral suasion, tremendous powers. As one of only four Swiss generals ever to serve, this commander immediately becomes a figure of history. His role and his function are precisely tailored to the emergency. He assumes his office on the day of his election, and he ceases to occupy it as soon as the crisis is over. Without intending to—at least, there is no evidence of this intention either from the 1848 or 1874 constitutional debates—the Swiss effectively created a way to have something like a presidential system, but only in times of need. To the extent that this device works, it enables the Swiss to enjoy the best of both worlds—in times of peace, a weak executive, incapable of becoming a tyrant; in time of need, a strong leader.

The Swiss defensive efforts in World War II are discussed in a separate chapter in Switzerland's role in that war, which became the source of controversy in the late 1990s. For our discussion of the workability of the executive, it is enough to note that Switzerland's exertions were remarkable, and suggest no weakness of institutional capability. Well before most other countries had begun to act, Switzerland began a series of what are probably the most extensive series of hidden fortifications in the world. More important, perhaps, Guisan understood the need of military men, especially Swiss, to have a true sense of idealism about their duties. One of his first acts after his election was to gather his top officers on the Rütli to repeat the oath of 1291. At his urging, the federal council more than once issued a declaration of neutrality that was so tenacious one could easily mistake them for a declaration of war. The declarations proclaimed that Switzerland would never surrender its neutrality to "any" attacker—there was only one real possibility—and go to some length to assure the people that, even if Switzerland was attacked and they heard that a surrender had taken place, it could not be true. By foreclosing any surrender option, Guisan not only encouraged the Swiss public and soldiers to prepare for fierce battle; he also signaled the Germans that any attack would cost many lives and would never lead to the kind of easy capitulation seen in France, Czechoslovakia, and other victims of Nazism. Guisan thereby raised the cost the Germans perceived they would have to pay to occupy Switzerland—and thus helped persuade even the mighty Wehrmacht that this was one country not worth attacking.

If the Swiss executive is highly flexible, of course, this is due not only to its own design but to other factors and institutions in the political culture. One is the nature of the army. Being a citizens' army, it reaches deep into the roots of the populace. Every third Swiss maintains a firearm at home, ready for duty in case of attack—usually within twenty-four hours. This type of army is extremely tenacious and ready; as Machiavelli observed, the Swiss fight "like no army since that of the Roman Republic" when defending their home. Yet, it is instinctively defensive; hence, the Swiss response to opportunities in the mid-nineteenth century. Until the great engine for the defense of the country is engaged, Switzerland moves at the deliberate pace to which its republican institutions are suited.

Similar factors are at play with the Swiss presidency during peacetime. It might not be too much to say that the Swiss presidency could never function were it not for the support of a whole battery of other institutions, and popular habits of mind, that enable this counter-intuitive executive by committee to function. Among these are the weakness of the other branches of government and of government as a whole. Members of the parliament and the judiciary, as we will see, are not highly paid, have tiny staffs, and, while certainly respected, are without the semiroyal privileges that one sees for a United States Senator or Supreme Court Justice. Hence the Swiss executive, while seeming trivial compared to chief executives in America, France, or even Germany or Britain, is not nearly so overshadowed compared to Switzerland's people's parliament and its efficient but simple justices. Likewise, the decentralized nature of authority—Switzerland's federalism—means that a less potent executive is less necessary. Switzerland has no great bureaucracy to buck and kick against the policies desired by the government.

On the negative side, there is less potential for nuisance to attract the vain and the ambitious. "We do not have enough spoils," as a member of the Swiss civil service told me, "to have a 'spoils system.'" As well, of course, since the executive branch is always headed by seven persons from four very different parties, the opportunities for favoritism are even smaller.

A more positive way of viewing the interaction of Swiss federalism with its minimalist executive is to understand that in Switzerland federalism does not merely mean a division of power in which cantons or even communities enjoy significant sovereignty and responsibility. Swiss federalism stretches down to the individual who sits on the school board, or helps run the library—largely volunteer activities in all but the largest Swiss communities. If we view the body politic as an actual body, this means that the muscles and the capillaries and the lungs of the Swiss system are constantly exercising and invigorating themselves. The Swiss executive draws on a more united, energetic body than other executives, whose people are less informed. The Swiss vote more, volunteer more—in short, they govern more. Hence they are more fitted and ready to unite behind their chief executive, divided though it is politically, whenever the times demand. And since the greatest strength of modern democratic chief executives is to thus channel the people's vitality— "to focus attention and set the agenda," as Doris Kearns Goodwin puts it—

the Swiss executive, in this sense, is one of the strongest in the world. When the executive—or the parliament or the courts—propose to act in accord with the popular wisdom, they automatically marshal an army of true citizens to their side, and can overwhelm any other branch that might oppose. (All the branches of the Swiss government are habituated to following the people's wisdom.)

Thus a more proper understanding of Swiss federalism lies in comparing not just the relative powers of the branches and levels of government in the abstract, but their capacity for action with popular support, popular indifference, and against popular opposition. With popular support, any branch of the Swiss government can accomplish nearly anything, for at every level there is the recourse to the ballot box. With popular opposition, almost nothing can be done. Only in the middle band, in the cases where the people are relatively indifferent, do the powers as such come very far into play, and in these cases by their very nature there is little need for a strong executive.

This combination has the additional benefit of rendering the Swiss relatively difficult to sway with sudden arguments, demagogic appeals, and slanted versions of the facts. Having never had a king or queen, they refuse to have a pseudo-king or Caesar to attempt to seduce or bully them. "Switzerland," as Lenin grumbled after living in the country for many years, "is the worst ground for the revolution."

Today, Switzerland faces no crises comparable to the Great Depression or World Wars. Paradoxically, however, many Swiss wonder if the institution of the corporate presidency may require mending.

The controversy over Switzerland's relations with Nazi Germany during World War II, for example, hit the Swiss hard. The Swiss were not prepared for the kind of international opprobrium heaped on them. Many Swiss still remember the sacrifices made during the war to keep Hitler out. When international press, and even the U.S. government, began focusing attention on dormant banking accounts, the Swiss wondered why no one mentioned the considerable resources they spent, and the dangers they accepted, in harboring more than 50,000 allied internees and nearly as many civilian refugees—many of them Jews or resistance leaders—from Germany, France, Poland, and elsewhere.

The Swiss wondered why their own government could not be more vigorous, in a double sense. First, why hadn't the authorities simply forced the Swiss banks to resolve the issue of the dormant accounts years ago? And second, why did its leaders seem powerless now to place Switzerland's sins of omission in context with her great humanitarian exertions? Naturally, much of this frustration found its object in the executive, particularly Flavio Cotti, now retired from the federal council, who served as president and foreign minister during the critical year of 1998.

In many ways, the Swiss had an easier time opposing Hitler than they do dealing with the Holocaust issue. Moral and physical threats cannot cow them; but confronting a complex series of factual issues, wrapped up in the bitterness and rage sewn by the Hitler genocide, are hard to come to grips with, let alone combat. This is a job for a national leader and communicator with both toughness and sensitivity, in the mold of a Ronald Reagan or Bill Clinton, and the Swiss model does not place politicians of this nature in the council.

Traveling in Switzerland in 1998 and 1999, an American was often engaged in discussions about the U.S. president. The Swiss were not much interested in Clinton's amours and other behavior *per se*; much less so than Americans and most Europeans. They were intrigued by the response of our political institutions in launching the country's second impeachment trial in its history. And if they understood the idea of a free people having a king-like president in the abstract, they certainly had a hard time "feeling it in their bones."

This was brought home to me during a visit to the Ticino in early 1999, during the Senate impeachment debate. My train stopped at Bellinzona, where a beautiful castle, Castelgrande, nestled between the river and the grassy slopes and ridges along the southern Alps, virtually compelled me to stop.

Some men at a café up the street were drinking a delicious type of "Russian hot chocolate" with liquor in it and, being unusually expansive for Swiss, invited me to join. We quickly came to discuss my reason for being in the Ticino, and thence, politics. The eldest of the three men, clearly the sort of leader of the group and not by chance the best German speaker, held forth on various issues from the World War II controversy to the recent appearance of Herr Blocher, a parliamentarian who is, roughly, Switzerland's Pat Buchanan in ideological terms, though a more powerful figure for having been elected to office many times and having led successful efforts on a number of referenda.

Eventually, here in the heart of the world's oldest democracy, our discussion of the great issues moved to the Lewinsky affair. The other two men brightened considerably at the shift of the conversation, either because there were some proper nouns they recognized—"Monica" was all one had to say in even the most remote village of Switzerland—or because there was an opening to talk about sex; probably both.

After soliciting my prediction on the impeachment question—which was that Clinton would not be thrown out of office—the two men settled down into a discussion of their likes and dislikes for various American presidents. Kennedy, Reagan, and Carter were the popular figures.

During this part of the conversation, the older man seemed not to be listening. He was frowning and deliberating, as if thinking through something he wanted to say just right, or working out a math problem. Finally he looked up and raised his thick, Brezhnevian eyebrows and announced his findings: "Such a thing just would not be possible in Switzerland—not even a part of it."

His companions looked at one another and me, a little confused. One of them took a drink from his mug and smiled, confident that there would be some punch line. The other one crossed himself—it seemed to be a gently mocking indication that his older friend, the conclusion-drawer, was a fairly orthodox Catholic and was making a point about the state of morals. That was my thought, too—especially from the earlier parts of the conversation, on the American television programming and its excesses, and from my rusty German, it seemed to me that he was trying to make a point about the sexual intrigue. It was either that "such a thing" wasn't possible because the Swiss had higher standards for their public officials, or that "such a thing" wasn't possible because there just wouldn't be such a fuss about consensual relationships.

Not sure what he was trying to say but not wanting to appear dense, the fellow next to me asked "why?" in Italian. The older gentleman smiled with satisfaction, as if having foreseen the query and, speaking to me in German, said "because so much power" could never be concentrated in one man. The Clinton-Lewinsky affair wasn't possible not only because a Swiss would probably not suffer from such hubris, but because the Swiss republic wouldn't place a man in a position to be so tempted by power. Nor would it have brought a young woman like Monica Lewinsky into the kind of hero worship that is made possible by such concentrations of power in one personality— this was my thought, but it was in the spirit of what the old man was saying. He nodded. "Not even a part of it."

One of the colleagues joined in. "This castle," he said, gesturing at the massive and largely undisturbed Castelgrande, "is not the rule but the exception." And he was right, both in the narrow and the broader sense. The Swiss probably have sacked more castles in their country, and tolerated fewer lords, than any other country of Europe. Where men and women are citizens, there cannot be lords and tyrants.

"Not even a part of it," the old man smiled, and leaned back.

Indeed, from the time of President Clinton's 1998 denial (January) to admission (August) and impeachment vote in House (December) was virtually one year. That is a full term in office for the Swiss president.

The Swiss constitution makes no provision for impeachment procedures. It was not thought necessary. This is not because Swiss human nature is better than others, or that the Swiss vainly imagine it to be so. It is because the nature of the office is different—less given to abuse in the first place, and more easily corrected when there is abuse.

It is difficult to picture this institution of a mixed presidency functioning in almost any place other than Switzerland. Therein may lie one index of just how successful its institutions are.

Note

1.   The *Vorort* was a precursor to the Swiss corporate presidency from 1848 to the present. The Vorort moved from city to city as the site of the Diet meetings, and hence the "capitol" of Switzerland itself moved. The Vorort was little more than a kind of secretariat to the Diet, though from time to time its members were able to distinguish themselves in diplomatic assignments. Among these was Charles Pictet de Rochemond, who helped negotiate European recognition of the value of Swiss neutrality at the Congress of Vienna.

7

Judiciary

"The judiciary in Switzerland," writes James Bryce, "is a less important part of the machinery of federal government than it is in the United States or in the Australian Commonwealth, and may therefore be briefly dealt with." [1]

This is certainly true in literal terms. The Swiss constitution grants the judiciary few powers, and these have not been expanded—neither by chance nor by legal cunning.

Yet the same initial observation might be made about the federal judiciary in Germany, France, or the United States. Their stated powers are few; their constitutional role, limited; their dependence upon the other branches of government, almost total. In these other cases, however, the role of judges and of the federal judges in particular have grown substantially since the foundation of those republics.

In Switzerland, by contrast, some combination of causes has rendered the judiciary restrained not only on paper, but in practice; the Swiss high court is limited not only in *de jure*, but in *de facto* terms. It is therefore worth some attention in its own right, and a useful tool for understanding the "machinery of government."

Housed in a comfortable but nonpalatial set of offices in Lausanne—the Swiss emphasis on keeping the government divided and diversified—the Swiss Supreme Court operates like few other federal appeals courts in the world. The Swiss allowed me to visit during public hours and even use the law library for research. There was the usual lack of fuss, fanfare, and bureaucracy: No metal detectors, no demand for i.d. papers. Both the chief of staff for the president of the court and two of the justices came through the library or cafeteria during my afternoon in Lausanne, and were happy to strike up a conversation about comparative legal systems. This air of informality in the halls of government is all the more striking in Switzerland because of the greater formality of the Swiss in general compared to Americans and even, in recent years, many Britons. The justices come and go with no formal robes and do not even appear to wear them in many Swiss courts, although there was no opportunity for me to see the federal court in session.

At a lounge up the street with a TV set, several Swiss lawyers—they did not seem to be professional staff or justices from the court, but in Switzerland, it is hard to tell—occasionally would gather to watch portions of the U.S. impeachment hearings. During one of the down times, a commentator began to discuss the elaborate robe tailored for the occasion for Justice Rhenquist. The Swiss thought it was mildly ridiculous but, perhaps out of deference to the obvious American nearby, did not go on about it for very long.

The Swiss federal court matches this spirit in its operations. There are thirty-nine justices on the federal court, another thirty-nine alternates and extraordinary alternates, and eighteen justices and alternates at the federal insurance court. The federal court is further broken down into nine divisions with particular specialties: there is a court for hearing criminal appeals, a court for disputes between the cantons, and others. The court as a whole handles about 4,000 cases per year. Justices are not given to long speeches or written opinions. "The parliament and ultimately the people write the laws and the constitution," a staff member who works with justice Nordmann-Zimmerman told me, "which frees our justices to decide particular cases. There is not a need for detailed instructions from our court on constitutional issues; Switzerland is a democracy."

By way of an overview, Table 7.1 compares some of the salient features of the Swiss judiciary with those of several other countries.

The combination of a large number of justices and the division of cases by type, as well as the limited powers of the court, have the effect of rendering it far less ambitious than many other federal courts. There is no striving upward, little calculation as to how to make great pronouncements or innovations in the law. The Swiss federal court is about deciding cases. This, in turn, has an impact on what sort of person seeks nomination to the federal court. It is certainly not coveted by the most brilliant attorneys as a kind of cap to their careers or an opportunity to make history.

Some of the persons nominated to the court, in fact, are not even attorneys but members of parliament, businessmen, and other professionals. It is not that these nonlawyers predominate; they constitute normally six to ten of the thirty-five to thirty-nine justices (much of the time, several seats are vacant). Their presence, however, has a leavening effect on the court, and the mere fact that there are some is a reminder to the attorneys who predominate that the law is meant to serve people from different walks of life. Ideas and concepts from outside the legal profession are able to make a regular entry, and thus help a little bit to prevent the high court from becoming an aloof oligarchy trapped in certain legal orthodoxies.

The sheer number of justices, as well, helps reinforce the idea of public service and, if you will, judicial humility. A body of some sixty persons, with

Table 7.1

Supreme Courts Compared

	Switzerland	France	Germany	U.S.
Number of justices	54*	11	11	9
Justices nominated by...	legislature	president	prime minister	president
Justices approved by...	legislature	legislature	legislature	2/3 of Senate
Length of term	six years	life	life	life
Percent of judges who are attorneys⁺	*less* than 80 %	*more* than 90 %	*more* than 90 %	100%
Power to declare local laws void	yes**	yes	yes	yes
Power to declare federal laws void***	no	(yes)	(yes)	yes

Source: Alexis de Tocqueville Institution, "Supreme courts compared," Research Memorandum, 1999, copyright AdTI, all rights reserved.

Notes: *—Thirty-nine justices on the federal court and members of the federal insurance court. Does not include thirty-nine "extraordinary" alternate justices for the main court or nine for the insurance court, which would bring the total to 92.

**—This power is used more sparingly in Switzerland than in the other countries; see chapter 13.

+—From last fifty justices for U.S. and Switzerland; current members of German and French courts.

***—French and German justices have rights of judicial review but it is more recent and less sweeping than the American use of the principle.

more frequent turnover, does not develop into the same sort of cozy clique as a body of a dozen or so persons typically serving thirty years or more on the bench. (Although it is rare for the justices to be rejected in seeking a reappointment, it does happen. As well, it happens frequently that a justice will stand down after two or three terms. The position does not carry the almost lord-like prestige of a position in other supreme courts, and the pay is at the same low level the Swiss extend to all public servants.)

The spirit of this supreme court was summed up for me by a Swiss attorney, Dr. iur. Wilhelm Boner, who studied comparative law at Tulane University in the U.S. before returning to his native canton of Aargau to practice law. Asked to review some of the more famous or important Swiss supreme court decisions, Boner said, "It is possible to name some, but it would be misleading if you mean 'great cases' in the sense of *Marbury vs. Madison* or *Dred Scott*. Our federal court does not exist to produce those sort of rulings, but to settle individual cases."

Likewise, the Swiss judges are denied the lifetime tenure that is accorded supreme court justices in most other developed democracies. They are not, however, subject to frequent partisan campaigns or bitter denunciation. In fact, by virtue of the number of court members, and the fact that they are not nominated for life, the nomination debates tend to be far more civilized than those commonly seen in the United States or Great Britain. Nor are the justices "lobbied" or pressured during their early years as they pursue reelection. Reelection is more or less assumed for good behavior; it is extremely likely. It is not, however, automatic. More than 95 percent of the justices who seek reappointment after six years receive it. But that 5 percent possibility is all that is needed to concentrate the mind of the justices. And the fact that most justices receive reelection does not alter the fact that they must periodically receive it.

The result is a judiciary much more attuned to the attitudes and wisdom, but also the whims, of the people. In other countries this might have proven a dangerous mix. In Switzerland it has not, both because of the limited powers of the judiciary and the relative conservatism—in the sense of having an aversion to radical innovations—of the Swiss people.

The most important difference between the Swiss high court and others, however, is its want of the power, common in Western countries, to void federal laws on constitutional grounds. As Bryce writes,

> The Swiss Tribunal cannot declare any Federal law or part of a law to be invalid as infringing some provision of the Federal Constitution....This principle does not commend itself to American lawyers.

This power has evolved in some countries, such as the U.S., where it was not specifically enumerated in the constitution. More recent constitutions have often tended to grant the authority explicitly, and some (such as Russia) even provide for a kind of judiciary veto—the opportunity to pass on the constitutionality of statues before there is an actual case in controversy, or even before the laws have taken effect. Why is it that in Switzerland the justices of the federal court have been so restrained?

Swiss federalism is a partial answer, but not satisfactory. Other countries enjoy various degrees of federalism, but regardless, have found irresistible the march of legal authorities to judicial constitutional review. Federalism can cut both ways, moreover. In the United States, judicial review was established in *Marbury* in what on the surface was an act of judicial restraint. The Dred Scott decision enforcing slave-holder rights even in nonslave states was put forward—whether fairly or not—as a matter of states' rights.

The culture of republicanism—the ethic of keeping powers small, ambitions in check—likewise is a part of the answer, but seems unsatisfying. Chance or necessity normally puts someone in a position to expand the powers of an office or institution, and human nature being what it is, some occupant eventually embraces the opportunity. As well, this consideration too often makes it necessary for the judiciary to exert power on its own, in order to block a greater accumulation or abuse of power by another. If the Supreme Court of the United States has acted with a heavy hand in matters such as Dred Scott, it has also blocked abuses of powers by Presidents Richard Nixon, William Clinton, and others, and been a bulwark for defending individual rights of all sorts against federal intrusions.

Another partial explanation can be seen if we look at the Swiss legal system from the bottom up. It is essentially a cantonal affair—recall that the twenty-three cantons each set their own rules for both civil and criminal procedure. Although there is increasing harmonization, there are limits to this, and the legal culture is still based on law firms doing the bulk of their business by canton or on a canton-by-canton basis. As well, Switzerland has a number of provisions that discourage professionals from thinking of legal practice as a way to amass great wealth or fame. There is a loser-pays provision for lawsuits: If Smith brings an action against Jones, and Smith loses the case, he not only does not receive judgment, but must pay Jones's reasonable attorney's fees. This discourages attorneys from rolling the dice and filing numerous lawsuits for large amounts on the hopes of cashing in on one or two big awards. It also toughens the attitude of defendants in such lawsuits; they know that if they can persuade the judge they have committed no grave harm to the opposing party, their costs in having to prove this will be partially covered.

As well, the Swiss mindset of *Willensnation*, its position as a potential gatekeeper, plays a role. The Swiss know that their position depends on providing the services of an honest broker if they are to be a trading, transportation, and communications hub. If its Swiss legal system were a capricious thing, given to change at the whim of judges or manipulation by highly skilled attorneys, Switzerland would be like a vending machine center which can't reliably offer change. Angry customers would turn away, or even kick the machines, and business would decline. All nations, of course, pay these costs when their legal system is unwieldy or their currency unstable, or any of several other vagaries. The Swiss, however, being so small, so strategically located, and so dependent on foreign trade, are acutely aware of these tradeoffs. This has helped restrain them in all manner of behavior.

To understand why the federal courts have almost no authority to void federal law and only limited authority to void cantonal statutes, it is helpful to remember who may: the people. This right to review laws, and change the constitution itself, is in use continuously throughout Switzerland. Thus the concept that a particular body would be necessary to protect the constitution is somewhat alien. To do so would be to protect the people from the people, the constitution from its authors. Of course, Swiss professionals engaged in international business, especially those familiar with the United States, understand the concept of judicial review as practiced here and in some European countries. Even for them, though, the notion is regarded as somewhat confused—and troublesome. For working-class Swiss, one must explain the doctrine many times to get it across, and even then one has the feeling that the concept is regarded as somewhat antidemocratic.

In the United States, there is much debate among legal scholars about what the "original intent of the framers" was regarding this or that clause—or even, whether this matter has relevance. In Switzerland, to a much greater extent, the "framers" are still alive and they are not a particular group of men, but all the citizens. There is no need to perform highly speculative debates about what they meant; and if an error is made, it is easily corrected by those same authors themselves.

A more positive way of putting this is to say that Switzerland has a Supreme Court for constitutional review—but it is the voters.

Note

1.   This chapter is concerned wholly with the Swiss federal court, its functioning, and especially its constitutional role. For a related discussion of the Swiss legal system at the cantonal and local levels, for civil and criminal law, see Chap. 13.

8

Parliament

At a glance, the Swiss parliament appears ill suited to govern any country, let alone one with the administrative, linguistic, and economic complexities of Switzerland.

Its members are numerous, and therefore, less remarkable as a group. For every million Swiss citizens, there are about forty members of the lower house of parliament; for every one million Americans, two members of Congress. This tends to reduce the prestige surrounding a citizen's holding seat in the legislature in Bern and also, by sheer rules of arithmetic, reduces the level of erudition of the group that is able to secure election closer to the societal mean. Most of the members are not particularly smooth in either appearance or speech.

"The debates," as Bryce noted in the 1920s, "are practical but not particularly distinguished." During a dozen or so sessions in the fall of 1998 and spring of 1999, one observed perhaps a quarter of the male members in well-cut suits of wool or some other natural material; about half in synthetics and knits with bad ties and shoes; and perhaps a quarter in blue jeans, corduroy-jacket combinations, sweaters, and the like.

It's common to talk with a Swiss for more than an hour—and in my case, most conversations quickly reached the subject of the political economy and culture—only to happen upon the fact that one's counterpart was a member of the national or cantonal legislature. In two long luncheon meetings, Franz Muheim never mentioned that he had been a member of the Swiss Senate from Uri. The "Who's Who" of Switzerland lists only a fraction of the current members of the two chambers; in America or Europe, only a tiny number of members (or even former members) would be so omitted. Asked to name a single important bill from Swiss history, such as "the Jackson Amendment," "Glass-Steagal," or "Kemp Roth," most Swiss, even the well read, cannot do so.

Switzerland's legislature meets four times a year for a period of three weeks, so the individual and collective expertise of its members on any issue are highly limited. Debates in the chamber are competent and businesslike, but seldom stirring or memorable, or even particularly clever or media grabbing like those in the U.S. Congress or House of Commons. The deliberations of the two chambers bear a faint resemblance to the pace and logistics of a meeting of the United Nations General Assembly. Although most members have some competence in two or more of the country's four official languages, some do not, and by law, individuals at such proceedings have a right to speak in any of the country's three official tongues.

As a whole, the body is respected, even revered. The Swiss make occasional jokes about their parliament, particularly the lack of special qualification or expertise by some of its members, or the presence of "so many lawyers," though in fact there are fewer attorneys than in most democratic assemblies. But the comments are of a "gentle wit," as Beatrice puts it in Shakespeare's *Much Ado About Nothing*, "stimulating without harming." Toward the individual members, in general, there is a tremendous affection. Visiting with a parliamentarian in his or her home town, one generally observes that they are known and liked. It is not the power worship or respect that would be given to a British MP, still less to a United States Senator. There is, however, a familial affection.

"We have to like the parliament, in a sense," as a newspaper editor told me, "because our parliament is us." It reflects, more than any other parliament, the people who elect it, and it enacts—especially given the many popular checks on it—laws that are closer to the heart and spirit of its people than in any other nation. For an individual, achieving a seat in the lower or even upper chamber is not on the level of distinction of other Western democracies. Members and former members make no fuss about their titles, and normally are not addressed as such. A Swiss who was a member of parliament and has a Ph.D. is nearly always referred to as "Doctor"—not "Congressman" or "Senator." When one Swiss person describes the achievements of another who spent some years in the legislature, it is not uncommon for them to completely omit the fact of their having served there—not by way of demeaning the body or the person's service there, but simply because it is not necessarily considered as important as their achievements in their business, their community, and their family. The reciprocal result, however, is that the Swiss feel perhaps less alienated from their politicians than the voters of any other country.

The election rules that produce these parliaments are also a mass of seeming contradictions. There are no federal term limits (at least one canton has a ten-year cap), and members enjoy a very high rate of reelection. Yet they generally step down after a period of ten or so years, being taken up with other pursuits. In many Western countries, the pattern is the opposite: Many politicians loudly proclaim the virtues of limited terms, yet decline to step down themselves after years in office.

The Swiss spend little on campaigns. For a seat in the national legislature, they consider any amount over $50,000 spent by one candidate to be excessive, and this invisible ceiling is punctured only rarely. For the cantonal legislatures, $5,000 or less per candidate is the norm. This compares to races in the millions for the U.S. Congress and state legislatures. Yet Switzerland has no limits on how much a candidate can spend, and none either on how much an individual can give to a candidate. Despite the seeming opportunities offered for even a small amount of money to influence the political system, the Swiss are plagued by few of the scandals and corruption that plague Washington, London, or Tokyo. In the early 1980s, a member of the federal counsel, the Swiss executive, was caught up in a financial scandal. She had alerted her husband to a pending investigation of a company on whose board he sat. The call in which she did so was leaked to the press. She resigned quietly in a manner of days.

"It is free," James Bryce wrote in *Modern Democracies*, "from even the suspicion of being used for private gain." The statement remains true today. Yet there are few checks of the type that in more corrupt states are deemed essential merely to restrain marginally the force of legislative malfeasance. Swiss members of the Congress fill out no forms disclosing their income and holdings, and release no tax records. Even their campaign spending is a private affair. Candidates normally (as a practice, not a legal requirement) report totals to the party but not the public. Nor are such figures leaked to journalists.

"There would not be a great need for those types of ethics laws here," as Hugo Bütler, the editor of the *Neue Zürcher Zeitung* commented, "because any question of corruption could immediately be remedied by the people," a reference to the referendum system, "and because there is a general respect for the parliament and its members as honest and just. For the Swiss, the parliament is *us*, a reflection of the people themselves." For that reason, it is difficult to quantify certain activities for comparison to other countries.

The Swiss have no federal term-limits on legislative seats, and although the turnover rate in the legislature is relatively low, they have few complaints about the difficulty of removing an occasional member who does not perform. "Our members of parliament tend to get reelected because they do a good job," as Christian Kuoni, a leading businessman, put it. "If they were not liked, people would not vote for them."

Who are the legislators, and how do they work? More than one-fifth are women: forty-four of 200 members in the lower chamber in 1998, and eight out of forty-six in the upper chamber. The most common profession among these members is lawyers, but this is true of only about one-third of the members, as opposed to half or more in a typical Western congress or parliament. A number of business executives serve, more than 15 percent in fact. This is down from perhaps more than a third in, say, the 1960s, owing both to the increasing demands of parliament and of business. A number of union leaders, teachers, doctors, and housewives also serve.

This diversity of professions has a number of important impacts. Naturally, the debates and discussion of the Swiss assembly are less precise and correct legally than one might expect among the more specialized legislatures of other developed countries. This renders the whole tone and art of governing somewhat rougher, less precise, and less bureaucratic—with advantages and disadvantages. Combined with the fact that there are six or seven parties represented, as well as the fact that Swiss's highly federalist structure refers many issues down to the cantonal and even communal level, the result is that a meeting of the Swiss assembly often has the feel of a city council. The discussions on the floor and in the chamber have the flavor, not of a separate society of persons all expert in the business of lawmaking, but of professionals and workers from different fields, all with different kinds of expertise. There is here more than any other legislature the sense less of a separate clique or society, and more of a chance assemblage of different persons, and a slice of the broader society at large.

During one session, the presiding officer of the Senate happened to notice an acquaintance up in the galleries. Without any great disruption in the proceedings, he called for one of his colleagues, a woman, to please take the chair, walked out the back of the room, and within a few seconds was up in the visitor's gallery to deliver a little briefing to his friends. Just as seamlessly, when the debate suddenly neared completion and it was time for a vote on a series of amendments, he got up and left.

The proceedings that day, by the way, were not some trivial vote on a nonbinding resolution or the like. (There are very few such resolutions in the Swiss parliament, by the way. "We have too much work to do in the time we have," as a member explained to me matter-of-factly in the outer chamber.) In fact, the Swiss were in the midst of a fiscal crisis. "All we have to do is cut a few billion francs," Carlo Schmid, a respected Senator from Appenzell, explained. Then again, this amounted to about 5 percent of the Swiss budget. Amounts of that sort have been sufficient to bring down parliamentary governments in other Western democracies and, at the very least, to produce a great outcry in the United States, with bitter discussions lasting until the wee hours of December 30. The Swiss, who in ten days were about to choose two new federal council members—in effect, two future presidents, and one-third of their executive branch—wrapped the whole discussion up in a few days, voted, and closed the budget gap with little fuss or fanfare.

The Swiss chambers thus operate in an atmosphere of relaxed seriousness. They form a true popular assembly, a people's parliament, which reflects and embodies the basic character of the nation itself. Much of this, as has been observed, flows from the broader political system that empowers popular wisdom. But there are particular rules and policies that play their role as well, operating themselves consistent with the broader political structure. It would be wrong to think that merely by copying these minor provisions, one would achieve the same spirit; but it would be equally wrong to ignore the democratic-republican spirit that pervades the Swiss legislature.

Approaching the Bundeshaus, a building of worn stones in the Georgian style that backs to a view of the River Aare, one sees indications almost immediately that this is a special kind of legislature. A public parking lot, no more than fifty feet from the main entrance, bustles with the cars of citizens. Up a simple set of stairs is a set of huge, beautiful double doors. Members of parliament come and go, leaving an outsider to wonder where the entrance is for "visitors" or the "general public." But here there is no great sociological gulf between the people and their representatives. "The entrance," explains a somewhat bemused woman in French, "is here," pointing to the obvious door a few feet in front of us.

Entering the parliament one sometimes encounters not a single guard (there are guards, but they often sit unobtrusively in one of two entry chambers to the side). There are no metal detectors or briefcase scanners. A group of two or three nice ladies, approximately forty to sixty years of age, generally approve your pass for the day. Usually, if one is going in to visit with a member of parliament, the parliamentary member will come down to meet the visitor. Up two broad flights of stairs—no special elevators for members—and one passes through a long, old-fashioned-type communal press room with big wooden tables and ample seating, but no special desks belonging to individual reporters.

Behind the press room was a wide, semicircular hallway, perhaps thirty feet wide and 200 long. Every fifteen feet or so on the inner side of the arc was a door feeding into one of the two legislative chambers. This archway served as a kind of grand lobby for members to hold meetings, make telephone calls (usually on a cell phone), and conduct other business. It was also, however, the office for most of the members. The typical parliamentarian has only a shared desk in this outer commons area, or at best, a cubbyhole at his party's office nearby. There are no paid staff, no special barber shops for members. Members generally eat in a cafeteria along with other members, visitors, and employees from the library and other government offices housed at the *Bundeshaus*.

As we sat in the cafeteria one morning, two members nominated for the federal council (the seven-member presidency) walked in. They were treated with respect, and a certain notoriety, but there was nothing out of the ordinary. In fact, they addressed several nonmembers of parliament by name, and carried on a conversation with them about the issue being debated that morning in the Senate. As in Swiss courts, in the great Swiss corporations, or on a Swiss sidewalk, there is a low-key absence of officiousness, and a constant emphasis on building a popular consensus.

This absence of pomp is not merely symbolic, and does not merely effect chance conversations or relationships in a cafeteria. The nature of the system helps promote this relaxed atmosphere among legislators. After all, there is little chance of sneaking any important measure into Swiss law by dint of a clever evasion or a raw-power parliamentary maneuver. There are too many checks. Policies are changed by people, elections are constant.

Senator Pat Moynihan once described the error of many Americans in thinking its legislators work by the "consent of the governed." In fact, as Moynihan aptly noted, they operate as they wish unless the people object. The same theme is woven through the memoirs of the late Tip O'Neill, *Man of the House*. The distinction is critical. As elections take place once every two years for the House, and every six for the Senate, there are few opportunities to object. And these are diluted by the fact that each member will have cast hundreds of votes. The voters, then, consent not directly to the thousands of small acts a government will commit, but to an amalgamated track record, a great average, for their own representative.

Among the Swiss parliamentarians, there is a kind of despair about the utility or possibility of manipulating other elites for political gain: What would be the point? That "despair," of course, is another way of saying, healthy respect for and orientation toward the people. Politics, then, is less tactical, more substantive. There are, interestingly, fewer appeals to "the people," and still less to opinion polls, than in a typical Western democratic assembly. In these, the regular citation of the people shows in a certain way that the people are taken into account, but also, that their voice will not automatically be heard. For many votes and issues, the people will never have a direct voice; hence their voice must be leveraged, inferred, or "brought into the discussion." In the Swiss assembly, there is a constant, pervasive knowledge that on anything controversial, the people will, willy-nilly, have the final say anyway. They are no more cited or appealed to than the air we breathe; they are simply there.

As for opinion polls in particular, there are remarkably few of them, and the Swiss of all walks of life hold them in contempt. "Polls reflect what men and women think when they are telephoned late at night and asked to spout off an opinion about something they may have no influence over," as one parliamentarian put it. "It is not the same as when you ask citizens to decide what the country will do: Then there is an informed choice, made in a serious and deliberative manner."

The parliamentary bodies also appear—based on attending some eight to ten sessions, over a period of several months, and reviewing press accounts of the proceedings going back a century—to be significantly less partisan. Debates are no less lively as to the ideas and principles involved, but less rancorous and accusative regarding alleged matters of personal or party bias. This probably has less to do with any of the particular legislators, or even the rules directly affecting the chamber, than with the general "spirit of the laws" which results from the Swiss system of direct democracy and culture of consensus.

In many democracies, the way one changes policies—often, the only way for major changes—is to win an election and with it a "mandate." The losing party is thus expelled from office, and begins its effort as the minority to defeat its opponent. Even where the individuals in this system are highly public spirited—as they usually are—the system itself brings them into constant conflict. There are many gains to be had by enmeshing this opponent in a scandal, or finding a way to neutralize that opponent with a clever parliamentary device. And, such change by realignment, with winner-take-all implications, tends to take place only periodically. To "lose the Congress," as the Republicans did in 1954 or the Democrats in 1994 in the United States, typically means at least five to ten years in the wilderness, and usually longer.

In the Swiss system, with so many controversial issues being referred to the people, there are many ways to achieve change without a single office holder losing his or her seat. The gains of defeating another party, particularly if it is by dint of some merely clever device of communications or investigative skill, are correspondingly minor. The popular orientation does not eliminate the competition over ideas; indeed, it heightens it. It tends to make party and personality a smaller factor, however. In the Swiss system, to gain such a minor advantage, even in the short run, would be roughly as important as winning the right to speak first or last in a debate or to sit on the right or left side of the room in the legislature. Such matters may matter, but in a world of finite time and resources, they are not what a prudent statesman spends his energy on.

Respect is obvious when listening to the Swiss people talk about their legislature, particularly as part of the broader system of government. Even more noticeable, however, is the respect of the lawmakers for the Swiss people. A Western politician who is defeated at the polls or who simply cannot get a particular message he desires passed into law will instinctively blame some flaw in the system, the people, or even the press—drawing any conclusion, almost, except the one that their initial idea itself was flawed. "We didn't do a good job of communicating what we wanted to do with this bill," is a common explanation. "Our message didn't get out," usually because of the "special interests." Sometimes the low opinion of the voters is stated straightforwardly, as in Senator Jack Danforth's 1984 proclamation that "the problem with this congress is that it is too responsive to the will of the people." Normally it is couched in more indirect terms, but the underlying assumption that the voters cannot sort out the demagogic appeals of others remains.

Swiss politicians take aim more often not at the messenger or their opponents, but at themselves. Andreas Gross is a well-known member of parliament and an author. He came to prominence by sponsoring an initiative to abolish the Swiss militia system of near-universal male service. If anything, one would expect an articulate and cosmopolitan member of parliament like Gross to have a certain stubbornness about admitting a mistake, and a great facility to explain how his ideas had only been thwarted by the Rich, the Military, the Press, or some other cadre. Instead, when asked what he thought of the initiative system given its rejection of his proposal some years ago, Gross said simply, "It is a good system—the best anyone has found. The people rejected our initiative, and therefore, it was wrong." When this happens, Gross continued, "you have to look at your own proposal again, see where you may have gone wrong."

Parliament's special character and reputation are partly the results of social factors and mores that can only be created through indirect measures over much time. Others, however, are the result of policy. These are not necessarily deliberate: The constitutional debates of 1848 and 1874, for example, give little evidence that the Swiss framers were setting out to produce these effects. They are, nevertheless, real results traceable of the acts of statesmen—not merely volcanoes or lightning bolts or other natural accidents.

One such effect is the result of the pay for members of the Swiss parliament, which is low compared to the rest of the developed world—as Table 8.1 indicates. The austere salaries are mirrored, or even exceeded, by the lean staff and perk structure. In the United States, even a junior member of Congress typically enjoys staff, office, and other privileges in the amount of $800,000 and up. This does not count the huge resources available to him directly through the ability to compel work by dozens of congressional agencies. Even in France and Germany, where the measurable legislative structure is more lean due to the parliamentary nature of the government, staff budgets dwarf those of the Swiss. The government provides no separate office to speak of, and no personal staff. The typical Swiss parliamentarian shares an

Table 8.1

Salaries for Legislators (ECU per month)	
Switzerland	2800
UK	5400
Netherlands	5200
Greece	5000
France	5450
Denmark	4950
Belgium	5600
Austria	8500
Germany	6300
United States	7250

Source: Alexis de Tocqueville Institution, from OECD data, 1998.

office, if that, at the party office within the capital. His cubbyhole resembles that of a congressional staffer in the United States.

One obvious impact of this low pay, in combination with the related factors mentioned, is that the Swiss regard service in that body as a real sacrifice. It is not as though the pay is so high in other legislatures that the money involved becomes a powerful magnet, drawing the most talented and ambitious to compete for the money involved. But neither, in combination with all the power and perks that attend to a position in the French or British parliament, or the American house or senate, can anyone pretend that membership there is anything but a boon to most of the members.

The impacts of this policy, or tendency, toward low pay for the members of parliament are not merely a matter of avoiding certain ills (e.g., reducing the lust to hold such office among the merely ambitious). It has positive effects as well. The notion that service in parliament is an act of citizenship has created a tolerant attitude among most employers toward the service of their members in that body. This, also combined with other factors—such as the campaign financing restraint—enables the Swiss parliament to achieve a much broader cross section of professional, racial, and cultural representation. It is important to note that Switzerland has moved somewhat in the direction of a more professional parliament and other functions of government in the last twenty-five years, a change some bemoan as insufficient, and some as having gone too far already. A mild reaction against this trend has set in. It is possible that the 1990s were a high-water mark of the professional politician, just as it is possible the trend will continue.

The citizen system has also probably played a role in the facility with which women have been able to move so quickly into the political structure in Switzerland. (Their presence is all the more remarkable if we recall that women did not even win the vote until a 1971 referendum.) "As a housewife on a farm, I have hardly enough time for the responsibilities in the legislature," as a member of the St. Gallen cantonal legislature told me. (The legislature meets ten weeks a year, about the same as the national parliament in Bern, but there are committee meetings and mountains of reading.)

The vast majority of parliamentarians keep their regular jobs, whether as homemaker or wage earner, at least to some extent, during the forty weeks of the year they are not in session. The result would be a conflict-of-interest nightmare under the extensive ethics-protection law common in other democracies. This disadvantage is compensated, however, by the culture of no-nonsense work that results. The Swiss parliament consists of citizens who live not with separate members' pension and health plans, special entrances and parking places and other perks, but will in fact be back at their workplace living under the laws they have created within a few weeks.

The Swiss system of government literally "by the people," from the community volunteers up to the national parliament, has not proven immune to erosion. The lament of François Loeb, a member of parliament who owns a prosperous department store chain, is typical: "I am able to maintain my business and take an active part in the assembly because my business is in good enough shape for me to be absent from time to time, and to delegate work to a competent staff. Not all the members are in that position, which means that their work in the parliament or their business must suffer, or both." Loeb worries that service in the parliament may become affordable only to the privileged in the future. So far, however, the Swiss penchant for moderation in campaign expenditures has helped prevent the legislature from becoming an aristocracy. The sons of former presidents and congressmen have fared better in the American electoral system with its spending and contribution limits than they have in Switzerland with its relatively lax rules, but public austerity. Anywhere the threat of a concentration of power raises its head, especially a political one, the Swiss instinctively react to bring matters under control.

There is a cost to the Swiss practice of giving scant economic support to its lawmakers. This was visible during visits to parliament in 1998 and 1999, as several of the more impressive members felt compelled to return to their private profession or business. The result is to deprive the Swiss people of the experience and intelligence of some of its more capable public servants. This turnover, on the other hand, has positive aspects. It enlivens the two chambers with periodic infusions of new energy. The impact, in combination with other factors, is to simulate something of the results sought by the device of term limits in some countries but without the imposition of a direct elite veto upon the man or woman who would otherwise be selected by the people.

Nearly as important as the parliament's lean budget is its limited calendar, which works in combination with these other matters to preserve the deliberate *amateur* quality of the legislature. Meeting only ten to twelve weeks a year, the legislators have little excuse to avoid centering their lives in their home district and, lacking the resources for the most part, only a few of them are able to become full-time socialites in Bern.

Likewise, the sheer numerousness of the representatives, in relative terms, helps keep the body from degenerating into arrogance. At 240 members with seven million people, the Swiss ratio of representation is the equivalent of a U.S. Congress expanded from its present membership of 535 to some 18,000. This is not a trivial effect. It renders the entire system more accessible, and thus reinforces the objective of maintaining a people's government that so many other Swiss institutions also strive to preserve. By diffusing power, it renders the legislature less vulnerable to manipulation, whether by wealth, particular interests in the press, or by other pressures.

"There is almost no lobbying," Bryce wrote, and this remains largely true today. One strives to find listings of firms even resembling lobbyists in the Bern telephone directory. Associations of employers and labor unions, industries, environmentalists, and other groups exist but bear little resemblance to their counterparts in Washington, D.C. Many of these offices did not even employ a single full-time lobbyist, where their U.S. or European counterpart would typically have a whole battery of them. The sheer size of Switzerland, to be sure, plays a role in this, as does its relatively small federal government. Wary of the dangers of power and privilege, Jean-Jaques Rousseau, the French philosopher who proudly signed most of his manuscripts "a citizen of Geneva," once suggested that republics move their capital periodically—disrupting the cozy inertia and special relationships that tend to build up in any governing city. The combined policies of the Swiss toward their legislature have some of the impact of that, at less cost.

Underlying all these effects, of course, is the system of initiative and referendum that affects the Swiss political economy, and in a sense the whole culture, so broadly. This system is often described, even by the Swiss, as a kind of negative check upon the other political institutions. It is certainly that. It is, however, more than that. It creates a spiritual bond, and a sense of responsibility by the people—turning them all, in effect, into part-time legislators since in their many votes each year they wind up functioning in precisely that manner.

In the Swiss parliament, the influence of direct democracy can be seen by a whole sociology of popular orientation. Each member of the assembly thinks of himself as a teacher, and a teacher of the whole nation of citizens. No teacher who holds his pupils in contempt will succeed, or even stay long on the job; hence the pedagogical impulse, healthy and strong to begin with, is reinforced. As well, a teacher with any wisdom soon realizes he has much to learn from his pupils. The instruction is no longer one way—particularly when the classroom is an intelligent one like the Swiss people, and the teacher a humble, part-time instructor who thinks himself a citizen, not a sovereign.

Thus, to attempt to transplant merely the policies that directly govern "parliament" itself, such as campaign finance or pay and staff provisions, to other democracies, might produce disappointing results if done without establishing some kind of initiative and referendum system, or other arrangements that would emulate its effects. One can make an excellent case for reforming the U.S. or the European legislatures even if only by means of some of those narrower measures. They would not, however, work in exactly the same way as in Switzerland, for there, every political relationship is subtly changed by the system of direct democracy.

It may be that the other democracies, given how far their institutions are from this populist faith in the wisdom of the electorate, must limit themselves to cruder measures. Or that to reach a state of refinement as great as the Swiss model, that they would have to pass through intermediary stages in which the faculty of popular voting and control could be built up gradually.

In a sense, the roots go deeper even than the practice of national and cantonal referendum. The Swiss institution of direct democracy, after all, stretches back over time, and at the same time is brought forward in the continuation of the ancient popular assemblies.

Carlo Schmid-Sutter, who has served in the national senate, has a grasp on the Swiss conception when he describes the *Landsgemeinde* as "the incarnation of the state, the place where all the citizens come together to act as a community." No representative assembly, however virtuous, can ever exactly capture that sensation. The Swiss, though, have achieved an unusually close approximation, in their parliament of citizens.

9

Referendum

"You don't believe in direct democracy unless you believe in it when you don't like the results." —*Andreas
Gross*

Referenda came into widespread use during the French Revolution. These
are not the most auspicious roots for a political device.[1]

The French held votes on taxes, church-run schools, and other issues in the
1790s, and these spread to Switzerland and other occupied territories in a
sporadic fashion in the late eighteenth and early nineteenth centuries. In fact,
the French conducted a referendum on a proposed Swiss constitution in 1802.
After it was voted down, Napoleon, who understood something of the special
Swiss temperament, wisely drafted a substantially different "mediation" constitution of 1803, consulting personally with a number of Swiss to ensure its
plausibility.

In the plebescites in Revolutionary France, votes often resembled those
98–1 or better affairs known in the North Korean legislature or the Cuban
vote on Fidel Castro's newest five-year plan. Taken in the spur of the moment,
with little real debate or presentation of alternatives, these plebescites revealed scarcely any of the deliberate sense of the people. They had all the
seriousness and thoughtfulness of an opinion poll taken over the telephone,
and gave to "plebiscitory democracy" the bad name it still has for many
today.

In Switzerland, by contrast, even during the French occupation, matters
were different. Though the French constitution was rejected, for example, the
margin was not huge. This was an indication that to the voters, the constitution itself was not that bad. There was bound to be a certain rejection of
anything French at that point; the interesting fact is that it was so small.
Debate on issues in the characteristically incisive Swiss press was in many ways
more lively than that tolerated within France itself. Not surprisingly the constitution, when imposed, did much better than the previous French efforts, largely by
returning a measure of the country's customary decentralization.

Once ensconsed in the Swiss mind, the referendum proved a difficult habit to shake. It is a tool of government very much in the spirit of the country's tradition. Switzerland has always had referendum and initiative of a sort. Its community democracies allowed citizens to meet and make laws directly. Only the form of the referendum, which allowed voters over a wide area to participate by casting a ballot, was different than the ancient *Landsgemeinde*.

And the referendum was, in many ways, an improvement. Popular assemblies require the transportation of a number of people for an entire day; they are becoming logistically difficult to hold once a year even for the small cantons. A referendum ballot can be cast in a few minutes at polling places dispersed throughout the district for convenience. This becomes an important advantage if one needs to hold follow up votes or discussions, say if one method of dealing with a problem is rejected, but the people wish to consider others. Because of this advantage in holding discussions seriatim, separated by an interval of weeks or months, the referendum is more amenable to a deliberative process. Popular assemblies, by contrast, must be carefully managed to avoid becoming a chaotic shouting match. And if they are managed too carefully, they may stifle the very process of give and take by the people they are meant to spur.

The long occupation by France, followed by the imposition of the constitution of 1815 by Austria, Russia, and the other powers, had given the Swiss a bellyful of foreign influence. But there were benign, even positive aspects of the French influx as well. It spurred a desire for equality among the people—and in Switzerland, with its traditions of self-reliance and economic opportunity, the emphasis was on legal and political equality, more than equality of economic result. Naturally the two intertwined and interrelated. The French occupation, and even its hated constitution, had proclaimed Switzerland "one Helvetic Republic." This had been the dream of classic liberal thinkers in Switzerland for some time. When the occupation ended, its imposition by the French did too, but the desire for a true Swiss nation did not.

When pressures such as these cannot be satisfied as to their direct object, they tend to move into secondary or "next-best" reforms. Like steam, they seek some crack through which to escape. In Switzerland in the 1820s, there was little hope of a Swiss nation, let alone a national political reform that would give the people direct and equal access to the law-making authority. At this time, the unicameral Diet still was merely a congress of cantons. Any ideas, any national reforms, had to pass through the sometimes undemocratic structures of the individual cantons to become law; and even then they would have only whatever force each canton decided to give them.

Naturally the reform forces turned, then, to the cantons. Some cantons were under no pressure, because the laws were already made directly by the people in assembly, such as Appenzell, Uri, Unterwalden, Glarus, and of course the ancient democracy of Schwyz. Others, though—notably Bern, Zürich,

Basel, and even Luzern—had no such tradition, and their representative democracy still had a substantially feudal character, with a large number of seats on the ruling council passing down by family. In Zürich, for example, the people were represented, but through the ancient labor guilds, who had their quota of seats among the old families. Bern resisted democratization in the sixteenth century, acceded somewhat in the seventeenth, and attempted to revert in the eighteenth century, as did the independent state, now a canton, of Geneva.

In 1830, events across Europe gave the democracy movement in Switzerland an assist. Poland, Spain, and southern Germany were in turmoil, a foreshadowing perhaps of the deeper unrest to occur in 1848. In Zürich, Bern, Thurgau, Fribourg, Luzern, Ticino, and Vaud, popular gatherings demanded greater voting rights. In general the demonstrations were not violent. They were called *Landsgemeinde* and modeled after them—political reformers cleverly simply convening these meetings to pass statutes that perhaps had no legal force, but had moral authority, and suggested the need for popular inclusion. Coinciding with the rewriting of many cantonal constitutions, the meetings had an impact. St. Gallen established a right for citizens to review and reject all laws in 1831. Zürich and Bern both not only opened up their council elections, but enacted a series of legal and political reforms that were approved in consultative referenda from 1832 to 1834. Every canton but Fribourg had established some type of direct popular legislative review by 1845, at which point the onset of deep divisions over the religious question put such secular concerns on temporary hold.

As the procedure spread, it produced forebodings of doom among some. "We are governed no better and now no differently than the hill people," a Zürich patriarch moaned in 1836. James Fennimore Cooper visited Switzerland during this transition to cantonal referendum and reported on a heated discussion of the referendum's spread that took place in a Brienz pub: "An Englishman at a nearby table began to cry out against the growing democracy of the cantons ... 'instead of one tyrant, they will now have many.'" Some of the shrewder members of the political class in the aristocratic cantons, however, saw the referendum as a co-opting device. Like some capitalists over Roosevelt's New Deal in economics, they may have calculated that a prudent concession to popular opinion was better than a revolution. Still others, of course, were staunch believers in the new creed. There was the peasant leader Joseph Leu of Luzern. An orthodox Catholic, Leu fought to have the Jesuits reinstated in the Luzern schools. But he also opposed the ruling families on political reform issues, and was a major force for the cantonal referendum.

Cantonal adoption of referendum was not enough to put to rest the feelings of religious enmity; no mere political device was enough for that. It was, however, available as soon as the Sonderbund War ended—as both a healing device and a means of establishing the legitimacy (or lack of it, if it failed) of the new constitution. Although there had been little experience with the device per se on a cantonal level, there was a consensus among the men writing the constitution in 1847 and 1848 that the referendum would prove a highly useful device for legitimizing their new structure of government—and therefore, warranted to be retained as a permanent part of the design. Evidently, the people had little objection to being consulted about the constitution initially, or about its provision by which they would be consulted periodically.

On September 12, 1848, the Swiss voted on the new constitution with its referendum provision, 145,584 in favor, 54,320 against. It was, fittingly, the first national referendum as such by a sovereign Switzerland.

As the referendum was working its way through the cantons and up to the federal constitution, a related but separate concept began to take hold—one perhaps even more important in its effects. This was the process of "initiative," by which citizens could bring their own proposals for new laws or constitutional provisions to a direct vote of the people. In canton Vaud (1845), any citizen obtaining 8,000 signatures on his proposal could put the matter to a referendum. From 1848 to 1860, the cantons of Geneva and Zürich added initiative. While the referendum offers the people an important veto on the acts of the legislature, the initiative allows them to force issues or ideas onto the agenda that their political elites might prefer to ignore. The one is a check and a brake; the other, a safety valve or a guarantee of access. Although this right was not in the federal constitution of 1848, the provisions for referendum were expanded in the new constitution of 1874. (This second vote followed rejection of a draft proposed in 1872 by foes of initiative and referendum.)

Finally in 1891, the right of initiative for changes to the federal constitution was approved by 60 percent of the voters and eighteen of the twenty-two (full) cantons. As a check against caprice, the constitutional referendum has always required approval by both the majority of the voters and a majority of the cantons.

At the federal level, there are three basic types of direct voting by the Swiss. This chapter does not label each one as such each time it discusses one or the other, but it is important to know that they exist and are distinct. As Wolf Linder defines these in *Swiss Democracy*:

> First, all proposals for constitutional amendments and important international treaties are subject to an *obligatory referendum*. This requires a double majority of the Swiss people and the cantons.... Second, most parliamentary acts are subject to an *optional referendum*. In such cases a parliamentary decision becomes law unless 50,000 citizens, within 90 days, demand the holding of popular vote. [In this case] a simple majority of the people decides whether the bill is approved or rejected.... Since the obligatory referendum refers to constitutional amendments and the optional referendum to ordinary legislation, the two instruments are often distinguished

as the "constitutional" referendum and the "legislative" referendum.... The *popular initiative*: 100,000 citizens can, by signing a formal proposition, demand a constitutional amendment as well as propose the alteration or removal of an existing provision... As with constitutional changes, acceptance requires majorities of both individual voters and the cantons. (Italics added.)

Table 9.1 lists some of the more important uses of the referendum power by the Swiss over the last century and a half. This need hardly be reviewed line by line by the casual reader. It is worth skimming, however, for items of interest. The text that follows will refer back to items in the table and to other Swiss referendum votes.

Looking at this 150-year history, the most important characteristic is probably something one does not see. There does not appear to have been a single *crise de regime* caused by the initiative or referendum policy.

This is saying a great deal, because one can certainly point to cases where the device helped defuse or prevent a crisis. That there are sometimes advantages in the most democratic approach is clear from the very premises of democracy itself. The case against this has always been based on the idea that, as a practical matter, it would lead to disaster or, over the long term, decay. Yet in Switzerland, there seem to be no gross errors, no irresponsible flights into the risky or the insane.

Opponents of the process, such as the great Swiss statesman Alfred Escher, had predicted a proliferation of ill-advised schemes that seemed likely to help the common people, but that ultimately were based on fad, envy, or greed. Perhaps even worse, Escher feared that the system would be corruptive—the process would become a cycle of passionate, demagogic appeals, fueling political extremism, and feeding back into still more extreme leadership. In these fears, Escher was solidly in line with the thinking of the Western political tradition, which from Plato to Rousseau feared democracy would end in envy by the poor, rule by the worst, and, ultimately, despotism. That pub Englishman who complained about Switzerland falling under "many dictators" anticipated by almost a half century an 1872 editorial in the *Neue Zürcher Zeiting* predicting a "tyranny of the many" or "dictatorship of the majority." This was exactly the possibility that American statesmen worked hard to prevent in setting up the U.S. Constitution of 1787. As a result, they carefully filtered any influence of public opinion through representatives and intermediary institutions, slowing it and making it more "deliberative" through the restraints of the constitution.

Perhaps the largest disruption of elite expectations through the referendum process took place in recent years when the Swiss rejected full political and economic integration into the European Union. One can argue the merits of this case either way. Even many proponents have the expectation, as investor and respected trade negotiator David de Pury put it, that "in the end, the referendum process will probably improve the terms on which Switzerland

Table 9.1

Direct Democracy in Switzerland

Proposal *or initiative* and thumbnail description or background.	Popular vote yes-no (percent)	Canton vote yes-no (absolute #)
(Where no cantonal vote total is given, the measure had already passed the parliament and therefore needed only popular approval. Where popular vote conflicts with canton vote, results are <u>underlined</u>)		
Constitutional revision (1848—yes) See discussion in Chap. 5.	73 - 27	15 1/2 - 6 1/2
Jewish immigration (1866—yes) Provided for establishment of Jewish immigrants with political rights and religious freedom. One of the only such laws in Europe prior to 1945.	53 - 47	12 1/2 - 9 1/2
Constitutional revision (1872—no) This draft would have virtually eliminated referendum and was narrowly defeated.	49 - 51	9 - 13
Constitutional revision (1874—yes) New draft includes referendum, consolidates federal military and foreign policy.	63 - 37	14 1/2 - 7 1/2
Bank note monopoly for the state (1880—no) Ultimately approved in 1891 after several rewrites.	31 - 69	4 - 18
Popular initiative (1891—yes) No longer limited to opposing laws they do not want, Swiss citizens could now propose constitutional laws they do want.	60 - 40	18 - 4
"Aufnahme des Schächtverbotes" (1893—yes) The first "initiative," regarding the butchering of animals.	60 - 40	11 1/2 - 10 1/2

Establish Bundesbank (1897—no) One of many proposals on central bank establishment and management rejected by the Swiss voters.	44 - 56	
Right to work (1894—no) Legislation limiting ability of trade unions to compel membership.	18 - 82	0 - 22
Proportional voting for Nationalrat (1910—no) Later approved (1918). Also a rare case of the cantons supporting an initiative, the popular vote having been against.	<u>48 - 52</u>	<u>12 - 10</u>
Proportional voting for Nationalrat (1918—yes) One of the demands of workers in the national strike—see Chap. 6, "Executives Branch."	67 - 33	19 1/2 - 2 1/2
Join League of Nations (1919—yes) A tentative step from pure neutrality—regretted when the Swiss see the weak reaction to Italy's 1935 war on Ethiopia.		
Expansion of employee rights (1920—no) Measure passed by parliament after the national strike, overturned by the voters. Elements of the proposal were later (1950s) adopted in legislation that was not challenged.	49 - 51	
New customs duties (1923—no) Postwar yearnings for a "return to normalcy."	27 - 63	1/2 - 21 1/2
Military training, building program (1935—yes) Principally to counter the Nazi threat. Note the year: At this time, Britain, France, and the United States all were rapidly reducing their defense establishments.	54 - 46	
Establish Romansch as a national language (1938—yes) One of several 1930s measures designed in part to solidify Swiss identity as separate from Germany. "Our diversity of people and language is a strength," a member of the national council said in advocating the measure—a pointed allusion to Nazi theories of racial and linguistic "purity."	92 - 8	22 - 0

Reduce "facultative" referendum (1938—no) As war neared, Swiss leaders felt hampered by the possibility needed laws would be overturned. Several national leaders organized an initiative to temporarily undo this string. Swiss voters strongly rejected this notion. This may have been one factor (among many) in stiffening the resistance of Swiss elites to the Nazis. Some historians argue this deprived Swiss leaders (if they ever had such inclinations) of the possibility of yielding to Hitlerian threats as others did.	15 - 85	0 - 22
Overturn military training law (1940—no) Attempt to block wartime training measures, increased drilling levels that had been approved by parliament.	44 - 56	
Increase power, discretion of national bank (1949—no) Helped force a resolution of the Swiss financial crisis in 1950 that put the country in postwar recovery—see next item.	38 - 62	1 1 ½ - 20 ½
Finance package for 1951-1954 (1950—yes) Followed the rejection of the government's austerity-minded budget and monetary plans of 1948-49. Coinciding with the start of the Marshall Plan and monetary reform in Switzerland and most of Europe (Germany 1948, Britain 1951), this helped launch the postwar *Wirtschaftswunder*.	69 - 31	20 - 2
Consumer protection law (1955—no) Would have been one of the earliest such statutes in the world. Also a rare case of popular support for an initiative (albeit narrow) being overturned by the canton vote.	<u>50 - 49</u>	<u>7 - 15</u>
44-hour work week (1958—yes) 1976 effort to reduce the work week further was defeated.	60 - 40	20 ½ - 1 ½
Voting rights for women (1959—no) Passed in 1971.	38 - 62	0 - 22

Raise daily stipend for Nationalrat (1962—no) Swiss officials continue to be among the lowest paid in the world in absolute terms, and are still lower measured against per capita income.	32 - 68	
Forbid atomic weaponry to Swiss army (1962—no) Supporters tried again with a more limited restriction in 1963, but failed (see next item).	21 - 79	4 - 18
Right of referendum before any decision to equip the army with atomic weapons (1963—no) The Swiss do not necessarily want nuclear weapons in their armed forces, but neither do they want to hamstring their leaders in a time of national emergency. One of many cases in which the referendum power declined to expand itself.	38 - 62	4 ½ – 17 ½
Liquor tax, other measures to fund efforts to combat alcoholism (1966—no) A rare case of tax or regulatory increase proposal coming from the initiative process.	23 - 77	n.a.
Tobacco tax (1968—no) Many of the parliamentary decisions overturned by "facultative" referendum have involved tax increases.	48 - 52	
Voting rights for women (1971—yes) See discussions in text.	66 - 34	15 ½ – 6 ½
Agreement with European Common Market (1972—yes) Regarded by some observers as relentlessly isolationist regarding international organizations, the Swiss voter in fact has a mixed, eclectic record.	73 - 27	22 – 0
New convents, Jesuits allowed (1973—yes) The vote ends a century and a half of official anti-Catholicism in the federal constitution.	55 - 45	16 ½ - 5 ½
Against "over-foreignization" (1974—no) Second of a series of measures to reduce immigration. All were defeated as one pro-immigration measure in 1981.	35 - 65	0 – 22

40-hour work week (1976—no) "We do not mind working only 40 hours a week," a worker told the *Tages Anzeiger*, "we just don't think it should be mandatory."	22 - 78	0 – 22
Civil service as a replacement for military duty by religious and ethical objectors (1977—no) Similar measure was rejected in 1984.	38 - 62	0 – 22
Against over-foreignization (1977—no) Proposal to further restrict immigration.	29 - 71	0 – 22
Value added tax (1977—no) Rejected several times; ultimately passed.	40 - 60	1 – 21
Rent control (1977—no) Other measures to protect tenants, approved by parliament and much less extreme, were approved in the 1970s.	42 - 58	2 – 20
Establish tight, federal air pollution limits (1977—no) Later measures for less extreme limits, administered by the cantons, were not challenged.	39 - 61	1 ½ - 20 ½
Legalize abortion nationally (1978—no) "Right to life" initiative to make abortion illegal on a national basis also failed, in 1985. Abortion continues to be a concern of the cantons.	31 - 69	5 ½ - 17 ½
Vote needed to build highways (1978—no) Note that the Swiss abstained from making its politicians obtain its permission for each proposed national highway.	49 - 51	9 – 14
Creation of canton of Jura (1978—yes) Swiss culture of consensus defuses a long-simmering dispute. Jura's desire to be independent of Bern had spawned the creation of a terrorist "liberation army" that killed dozens during the 1960s. Interestingly, more than eighty percent of Bernese voters supported the initiative.	82 - 18	22 - 0

Create federal security police force (1978—no) Proposed specialized, central police forces to protect against terrorism, Soviet espionage, and other threats. The Swiss feared such a move undermined federalism and was a slight but real step toward a police state.	44 - 56	
Lower retirement age for social security (1978—no) Would have provided state pension benefits to men at age 60 (instead of 65) and 58 for women (instead of 62).	21 - 79	0 - 22
Value-added tax (1979—no) One of several taxes or regulatory initiatives rejected but ultimately passed if political leaders made a persistent case of its necessity. Stronger rejection than in 1977 was in sympathy with global move towards lower taxation rates.	35 - 65	0 - 23
Abolish state support for religion (1980—no) Would have established U.S.-style "separation of church and state," preventing cantons from using tax dollars to support religion, blocking religious teaching in state schools.	21 - 79	0 - 23
Seatbelts mandatory (1980—yes) Also requires helmet for motorcycle riders. This was a challenge to a law already passed by parliament. Initial surveys suggested overwhelming support for overturning the law, but the politicians convinced the people.	52 - 48	13 - 10
Immigration liberalization bill (1981—no) Would have eased restrictive limitations on guest workers, providing a right to remain in Switzerland even for guest workers no longer employed.	14 - 85	0 - 23
Equal rights for men and women (1981—yes) Similar in language to failed U.S. Equal Rights Amendment.	60 - 40	15 ½ - 7 ½

"Verhinderung missbräuchlicher Preise" (1982—yes) One of the few initiatives to pass in the last 50 years, a consumer protection vote against corporate cartels.	56 - 44	17 – 6
Civil service as a replacement for military duty by religious and ethical objectors (1984—no) A similar measure later passed.	36 - 64	0 – 23
Loosen banking protections (1984—no) One of many incremental erosions of bank secrecy protections passed in 1934. All were defeated except those having to do with drug dealers and other alleged international criminals.	27 - 73	
"Right to life"—outlaw abortion (1985—no) Left cantons free to legalize or continue to restrict abortion. 1978 measure to legalize abortion nationally also defeated.	31 - 69	5 ½ - 17 ½
Join United Nations (1986—no) The Swiss do not hesitate to involve themselves in good works internationally (the Red Cross) but are chary of any involvement in organizations that might compromise their neutrality.	24 - 76	0 - 23
Abolish the army (1989—no) See comments of Andreas Gross in chapter 8.	36 - 64	1 ½ - 21 ½
Join International Monetary Fund (1992—yes) Swiss concerns about neutrality are lower regarding fundamentally commercial or monetary organizations. Even so the country did not join the IMF for a half century after its founding (1943-44.)	56 – 44	
Full entry into the European Economic Area (1992—no) Swiss leaders immediately set about negotiating a series of bilateral treaties simulating entry for trade and other policies, completed in 1999. Political union is a live issue for the future, likely to arise again in the 2002-2003 range.	49.7 – 50.3	7 – 16
Ban purchase of U.S. F-18 fighter (1993—no)	43 - 57	4 – 18

Increase value added tax (1995—yes) Brought the Swiss closer in line with European Union countries, but not yet "harmonized."		
Approve new (consolidated) constitution (1999-yes) Substantively, the constitution was essentially a more tightly worded version of the old constitution, designed to convert various secular measures into laws and reduce the constitution's length. Late in the process, a lively debate ensued about the meaning of various phrases in the preamble, such as commitments to international law, but the draft still passed. (See chapter 5.)	59-41	13-9
Restrict foreign-born share of population (2000-no) Most recent in a series of generally moderate, pro-immigration votes by the Swiss.	36 -64	0 - 23

enters the EU, and the period of discussion and education that will go on will be beneficial to us. We will enter on much more solid ground than if we had not gone through this process, troublesome though it is to some." Whether the decision was wise or ill advised, however, it clearly was no Armageddon for the Swiss political economy. After an initial slump, the stock market and currency soared in the years following Swiss rejection of the proposal.

On foreign affairs, there has been a lively debate as well. Periodically the Swiss voter blocks the desire of its leaders to join an international organization (such as the United Nations) or take other actions that might incrementally impinge upon traditional Swiss neutrality. There is strong agreement among both leaders and the people that the neutrality policy is wise. But what does neutrality mean? Here there is much back and forth, as the Swiss sometimes choose to join in international organizations, and sometimes they do not. Even questions primarily "about" other subjects, such as environmental policy, often have reference back to neutrality.

Insofar as we can draw any general conclusions about the process and foreign policy, it is that the voters guard Swiss neutrality but are willing to allow for an activist version of it if they hear a sustained, intelligent case. Thus, over time, the voters acceded to Swiss entry into the World Bank, the International Monetary Fund, and various European economic organizations.

They may well someday join the emerging European state and the United Nations, but the people require more convincing.

Domestic policy reveals more of the tendencies of the referendum. It is also, numerically, the more common theatre of action for the referendum—depending on how one classifies such matters as military service, domestic issues comprise about 85 percent to 95 percent of the material of popular votes since 1848. We can divide these still further into subject categories as follows:

- *taxes and spending* (about 20 percent of all Swiss domestic issues);
- *other economic issues*, e.g., central bank management, social welfare programs, and others (15 percent);
- *political reform* (about 20 percent—the fairly well-tuned Swiss machine is constantly checking its own oil);
- *procedural matters*—"the government may finance its capital budget over seventeen years instead of fifteen years," the cantons must provide environmental reviews—(about 15 percent);
- *social-moral issues* such as abortion, the prohibition of absinthe, decriminalization of the Jesuit Order (15 percent); and
- *eclectic matters*, such as the vivisection of animals, or outlawing cars one Sunday of each month (10 to 15 percent).

On largely administrative issues, the Swiss have proven amenable, even facilitative. This becomes less so in proportion as any given proposal is seen as being not merely technical, but having broader implications. A good example would be initiatives regarding the military organization, male service, and other such matters. The Swiss have readily supported expansion of military capability when the country is under threat, as in the 1930s, and offered no resistance to increased drilling and other sacrifices during World War I and World War II. They have turned down a number of proposals for changes in military service, including some rather minor ones, however, apparently viewing this as a kind of moral issue and something sacred to Swiss citizenship. And they voted no on a proposal to weaken the facultative referendum during World War II—as if aware that, while they would never stand in the way of a legitimate necessity, they nevertheless wanted their leaders to operate under the knowledge that arbitrary actions could still easily be challenged.

The referendum power is even, in a sense, self-denying. Far from grasping for power, the people have periodically denied it to themselves—if, again, the matter is one they deem best handled by their politicians. In the 1960s, the Swiss even turned down efforts to require prior consent by referendum on nuclear weapons, and in the 1970s, rejected a similar proposal that would have made it easier to use the process to block highway construction projects. It is not that the Swiss, who are generally pro-environment, care nothing for the state of their roads or the communities they go through. Indeed, one of the major controversies in Switzerland in the 1990s concerned how to control the large, smoke trucks that pass through the country between Germany, France, Italy, and Mediterranean Europe. Rather, the Swiss have a capacity for self-denial and prudent forbearance, even where their own power is concerned.

This characteristic is, in part, especially Swiss—tied up with the concept of neutrality, of a self-conscious inability to influence certain great affairs, and a positive desire not to try. The sensibility is also, however, the product of institutions. It can be imitated by others, and inculcated by the right set of political arrangements.

Always interesting, and in fact also instructive, are the somewhat off-beat proposals that occasionally come up for a vote. Most of these are placed on the ballot through the initiative process, which allows any citizen to bring a constitutional amendment before the country, provided he can collect sufficient signatures to show some serious level of support.[2] Only rarely do such measures—such as 1977's proposed prohibition of automobiles on the second Sunday of every month—pass.

One is tempted to dismiss them as insignificant, and in direct legislative terms they are. They may also illustrate, however, that some of the system's most important impacts may be indirect or unseen. The power to bring a strongly felt proposal on to the national agenda, and have it debated in the press and voted on by the people, is an important one, and one the Swiss cherish. It defuses passions, and gives the angry and the enthusiastic an outlet for their energies. "Many of the people who worked on our initiative," as Andreas Gross put it, "became active in politics or in the society in other ways. Even though we were defeated, they were not alienated." A movement that has its measure rejected by Congress or vetoed by the president is likely to feel they were thwarted unfairly, that the will of the people was twisted by lobbyists and slick communicators. The Swiss whose initiative does not pass may feel some of this anger, but knows that his case has been judged directly by the people. He may feel he has helped educate the society, and probably has: All the articles about immigration policy in the Swiss press, while they have not enabled anti-immigration measures to pass, have provided information that the proponents are eager to see disseminated. The educational process works in both directions, too. Often the movements that propound radical ideas are able to refine or moderate their positions and become more effective. Politicians who misread the popular mood, meanwhile, can go back to their office and rethink their approach.

And those who persist in the process do frequently prevail. The "radical" cause of women's suffrage, rejected many times in Switzerland, did pass in 1971. Consumer protection legislation, defeated in 1955, became law several years later, and a significant extension of the legislation by parliament in the 1970s was ultimately approved when challenged by a facultative referendum.

The sheer volume of initiatives and referenda can tell us something about the state of Swiss affairs, and has offered information to all Swiss politicians who were intelligent enough to pay attention. In the 1970s, for instance, there was a sudden flurry of initiative making and referendum challenges—more than triple the average number of votes seen in other decades of the twentieth century. Putting aside the substance and the results of all this activity, it certainly suggests a restlessness on the part of the people and a preoccupation to improve the performance of their institutions. The Swiss do not lightly rouse themselves to such activity; they are happy to pay the price of citizen's government, but not looking for needless opportunities to fill up their evenings with political meetings. A large number of the proposals were environmental in nature—to block nuclear power, limit automobile emissions, and the like. Yet even though most of these were turned down, they helped produce policy changes in the 1980s that enacted some of the laws sought by the initial activists. Unable to persuade the people directly to adopt all their proposals, the environmentalists nevertheless generated a large discussion in the public and the press, and the parliament, reflecting this slow change in attitude, adjusted.

There are, finally, all the cases in which the initiatives and referendum process "created a law" without a specific referendum ever taking place. This happens when the politician in Bern, sensing popular concern and anticipating an initiative by the citizens, proposes and enacts a law addressing the problem before the initiative is necessary. Or when legislators, knowing a certain proposition they may admire will inevitably be overturned by a facultative referendum, vote against it themselves. This can happen in a purely representative democracy too, of course, but notice how the effect is stronger and more direct in the case of initiative and referendum. The member of Congress who casts an unpopular vote may jeopardize his own reelection, but of course the voters will render their judgment on that based on hundreds of votes. A Swiss parliamentarian likewise can vote for an unpopular measure out of personal conviction or misguided judgment, but he has even less incentive to, since the measure, if truly unpopular, will almost certainly be overturned. It is a much higher certainty than in systems where elites have greater discretion to substitute their own judgments.

In any of these cases there is no referendum to refer back to now. But it is certain that the referendum helped to produce the result—may even be, in some cases, the immediate cause.

Taxes and central bank policy are the issues on which voters have proven most troublesome to their leaders through the referendum. Here, too, they might have done serious damage. The Swiss turned down tax increases in every decade of the twentieth century, and the referendum process directly, or by indirect pressure, helped bring about significant tax cuts in the 1920s, 1950s, and 1980s. Partly for this reason, Switzerland has developed a deserved reputation as a low-tax, low-spending country. This is generally true of its combined government budget, but is especially true of its central government, which consumes only 30 percent of government activity (the cantons, 40 percent, and the communes, 30 percent—resulting in a 30-40-30 "formula" of the sort the Swiss cite often with satisfaction). The Swiss, as we will discuss in more detail, do not even have an agency that corresponds to the U.S. Internal Revenue Service—and when measures even resembling them are proposed, they are soundly rejected at the ballot box.

On the other hand, the Swiss are not reflexively against all taxation or still less all government. At first skeptical about train travel, the Swiss today love their national train system—and rightly regard it as a prudent investment that helped fuel the country's booming growth in the nineteenth and twentieth centuries. They eventually approved excise taxes on liquor and cigarettes that they at first turned down, although the final outcome was no doubt less than many politicians—particularly of the center-left—might have hoped for. Switzerland adapted itself to European protectionism in the 1920s and 1930s, though the Swiss raised tariffs later, and less, than other countries. The Swiss eventually adopted a payroll tax and an income tax, though they jealously watch to ensure that these are administered by the cantons and communes. And they allowed a Value-Added Tax on the fourth or fifth try—but it is less than half the rest of Europe's.

"Switzerland grew out of a tax revolt, in part," as Senator Franz Muheim told me at a meeting across from the Luzern train station, "but it also grew out of that bridge that the people of Uri built and maintained with their own community effort." Such taxes, in fact, bought Uri's freedom. As this historical analogy might suggest, taxes have generally had a much better chance when they are linked to some project or benefit, either directly or as a general matter of need. The Swiss are not fond of spending merely for the sake of spending, however, and are especially tight-fisted about transfer payments and other programs not linked to production. By contrast they are more willing than other countries, as a share of what the government does, to commit resources to education, transportation projects, and other goods perceived as stimulating production or efficiency, or aiding the community generally, or both. In part, the Swiss are merely fortunate in being able to devote themselves to such projects, and reject programs that merely pass around money and the taxes needed to fund them. They suffer few extremes of poverty or wealth, and in the general condition of rough equality that results, have less need for such palliatives. To an extent, however, the shape of the Swiss fiscal picture is creditable to intelligent choices by the Swiss. The initiative and referendum process made a contribution to this, both as a general matter and in the visible ways in which certain programs were adapted.

For example, the Swiss turned down a proposal to move back the retirement age to fifty-eight and sixty-two—an attractive-looking proposal at the time, but one whose rejection now appears quite shrewd as aging populations stress other government pension systems throughout Western Europe, and are literally crippling the economies of Russia, Poland, the Czech Republic, and the rest of the former Soviet bloc. The Swiss have also maintained lower income and consumption tax rates than the rest of Europe, helping them to continue to attract many of the most enterprising minds of science, finance, and manufacturing. Direct democracy is the greatest single cause of these economic policies that have helped Switzerland grow so rapidly over the last century.

Switzerland's affection for taxes is nearly matched by its love for a powerful, unaccountable central bank. On at least six occasions they rejected government proposals for central bank management. Yet this tendency seems to have done no harm, and arguably has done good. Twice in the nineteenth century (1876 and 1880), the Swiss refused to even allow the central government a monopoly on bank notes. When a third effort was started in parliament in 1887, signatures for a facultative challenge gathered so fast that the effort was dropped. The political leadership finally drafted a proposal that made sense to the electorate, and in 1891 a more limited authority was granted than existed in the United States or most of Europe. In 1897, the proposal was approved and the government had the authority to set up a central bank. But it was still another decade (1907) until a workable design could be found that was not threatened by immediate rejection by the voters.

When the national bank was created, it was one of the "weakest" such structures in the developed world. Even today the National Bank's role is strictly limited to monetary policy. The bank is a private entity legally, with a small staff and limited powers. A majority of the bank's stock is held by the cantons, the cantonal banks, and some several dozen other public bodies and institutions. In the early twentieth century the Swiss turned down one proposal to allow the bank greater latitude in conducting open-market operations. Other ideas were stillborn in parliament when the representatives considered how chary the voters had been in earlier bank votes. Their denial of this flexibility, coupled with Switzerland's low-deficit fiscal situation, may have helped soften the Great Depression, which in Switzerland was a blip of unemployment that never topped 5 percent, and a "growth recession" in which output did not decline, but expanded only 1 percent cumulatively from 1930 to 1934.

In 1949, frustrated by the government's failure to "get with" the emerging monetary order, voters resoundingly rejected another proposed change in the national bank. The result was something of a crisis, but forced the government to revise its financial austerity package into a growth initiative built around postwar tax relief, monetary stabilization, and public works programs such as road construction. The combination helped pull Switzerland out of the European malaise of the early postwar years.[3]

Again in 1961, the appreciation of several European currencies threatened Switzerland's monetary order. The government floated the currency and, after a long struggle, redesigned the bank. Most leaders of industry consider the design of the Swiss central bank to be a major asset, and that design is in no small way attributable to what one Swiss investor calls "the people's wonderful stubbornness on financial issues." Over the last 150 years, the Swiss have been less troubled by the wild swings of inflation and deflation seen in the world at large than almost any other country—even including the United States.

The experience with issues of banking and taxation illustrates some important points about the referendum process itself, especially as it has evolved into something of an art form over long experience.

The first is that the process itself has become deliberative. The effort by political leaders to secure arrangements for a central bank, or funding for desired projects, became an ongoing conversation. Political leaders first press one way, and then, finding there is insufficient support for a particular conception, they lead in another. The Swiss have seen this process in recent years regarding the debate over entry into the European Union: Proponents have had to rethink their arguments and their premises, and adjust their proposals and policies, in order to persuade the voters. In this, they naturally confer and deliberate among themselves, too, though with the people constantly in mind. Thus the process of establishing a national bank became a forty-year dialogue, and the value-added tax, one of almost twenty-five years.

This is in marked contrast with traditional Western thought about the strengths and weaknesses of popular legislation. During the debates over the American Constitution, one of the advantages proposed for America's legislative system, in contrast to the more direct democracies of classical Greece, was the idea that a body of lawmakers would be able to consult, think, and craft the laws—to become a skilled profession, of sorts, and to be removed, at least to arm's length, from the passions of the people. Proposals would benefit from having been forged, refined, and crafted over time. Indeed the framers were so concerned about the popular whim that they feared the "rashness" of even representative assemblies (*Federalist* 63). One of the main arguments for the Senate was that this more senior body would impose something of a check on the possibly unruly House. The presidential veto, in turn, was set atop of both houses, and provided a still further check. Many hurdles were set up in order to filter public opinion through experts and seasoned officials, and to stretch the process out so that decisions would reflect the *"deliberate sense"* of the country, rather than mere waves of passion.

In Switzerland, though, direct democracy turns out to be significantly deliberative. "In our system," as federal counselor and 1999 President Ruth Dreifuss explained to a foreign journalist asking about the process of Swiss entry into the EU, "things take time." Indeed, the most common complaint about the system, as it has actually operated, is that the Swiss referendum process slows things down too greatly. The people turn matters over and become part of a legislative process—especially when, as in Switzerland, they are placed in a position where they are, in effect, lawmakers.

This raises a second point about the Swiss system and about popular politics generally. The people's opinion on a given matter, requested under one set of conditions, is not necessarily the same as their opinion on the same matter, but under different conditions. A system of referendum does not yield the same results one would have if one polled the people about the issues on the referenda—because when someone knows he is going to be asked to render an opinion, and that opinion will become law, he treats the matter more seriously. This does not mean that public opinion polls are wrong, or meaningless—it just means that they measure, normally quite accurately, something that may differ significantly over time or over different conditions. Nor are the people fickle in this, any more than water is capricious because it is a fluid at one temperature and a solid at another. They are, in fact, wise, economizing on their need for information and thought about subjects depending on whether their opinion will have some tangible influence. Members of a jury treat a case differently than members of the general public, and by the same token, voters and lawmakers regard it otherwise than if they were mere bystanders.

In the Swiss case, this differential is more important, but less observable, because the people are now long accustomed to being lawmakers. It is probably one reason, for example, that the Swiss are voracious readers of newspapers and that their newspapers, in turn, offer some of the most serious coverage of political policies and issues in the West.

A good illustration of these tendencies, in both Switzerland and the United States, is the sensitive issue of immigration. Like the U.S., Switzerland plays home to a large number of foreign-born workers and their families—close to 20 percent of the population for the Swiss. In a country already trying to assimilate three major languages across mountain ranges, this is a significant tax on Swiss resources and patience. One frequently hears complaints by the Swiss about the immigrant population, and it is one of the most frequent subjects for comment in the graffiti in the train stations and on the streets. (Switzerland, a generally orderly and one might even say extremely tidy country, has as much or more graffiti than any other country in Western Europe; it is close in most cities to New York City standards. The graffiti about foreigners, as one might expect, is especially unkind.) Public opinion polls, though taken much less seriously in Switzerland, indicate that by margins of about three to one the Swiss feel there are too many foreigners, they cannot be assimilated, and something should be done about it.

Yet when confronted with the chance to reduce immigration through policy, Swiss voters have consistently rejected the proposals—and by large margins.

Anti-immigration measures failed in the 1960s, 1970s, and 1980s. These measures were well financed by supporters and most of them were not extreme by comparative standards. That is to say, if passed, they would not have moved Switzerland to the bottom or even the middle of Europe in terms of accepting immigrants; they would only have reduced the country's lead, in percentage terms, of acting as a home to the foreign born.

The sole victory by the anti-immigration forces was their defeat, albeit also by a large margin, of a 1981 initiative proposing to significantly liberalize immigration. The measure, however, would have had as large or larger an impact on the composition and incentives of immigrants as on their numbers: For example, it reduced requirements for work, and increased the availability of welfare and other services. Thus even many advocates of increased immigration levels were lukewarm or opposed to the proposal.

The persistence of this dichotomy suggests that the Swiss voter is not behaving in a fickle manner. There is no swing from one attitude to another, but rather, a steady pattern: Swiss attitudes on immigration are fundamentally negative; Swiss votes on immigration policy are fundamentally liberal.

(One finds a similar dichotomy on immigration in the United States, although, since there is no national referendum or initiative, it is more subtle and difficult to read. Voters answer polls negatively about immigration generally. But in large numbers, Americans support the admission of immigrants who are highly skilled, or who will take jobs that Americans won't, or who are reuniting with families. Since these groups comprise about 90 percent of immigrants, there is latent support for a liberal policy. In numerous congressional votes over recent decades, proponents of high levels of immigration held their own, and politicians who ran on broad antiforeign themes fared poorly: Richard Gephardt, John Connally, Ross Perot, George Wallace, and Patrick Buchanan all garnered a few primary victories, or made it close to 10 percent of the popular vote, but did no more. The only major immigration referendum in the United States, in the state of California, was passed, and was described as a major setback for immigration nationally. It was politically, perhaps, but the measure had no direct application to the number of immigrants accepted, a federal concern. Rather, Californians voted to reduce welfare and other services offered to legal and in some cases illegal immigrants. One can argue the fairness of such measures, as one can make a case for them on incentives grounds. They do not, however, constitute a direct vote for lower immigration levels, any more than requiring cars on the street to drive on the right side is "antitraffic.")

The effects of the Swiss system appear to be somewhat different from the process of initiative and referendum in various states in the United States. Several other factors, of course, are different as well—the party structure, the political system, and others. And it is difficult to say which of these differences are causes, and which are effects. On the whole, however, the initiative and referendum process in the state of California—familiar to me from having lived there for some six years—is somewhat less deliberative, and more impulsive, than in Switzerland. Part of this is due to the difference in the political party structure and tone. In the U.S., since there is no national initiative or referendum and since there are two dominant parties, it is much easier to bottle up issues or proposals for years. They can still be forced out by a well-timed referendum or initiative. Proposition 13 in 1978, for instance, put the idea of tax reduction on the national agenda. But the process is more problematic. In addition, the whole tone of discourse on political issues is more divisive in the U.S. than in Switzerland, and in particular the motives of parties much more likely to be impugned than in Switzerland. When groups lose or win a struggle in a particular state, they are much more inclined to merely resume the battle elsewhere, and their politicians, being more of a professional class than mere citizens who happen to volunteer services to the government, view the struggle as a war that must be fought and won.

There are other technical factors as well. The courts in the United States are more powerful and more inclined to throw out the results even of a popular vote, than in Switzerland. In California and Massachusetts, referendum results have been disallowed frequently by judges after the fact, or their placement on the ballot made difficult by arbitrary signature requirements (i.e., if there is one smudge on a sheet of paper with thirty signatures, all the signatures are invalid). This makes the process, like the parties and the power structure, less direct and certain in its impacts, and hence, turns the referendum and initiative into more of an extension of politics as usual than a reliable process for making the voice of the people felt. As well, while California and many states have both initiative and referendum provisions, there are few referenda as such, and none required. The process is certainly less regular than in the Swiss cantons, in some of which every significant law must be approved by the people. This has the effect of rendering the process more exceptional.

Because of many stages and iterations in Switzerland, the referendum process is not one shot—it's more deliberative and seriatim. The Swiss referendum process is more like the *legislative* process in the U.S. The American initiative and referendum process sometimes can become more drawn out and deliberative, but, for other reasons, it has tended not to be. In addition to those already mentioned, the sheer expense of collecting signatures in California, and the large amounts of money spent on demagogic appeals—which the voters, being less trained as legislators than the Swiss, are more susceptible to—has rendered the process more like what the American founders feared for direct democracy, than it is like the Swiss alternative.

Overall, direct democracy infuses and pervades Swiss institutions through all levels of government; in the United States, direct democracy has been an occasional tool used in some places in limited fashion. The U.S. system might be called a "weekend athlete" who, while not necessarily being fat, does not train regularly and has not honed his or her skills to their potential. The Swiss are direct democracy professionals, working out regularly. The typical Swiss citizen votes on a constitutional amendment about once a year, and votes several times on cantonal laws, initiatives, and amendments. He takes public issues seriously as issues; like a mini-legislator, he will have to "vote" meaningfully on their resolution.

The communications class—politicians, press, business leaders—take the importance of the people into account in everything they do. An American friend of mine who complains frequently about the massive efforts made to "lobby" members of Congress in Washington, D.C., asked me after a visit to Switzerland what possible difference it would make if the United States were to have an initiative and referendum process similar to Switzerland's. My response was that there would probably be, to her disappointment, as much or more lobbying as a matter of volume—but that a much greater amount of it would be directed at the people. "Imagine if all the effort and money spent in Washington went towards educating people—and listening to them." She agreed that this would be a substantial change.

The use of direct democracy with this frequency and at this level of importance creates the effect, almost, of a different system of government. There is far less difference between Switzerland and the United States than there is between the United States and, say, one of the Arab countries or the authoritarian government of Indonesia. But if we were to take a constitutional monarchy, such as Britain's, from the nineteenth or even eighteenth century, with an elected legislature, it is arguable that the U.S. democracy of today is closer to it, institutionally and certainly in spirit, than it is to democracy in Switzerland. When an American visitor to Switzerland told his hosts in 1999, "You have a democracy; we do not," he went too far. It might not be saying too much, however, that these two types of democracy are so different they might be classified as separate species with certain common ancestors and ideas.

Some of the disadvantages of the referendum system are peculiar to Switzerland: For example, the diversity of language sometimes yields drafting imprecisions in the wording of laws and resolutions, and renders political debate and discussion more difficult as well. There are other disadvantages to it, however, that while felt in Switzerland, might be even more acute for the United States and other powerful republics.

Critics of the system of direct voting generally fall into one of two categories.

One group consists of those who don't like the results of direct democracy. This is seen in representative elections too, of course: It is tough to see your ideas lose, particularly when votes are close. In the Swiss system, given that the voters have demonstrated a certain eclecticism and balance in their actions—supporting some government programs, opposing others; keeping out of some international organizations, but supporting some as well—most groups have suffered enough defeats, but also won enough victories so that the "losers" don't comprise a consistent or solid ideological bloc. Business interests, for example, have lost many votes on environmental policy, but have won others on taxes. The left has been unable to push certain spending schemes, but has enjoyed victories on pension and health care policies.

This does not mean, however, that such groups might not form, or have not partially formed already—creating a potential threat to the system by fostering a small, but hard-core lobby, dedicated to incessantly seeking opportunities to overturn the system so it can finally win passage of a particular economic or social agenda. One such group would be the Swiss, including centrists in the government and members of the manufacturing and other non-banking sectors, who are keen to have Switzerland join the European Union. Many of those who favor such policies—indeed the majority—nevertheless are willing to hew to the long and patient task of winning a majority of the Swiss over to their point of view. But there is a quiet resentment of some of the elite that this is a necessity, and that, of course, it could be that they will never win popular support for their policies despite their best efforts to explain why they are right. This sociological effect—the feeling of superiority and condescension by some Swiss elites—could be important in the long run. If direct democracy is ever to be overturned, it might well be that it happens as a result of a long, concerted effort by embittered business, political, or other elites.

A related group would be critics of the regime in accord over Switzerland's role in World War II—those who want to see further apologies, and payment of reparations by the Swiss, or, in some cases, demand that banking privacy and Swiss neutrality be done away with altogether. But again, even these critics, who often smolder with resentment over the stubborn resistance of the Swiss to clamor to their view of the war and related issues, are of mixed minds when it comes to direct democracy itself. When I visited one such critic, Jean Ziegler, in his office at the University of Geneva, I expected to hear a jihad against the direct democracy. Ziegler's assessment was that his proposal for a Swiss apology for the country's part in World War II would lose about 90-10 in a national referendum. Yet he does not propose to overturn the system as such. "There has to be a way to persuade people," he says, confidently. Others in Ziegler's circle, of course, may not take such a patient, long-run view. For the most part, however, it is notable that even many of those who find much of Switzerland corrupt—"like a girl who works in a whore house, but wants to remain a virgin," in the words of Ziegler's *The Swiss, the Gold, and the Dead*— accept the discipline of direct democracy, which forces them to treat each Swiss man and woman as their equal. "Change of the kind we are looking for takes time," Ziegler comments.

A second type of critic is more philosophical. One of the more serious is Beat Kappeler, a long-time labor union leader, and now an editor for the weekly journal *Weltwoche*. Kappeler's arguments for an adjustment in the Swiss system are varied, and his manner smooth and polished. Seemingly superior, on the one hand—he decries the notion that the system encourages voter study of the issues as "the ill-informed myth about well-informed Swiss voters"—he is, nevertheless, anything but an elitist. Kappeler recalls how, as a prominent labor leader, he eschewed first class on the Swiss trains in favor of second-class section. "It wasn't out of economic reasons, although it saves a little money," he concedes. "It's the fact that elites who travel in first class feel free to interrupt you and barge right in on you. People in second class leave you alone."

As theories of representative democracy are likely to be in the future, Kappeler is especially critical of the impact of direct democracy on legislators and the legislative process. In a short but cogent book, *Regieren statt revidieren*, he lays out the case that initiative and referendum have weakened the Swiss parliament and hampered it from making tough choices and providing meaningful leadership. (Weltwoche, Zürich, 1996.)

The weaker of Kappeler's two main criticisms is that direct democracy has perverted the legislative process by placing it at the mercy of special interest groups and well-heeled lobbies, who can "block almost anything" early in the process. Switzerland certainly has pressure groups, but how do they compare with other countries?

"We have lobbies, but they are not anything like the full-time armies you see in Washington," comments Casper Selg, host of the German-language news broadcast on Swiss public radio and a former correspondent in Washington, DC. "UBS does not have 10 or 20 full time staff working in Bern." Another correspondent, Swiss television's Hans Bärenberger, is likewise an experienced reporter in Bern. "Lobbying hasn't really become a profession the way it has in Washington and other capitals," he notes. "There are some hired guns, but I don't think I could name more than two or three. There are pressure groups and the parties, but these don't seem to be stronger than elsewhere, and I would guess they are weaker."

At the least, the referendum and initiative process provides a check on these groups. If Kappeler doesn't like their influence, why doesn't he challenge laws, or propose new ones through the referendum? Kappeler's answer, and it is a fair point, is that this tool, while always present in theory, cannot always be used in practical terms after the long period of building a complicated set of policies or interconnected programs. The voters in Switzerland do rely on legislative expertise, and do tend to give their elites the benefit of the doubt—approving the vast majority of laws passed by parliament that are challenged.

As well, Kappeler argues, money plays an unhealthy role in the referendum process itself. Often one side outspends the other by a factor of 5-1, 10-1, and more, and the record of success by groups at the low end of that figure is not long. It is not, however, non-existent. When Kappeler met with me at the Bern train station, a national vote by the Swiss on reform of the military was only a few days off. Powerful forces, led by Christoph Blocher on the right and the Green Party on the left, were opposing a proposal to allow Swiss forces who volunteer to go abroad to carry arms.

Having watched Blocher's fund-raising efforts, and a sophisticated media campaign to accompany it, along with what he called the "very poor" effort of the government to rally support for its own proposal, Kappeler's assessment was that the opposition was likely to win. I ventured the opinion, taken from Jeff Greenfield's concept of "political jujitsu," that the very fact that the opposition had so much money was being turned into an issue by the government. It also seemed to me that the federal council, in particular President Moritz Leuenberger, had in fact waged a reasonably skillful counter-effort, and would probably pull out a win. My guess turned out to be right in this case, though the win was only by a slim 51-49 margin. Nevertheless, the result suggested that money, in referendum politics as in other votes, can be a two-edged sword.

Kappeler's second argument, that direct democracy tends to produce a weaker brand of leadership, is more difficult to deny. This has been observed in the U.S., for example, in the state of California, where governors and legislators have often seemed ineffectual, dating back to the populist uprising that took place in the state during the 1978 Proposition 13 tax cut.

"We don't have a government," Kappeler argues. "We have a toy government." Most members of the Swiss executive, let alone ordinary members of parliament, have little experience and no competence, in Kappeler's eyes— let alone strength, or polish. "It is not quaint any more," he adds with a smile.

In making this point, however, Kappeler and the defenders of direct democracy find themselves in rough agreement. Both he and the system's supporters find that the referendum system tends to produce a less agile, less polished, less independent legislature and executive than would otherwise be the case. Kappeler believes this to be a political ill. Supporters believe it is a political good. At least, they share the same assessment of its impact.

Even enthusiastic Swiss are sometimes weary of their democracy—and the referendum system is a partial cause of this. Turnout levels in Switzerland have reached U.S.-like levels of 50 to 60 percent in national elections and 30 to 40 percent in cantonal elections. It is, in fact, work. "You must remember, we have to vote three or four times a year, sometimes more," as the late Dr. Paul Jolles, the former Swiss Secretary of State, put it. "Some people are tired of it. That is the price of citizenship—it is work sometimes."

This phenomenon is not to be overstated, however, especially in comparison to other affluent societies. The Swiss are uniquely proud of their political system, as survey data show, and as American sociologist Carol Schmid, cited previously, has demonstrated in depth. If the burden placed on the Swiss citizen is high, it is also true that his capacity for bearing such burdens appears to be high as well, provided that they are the reasonable duties of citizens. Their weariness is that of some Americans when called for jury duty. If they are busy people, there is a certain natural reluctance to have to spend days or weeks at a trial. But if they are patriots, they are willing to do so, and may even wax nostalgic about this exercise of a right their forefathers fought and died for.

This drawback, the desire to be less involved in the details, is merely the unavoidable flip side of one of the system's striking advantages—its precision. The Swiss system of citizen legislation facilitates a much quicker and more accurate matching of public policy to the will of the electorate. The difference between it and purely representative democracy is illustrated if we imagine a system in which you could pick only which grocery store someone else would shop at for you—or, still further, if you could select between three or four carts that had been previously filled by people at the store, but could not stock the carts yourself. It is possible, particularly if leaders are respectful of the popular will, to communicate what groceries you want to the cart fillers. Over time, you might find one of them consistently putting eggs into the cart. But even if he did, he might also tend to purchase $20 worth of Spam, which you don't want, or to buy 2 percent milk instead of your preference, skimmed. There would only be very rough approximations of your desires, though. And in a system of representative elections, remember, the voters are only able to communicate with the "cart stockers" once every few years and when they do, rather than giving elaborate instructions they vote yes or no for one of them, accepting all the choices they didn't like in the bargain.

Imagine if, after acclimating yourself to this system, you were suddenly allowed to make periodic trips to the grocery store yourself, and pick out your own items. You would have an immense feeling of relief as you knew that, from time to time, you could take care of some of the neglected items. Sophisticated grocery stores would watch carefully to see what you picked out when you had a chance, and use this as a signal to improve their own purchases. In thinking about the Swiss system, and watching it in action, one feels something of the sense of exhilaration that that shopper would feel. It is far from perfect, and there are many mistakes made. But the mistakes you make are yours. It is a gulp of oxygen; a sip of undiluted democratic spring water.

Professor Wolf Linder of the University of Bern, a leading analyst of the referendum and initiative process in Switzerland, offers a contrasting metaphor. "I think it is true, and a good image, that direct democracy is, in a sense, much like this grocery store," he suggests. "But we might say that representative democracy presents a different image, and it has some advantages.

"Suppose you would like to buy a computer. You face many different choices, and you know there are many good models, but you want to get one that is right for you, and at a decent price. What do you do? You have a nephew that knows a lot about computers, so you ask him to help you. You tell him what you want—'I want a computer that does this, and this; I don't care about a lot of storage, but I want a fast model,' and so on. He then knows what you want, but he also knows about the different computers that can do this.

"So he selects the model for you. He is, in effect, your representative."

This is a just and persuasive summary of the representative model. It relies, of course, on the same kind of hybrid as my own image of the grocery store does—combining politics on the one hand with consumer choices in a market on the other hand. In politics, of course, even democratic politics, we cannot each select our own nephew to buy the particular type of government we want. Rather, say in a town of 10,000 people, all of us select one person to buy a computer for all 10,000 of us—a loss of intimacy and of control on our part. Furthermore, in a real-life grocery store, there are, in fact, elements of representative government. We rely on the grocer to select various items to put on the shelf for us, and a whole range of government inspectors and regulators to make sure—hopefully—that the food we buy is accurately labeled, properly handled, and safe.

Nor can we all go to the grocery store and buy whatever we want, individually, you selecting snow peas and your neighbor preferring corn on the cob. However many choices there are before a law is made, once it is made, it is the law—for all of us. Jude cannot pay taxes under one code, while Jeff pays taxes under another. So, to the extent that either image relies on the desirability of making individual choices, they somewhat miss the mark.

Even so, on the central matter that is being compared, the two illustrations are illuminating. Representative government, to an extent, relies on expertise of someone—your nephew, a consultant, your congressman—to make decisions for us. Direct democracy, to a greater extent, lets us make choices more directly, with less intervention by experts. In the case of initiative, it even enables us to "place an item on the shelf" that the store manager, or our nephew the computer nerd, has declined to do, whether out of stubbornness or ignorance or because they simply aren't hearing us very well. This advantage may be less or more acute depending on many other factors. For example, in many countries, multiparty systems create opportunities for voters to choose their representatives, at least to select between several different models. In the United States, a strong and somewhat exclusive two-party system means that in most cases, the choice comes down to brand X and brand Y.

These illustrations also remind us that neither Switzerland, the United States, nor any other modern democracy we see today is purely "representative" or "direct." The systems we observe, and are likely to observe, are mixed regimes. They vary in degree, more than in kind. Still, most of the world at present tends to lean far more toward the representative model. And Switzerland uses the instrument of direct democracy more extensively, indeed far more extensively, than the others. Anyone who wants to know what European or U.S. politics would be like if direct democracy were employed more extensively will surely wish to study this convenient political and social test case.

Whether such a system is suitable for other countries or not, the Swiss use of this device, over a substantial period, is a valuable departure. Other democracies rely almost exclusively on representative methods of securing popular consent. The Swiss alone have taken this more direct route. This is not to say that the other democracies are wrong. The fact that Switzerland is virtually alone suggests prudence may argue against its innovation. It is, at the least, something different.

If we glance at how the initiative and referendum process has performed, now a 150-year experience, several patterns become readily apparent.

Even those who are skeptics of the benefits of referendum, of whom there are few, concede it has committed few if any drastic wrongs. The most common complaint against it among the small number of critics is that having worked well, it is now "out of date" because it hampers entry into the European Union and other desirable outcomes. (And many of the staunch advocates of full EU entry, which the Swiss have declined for the present, say that the referendum process would need only adjustment for that end, along the lines of the Swiss entry into the League of Nations, and not a complete overhaul. That is a separate debate.)

In short, if the general presumption is in favor of the most direct means of popular control, subject only to checks on the people as might seem necessary, the Swiss experience seems to suggest the need for such limits is small indeed. We may conclude with Viscount Bryce that the Swiss have used their power of initiative and referendum "responsibly and well," and certainly without gross disaster or inconvenience. Having asked dozens of Swiss what the worst result initiative or referendum has produced, most of them answered "none" if the question meant has there been a single grave error or result. The respondent will then point to a particular referendum he or she did not agree with—but will hasten to add that this is only their personal opinion.

Importantly, when commenting about "mistakes" by the voters, most add one of the following two points—or both. First, nearly all will say that the result "is not final"—that if they and others who agree with them are right and can marshal the facts, the public, being reasonable and indeed astute, will eventually agree with them. Second, many—especially politicians, such as Mr. Loeb, Mr. Gross, others—will have come to the conclusion that because the people disagreed, their own initial opinion must have been wrong. So far from feeling any contempt for their fellow citizens as ill informed, the Swiss—even the most brilliant—regard the voters as a standard of judgment, more than an object. In most countries, as the former economic and political guru to Jack Kemp, Jude Wanniski, has observed, the voters as a whole are smarter than their leaders. The difference may be that, in Switzerland, most leaders believe the people are smarter.

As a result, there is perhaps less of a gap between elite and popular opinion in Switzerland than in any other country. There is, when such gaps occur, less arrogance felt by the elites and less frustration by the people than perhaps mankind has ever seen over an extended time under any other political system. The chief institutional sources of this distinctive level of mutual respect, in my observation, is the federal and cantonal initiative and referendum process, and community democracy.

Notes

1. The history of the instrument and the term are under debate. A case can be made that the word itself derives from a practice in the Swiss Diet, predating the French Revolution, of "referring" questions back to the cantons. A number of cantonal constitutions required this (as did the colony of New York in the U.S. Continental Congress). But there are many acts of "referring" questions to other branches and authorities in politics. In the Swiss case, some of these referrals might issue forth in a popular assembly; others would not.
2. The level as of this writing was 100,000 signatures within an eighteen-month period, though there is discussion of raising these and other signature requirements to reflect growth in the population and the size of the voting public since those levels were established.
3. Gregory Fossedal, Richard Holbrooke, and Paul Nitze, "How the Marshall Plan Worked," Research Report 05-997-02, Alexis de Tocqueville Institution, June 5, 1997; and Gregory Fossedal and Richard Holbrooke, "Will Clayton's Genius," *Houston Chronicle*, 2 June 1997.

10

Communities

Yves Christen is something of a contradiction—or maybe the right term is hybrid. He is trim, of average height, and well-groomed, and has blondish-brown hair with grey streaks. Jack Kemp would covet Christen's blowdryer. His sharp, alert features and smooth, precise gestures suggest a French bureaucrat. Yet there is a dash of uncalculated hail-fellow-well-met as he strides into and through the restaurant: a pinch American, even Bavarian. Christen glances around confidently. His eyes take in a number of friends that he knows, but is not afraid to make contact with the occasional stranger.

Christen's words are measured, his voice soft. Answering questions he speaks smoothly, but without that intangible, tenth-of-a-second mental look upward that one feels with an American politician—the moment when everything seems to go through a little high-speed computer before the slightly fabricated answer is meted out. Christen looks you in the eye and answers; you are talking to *Christen*. His native tongue is French but his German is good, his English stops for the right word twice or so a sentence, but is passable.

In other words, Christen is a little bit, in the best sense of the word, of a mutt—a polyglot man in a polyglot nation. He embodies something very Swiss, the blending of diversities. You can't understand the Swiss democracy without going to its communities, its communes and cantons, and meeting its part-time mayors, its housewives, and police chiefs.

Christen is the town council chairman of the city of Vevey. He is also a member of parliament. We saw him earlier on the same day, voting for the two new federal council members, the future presidents of Switzerland. Christen also has a law practice or some small business to make ends meet—another citizen lawmaker in a nation of them.

One cannot understand Switzerland without getting down to the particular canton, its communes, and the specific people who make up the communes. In any country, as Mark Twain observed, "The people are the real thing... the country itself." Christen is a sort of embodiment of this, although, in Switzerland, they have several million embodiments of it. He would be the first to deny there is anything special about him.

Vevey

Tonight, Christen and the other council members will vote on five new Swiss citizens—that is, on whether five foreign-born families may become citizens. There are other matters on the agenda for the meeting we'll attend, including the one that was on the front page of newspapers across the country: the fire that destroyed a block of low-income housing units just days before. Reading the small schedule of items to be discussed from the local paper, however, the matter of the immigrants struck me.

Here in Christen was one official, on the very same day, participating in one of the "highest" acts of state, the choosing of a future president, and one of the most humble (in the literal sense of the word) or basic, deciding who is a Swiss citizen and who is not.

The item was around the middle of the official notice of the "Conseil Communal de Vevey" in *La Presse de Vevey* a few days before:

9. Report on:

Request to incorporate (*agrégation*) the residents...

1. M. Tekik Djikoli and his minor son, from Yugoslavia

2. Miss Deborah Melchiorre, from Italy

3. Mrs. Sebastiana Pinieri and her three minor children, from Italy

4. Mr. Gheorghe-Gavril Pop, from Romania, and his spouse, also from Romania.

5. Mr. Gian Franco Sentinelli and his spouse, from Italy (1/99).

In importance and symbolism, of course, the council will be committing one of the quintessential acts of statecraft. The question of who is a citizen goes to the heart of what a citizen is and, therefore, what the country itself is. This issue has been fought and died over—the American Civil War, for instance—and with good reason. From antiquity, it meant something to be a Roman citizen, a member of the commune of Sparta, a burgher of Switzerland. Jean-Jacques Rousseau took the matter seriously enough that, years after becoming an expatriate, he proudly signed his works "citizen of Geneva," and John F. Kennedy stirred souls around the world by declaring himself a "citizen of Berlin."

That the Swiss handle it this way—at the local level of government and indeed in a kind of election—is rich with meaning. The decision was to be handed down not by a bureaucrat applying rules and stamps in an impersonal office. Instead, in Switzerland, the prospective fellow citizens of these applications were meeting in the open to discuss the matter and vote. "It is simple," a member of the town council explained as we milled around outside the hall. "Citizenship is conferred by citizens."

Vevey is a city of approximately 15,000 persons located on the North side of Lac de Leman, or the Lake of Geneva, perhaps thirty miles West of the lake's Eastern tip. Though Vevey plays home to the headquarters of Nestlé Corporation, the giant food products and pharmaceutical company, it has fallen on something of a recession. Vevey suffers one of the highest unemployment rates in Switzerland. Being Switzerland, this means it is at or even over 5 percent, but being Switzerland, this is an unusual and troublesome figure. This economic reality adds perhaps a slight edge to the proceedings regarding the applicants for citizenship. One of the most common complaints of proponents of reduced immigration is that foreigners are "taking up jobs" or, if not this, the related argument that they "drive down wages" by offering their labor cheaply.

We file into what seems to be an old church or theater with high-backed wooden benches. (The room reminds me of the meeting hall at the Grafton County Theatre in Hanover, New Hampshire, where then-presidential candidate Jerry Brown gave a speech during my junior year at college.) There are 100 members of the council, Christen told me earlier; today, there are (by my count) 82 in attendance. About 50 members are men—10 or less wear suits and appear to be professionals, the rest dress more casually, and there are perhaps 7 or 8 in work outfits or uniforms. The other 32 are women—approximately—and they are dressed at roughly the same level of formality as the men. Some nonbusiness-suit dresses, more pants, corduroys, and blue jeans. There is one woman who looks credibly like the comedienne Gilda Radner, and one fellow in a very expensive pin-striped suit. Other than that, most of the council members are not striking in appearance. There is also a young fellow in a green rugby shirt, about 25, sharp, articulate—just watching his movements, and the way he makes careful notes during some of the early proforma introductions, it strikes me that this is likely to be one of the more active members. "Rugby shirt guy," my note pad dubs him: RSG in notes.

The first few items on the agenda are procedural—filing reports for the public record, approving minutes, that sort of thing. During the new business section, a man in a yellow shirt ("leading socialist," my guide for the evening whispers) stands up to complain about the smoking habit of the local school principal. "It is not a bad thing from time to time," he says. "But the man who is advocating this is in charge of our children at school." There is scattered applause from about one-fourth of the members. A note on my pad: "Swiss federalism also means power to set standards."

There is some shuffling of papers up front and a very mild hum on the floor as everyone realizes there is no specific resolution to be voted on, but the fellow in the yellow shirt seems to want some sort of acknowledgment. Rugby shirt guy stands up to say, "If someone on this council did something as stupid" as the principal, they would be chastised roundly before the council. Soft laughter and nods of agreement. The council member with the yellow shirt looks over and smiles appreciatively. "Still, the man is not here, so we should probably let this go. The government should discuss it with him"—by which he probably meant the executive council or the mayor's office.

Soon we were up to item nine, the immigrants. Someone in the front reads the names, as if in an introduction. Are they going to appear, be interviewed perhaps? No, the chairman is only giving a few scattered details from the report by the council's committee on immigration matters.

We glance over to the right at a group of ten to twelve people in the back observation area with us; from the complexions and their interest in the proceedings, they could be some of the immigrant families.

Some questions go up to the chair.

"These are all recommended?"

The chairman confers with his colleague.

"Yes. I thought we had said that"—he had, actually—"but I was checking because you asked."

A woman in the front talked about the difficulty in the schools assimilating different language groups. There were some nods of agreement, but no great stir.

Rugby shirt guy whispered something to a female colleague of his in the row in front; it seemed not to be about the immigrants but about the forthcoming issue, the fire, from the way she nodded and then looked back at the proceedings—as if changing the subject.

This had the feeling to me of a ritual in which everyone knew how the votes on such things tend to turn out, but was respecting the need to ask some questions, make a few remarks—like a shopper who knows what car he wants, but feels he should spend a few minutes kicking the tires commenting about the mileage just to make sure he is being thoughtful and responsible.

Ballots (slips of very cheap paper; this is Switzerland) are passed around for the council members to vote on. There is low-key discussion as the members write down their votes on each applicant, but less movement than, say, during a typical vote in the U.S. Congress or a state legislature. The chair expects the procedure to last two or three minutes, not fifteen. He is not rushing anyone—that would make it feel like a vital decision was being made hastily—but there is a shared feeling that people will vote and the matter move on.

The ballots are collected and there is some brief discussion among those of us in the back. Will they announce the votes right away or wait until the end of the meeting? "Oh, no, it takes four or five minutes, they will just do it now. Everyone wants a little break before they discuss the fire anyway."

Over to the right, a woman—Mrs. Penieri? Miss Melchiori? she has no children with her—shifts a little bit on her seat.

The gavel up front bangs softly and the chair prepares to read the results. He confers one more time with a woman on his left, the deputy chairman, and the room quiets down. A man in the back section with us stands up, apparently to hear better. He has dark, Mediterranean skin; probably another immigrant.

"*Monsieur Djikoli et son fils ... Oui ... septante-trois ...* "

Seventy-three yes—that should be plenty if my count of eighty-two members is anywhere close to right.

"*No, sept.*"

So the count is 73–7; Missouir Djikoli is a Swiss citizen.

And make that eighty members, not eighty-two—unless a couple didn't vote. My count was not exact, but darn close.

During the slight buzz my attention was distracted from the vote on Ms. Melchiorre, but the chairman is now summarizing that vote again—it appears to be 75–7. Since her status is very different from that of Mr. Djikoli, the implication is that most of the members have a certain take on immigration and they vote for or against, with occasional exceptions.

The fellow on the right is sitting down now. Djikoli, perhaps? He is in the back by the coatroom talking to a boy with his hand on his shoulder.

"*Madame ... Pinieri ... et ses trois mineures ... soixante-six.*" So Mrs. Piniere was in; good.

"*Pop ... soixante-cinq. ... Sentinelli ... soixante-cinq.*"

So on this night, all the immigrants were approved. Vevey now had another eleven mouths to feed—or, depending upon your views of human potential, another Henri Nestlé or Albert Einstein.

The council members seem optimistic. There is warm and sustained applause for the vote, something that did not take place during the rest of the meeting, nor at any other official function we visited in Switzerland except during the speeches and announcements at the federal council vote earlier that day.

One of our friends from the dinner whispers something to my traveling companion.

"This is unusual," my friend passes on the comment. "Most are accepted, maybe 80 percent, but usually not all."

Indeed, in the mid-1980s, Carlo Schmid invited Aleksander Solzhynitsyn to the Appenzell *Landsgemeinde* and to various community meetings to observe democracy in action. Appenzell (Innerrhoden) is a *Landsgemeinde* canton, so all the laws of the canton and important decisions—such as citizenship—are in fact taken at the annual meeting.

When it came time to vote on the applications for citizenship at one of the meetings, Schmid apologized to his guest for the seeming crudity of what was about to happen—a fraternity popularity vote, perhaps, with people's lives in the balance. As the votes came in, about a third were negative, and Schmid explained again, afraid that the great Russian writer would think something less of Swiss liberalism to see such a display.

"No, you are wrong to apologize," Solzhynitsyn reassured him. "This is the way citizens should be made—and not made."

There is the same simple but electric radicalism one sees in so many Swiss practices—that pervasive, unrestrained democratic faith.

Lugano

As we pull out of the Lugano train station, there is a low thud.

A sideways movement, and then the taxi cab slides to a stop. We have hit the car in front of us in its right rear bumper.

A man, about age sixty, looks back out of the car in front. His license plate indicates ("BE") he is visiting from Bern. The taxi driver looks at me and says something in Italian. My eyes glaze and he tries again. "I have to go talk."

The driver gets out of the car and walks unassumingly but directly up to the car in front. The driver of the other car gets out with a weary smile. A good sign: He's not happy to be doing this, but at the same time he's decently cheerful about it. Well, this is Switzerland—hopefully we can get the matter taken care of in ten or fifteen minutes and be on our way.

Where is my laptop—here in the back seat or in the trunk? Good—there it is in its little black case. My hand reaches down to split open the case and turn it on, and the reassuring humming begins.

My driver and the man from the car in front seem to be talking politely but not yet agreeing on anything. No one has called the police, but a couple of horns toot behind us. The two men walk back now to look at the dent, and my driver is reaching for his wallet, a good sign.

As they reach the back of the car, their voices become more audible. They are speaking German; evidently the Bernese man is not fluent in Italian. Meanwhile, the computer is asking me something about "Scandisk" —evidently my Windows program did not "shut down properly." This happens from time to time. "Y" for yes, "Y" for yes, "D" for delete, "S" for skip the undo process—my left hand types the answers to the queries as my right hand jots fragments from the conversation up in front.

"There is some damage, I told you this. ... Yes, there it is. That would normally cost about 100 francs to get fixed."

The other man looks skeptical. He doesn't appear to be bargaining or anything for the sake of bargaining; he just doubts the dent he sees can be fixed for 100 francs (about $63).

"Well, where I take my car I would say it's more like 200 francs."

The cab driver looks back at me in the car. My computer is scanning files, moving into that phase where the file names roll by very quickly.

"If you take that to so-and-so in the suchlike district, they will fix it for no more than 150 francs," the cab driver offers hopefully.

"Maybe, but you are talking about a forty-five-minute drive each way. In this bad weather." It is raining in the Ticino—much warmer than the rest of Switzerland in March, about 50 degrees today, but wet.

"How would this be? We split the difference, it is 175 francs."

Icons are starting to appear on my computer "desktop." It's just about ready for me to start typing notes.

"I think that is fair," the driver of the other car says.

"Okay," the cab driver says in English. He looks back at me for a second and then does some shuffling with the bills in his hand, pulls out a few coins (probably five franc pieces to make the twenty-five francs over 150), and hands the mass to the other man.

Looking down, it strikes me that we are about to take off now and it is time to shut down the computer. The driver climbs back in. "Please wait," the computer screen tells me, "for your computer to shut down."

"Now, where we go?," the driver asks.

"Just a second—*momentli bitte*." There—ta dah, the little Windows tune plays—the computer is shut down, it's ready to be closed up.

As we pull away to my next stop—the office of a newspaper editor—it strikes me that the two men have solved their problem in about the time it takes my laptop to boot up. With a Scandisk program detour, that's about 150 seconds. The principals were a taxicab driver and a tourist, who speak different first languages, at a fairly busy train station. No insurance forms were filed, no information exchanged.

We pull around a kind of circular drive and do a 180-degree turn. As we pass by the station from the other angle, it becomes clear that there is a policeman directing traffic, though he is not very busy. There is some kind of minor construction at the end of the street. Evidently he saw no need to intervene, and the two drivers felt no need to involve him.

Hittnau

There probably is no such thing as a typical Swiss town, but if a composite were formed, Hittnau would not be far off. The town, not quite 2,500 in population, is not far from Zürich—perhaps forty minutes away. Most of the townspeople work in the city or in its periphery of offices. Our hostess on the church council is employed at an asset management company. Long commutes are not nearly as common in Switzerland as among the Americans or even the British, but land is scarce and as families grow, if they want to own a home with a stretch of grass around it they must go to places like Hittnau.

We arrive late in the day; it is hard to see much, but from the age of some of the buildings, and the clientele at the local tavern we visit for dinner, it seems clear that there is a substantial "native" population of people who grew up here and who probably have children and parents here too. One is reminded of (say) Greenwich, Connecticut, or McLean, Virginia—on a smaller scale, of course. Many of the people you see, probably most, work in the city, but the bartender or owner of the restaurant you are in might be a fifth-generation native, or a second-generation immigrant, who seldom leave the town. Though we are in the heart of German-Protestant Switzerland, under the shadow of Zürich and Zwingli, the town is diverse. About one-fourth of the people are Roman Catholic. There are some immigrants, though not as many as in the large cities.

We arrive at what appears to be a school or office building—flat, bricks; it is in fact the community hall—and hustle in through a back door. It is 4:28, we are twenty-eight minutes late for our meeting, and everyone is seated around a table, ready to go. Around the table are five of the members of the town council or other leading members of the town: a member of the church council, Mrs. Buhrer, and her husband, Dr. Buhrer; two of the ladies from the town council; and a woman who is active in the school management, though not a teacher, as well as in the operation of the town's (one, Protestant) church. There was going to be someone from the police force of one man, part time, who makes calls in Hittnau when needed from the next town, Pfäffikon, but he could not make it. Not that there has been a mugging or a robbery. "Most of his time is spent looking for a few road violations or handing out official documents," the lady from the town council explains. "We do not have much crime," the schoolteacher smiles.

Several of my questions sent in advance have had to do with the intermingling of church and state in Switzerland. This, of course, is very different from what one would see in the United States of the late twentieth or early twenty-first centuries, and one sees it most clearly in the towns. Accordingly they begin with a brief series of presentations on this issue. There are more of the hand-written graphs and flow charts, not done on a computer but carefully drawn with ballpoint pens and rulers.

Dr. Buhrer seems somewhat apologetic, explaining that the taxes going to the church (about 10 percent of the community rate) are optional and can be avoided by filling out a card. Many people who are not active in the church, he says, continue to pay the taxes out of a desire to contribute something, even if they are not religious. He anticipates my next question by adding, "There is a Catholic Church about twenty minutes over. I do not think there are Jewish people in Hittnau, but the people who practice other religions tend to do so in the cities—for us, Zürich."

Like many of the churches in Switzerland, and particularly in Bern, Geneva, and Zürich, the Hittnau church seems to be functionally similar to the "civil religion" that Rousseau speculated about as the ideal for his small, virtuous republic. Religion has been integrated with, almost subsumed into, the Swiss democracy—it is partly secular. The faith is not highly partisan or even doc-trinal in character, certainly not here in Hittnau.

"What is the biggest controversy you've had here—have there been any divisive issues in Hittnau?" My traveling companion scrunches a little bit, as if thinking, here goes the American journalist again, asking about a scandal in the church choir or a kickback scheme at the zoning board. My interest in controversy, however, is not morbid, nor focused on ethics. One learns a lot about a system when it is under stress—its flaws and strengths sometime come out in relief. What do the Swiss do when they have a political *problem*?

Our hosts from Hittnau were nonplused, but no one had a ready answer. Mrs. Buhrer smiled and looked around the table and the others smiled back, apparently trying sincerely to remember anything that had gotten heated within the council.

Then one of the council members explained, "about three months ago, we had a vote that was four to three. This happens from time to time. I think in this case it was about something in the school, not something people were angry about, but just something where there was a close difference of opinion."

"But you must realize, in these cases, what happens is that everyone on the council defends the decision, and there is no sniping or attacking of each other. We have a strong culture of consensus, a tendency to try to work things out on a solution that we can all agree on in the end."

This phrase about consensus comes up often in Switzerland; it leaves me skeptical. There is a faint aroma of the mysterious way people used to talk about Japanese society—before the collapse of its economy made this rolling "consensus" seem less robust than hapless.

"It seems like people everywhere would like to have this kind of approach. People in Bosnia would like to have this kind of harmony, they just can't get it. Are people in Switzerland just very nice, very cooperative? Or are there things that you do that facilitate this?"

My companion seems to like the question. "Gregory is trying to get an understanding of *why* it works this way—how is *this* possible?" Again there are some mutual looks across the table, but some nods and mild thought frowns.

"I think part of it is, we work with everyone in the town—there is broad consultation," answers Mrs. Buhrer. "When you have a small town like this and many things are done on a volunteer basis, you work that way."

"Another factor you have to remember," her husband adds, "is that many of these things are referred to the people anyway."

In Hittnau, as in nearly all the communes, everything from the town bud-get to the creation of a no-smoking zone near the train station is voted on by the community. Someone slides me a small booklet with the town budget, which appears to be mass-produced for the voters. "This gives you a certain notion—well, it causes things to be done with them in mind. I do not mean that negatively, that people are looking over our shoulders. I mean that there is a certain reality, a certain rough sketch you could draw of what people basically want. It is there, whether someone disagrees with a part of it, it is there. We view our job as trying to approximate that picture."

The picture he is talking about, in fact, is going to come into being in rough terms anyway, at some point or another, because the system almost cannot resist going to it. The discussions, the meetings—they all end, politically and therefore psychologically, at the people. Consensus building among elites, in this sense, is merely a faster way of bowing to the inevitable. Of course, it is more than that; there is a sincere interest in the faces around me in cooperating with one another. But it is not less than that. The system itself encourages, rather than discourages, this nonpartisan approach.

Thus the "politics of consensus" is, in part, a concomitant of direct democracy and decentralization. It defuses personal disputes and zero-sum competition between leaders, and at the same time builds a culture of collaboration between the people and their politicians. (Under the militia system and at this level of government especially, the people are the politicians.) Notice that while there is nothing to prevent this from happening in representative democracy, it is less automatic. The legislator may hope to please all constituents by working the system to take contradictory positions on different bills; the bottom line is more confused. He does not, in any case, feel with any certainty that any particular issue he is deciding may be referred to the people—in fact, it almost certainly will not be, in a direct sense, and even in an indirect sense, of a particular issue becoming important in his next election race, the odds are rather remote.

Mrs. Buhrer, who (we later found out) was going into the hospital for surgery the next day, sensed my interest in this connection between consensus politics and direct democracy. She explained, "We view ourselves as trying to bring about..."—she looked over to a colleague for the right word—"trying to *facilitate* choices, do what the people want. It is our job to do this well and offer intelligent choices."

Hugo Bütler told us a few days later about the case of a church in Stein, a small Rhein town, where an influx of Italian immigrants took place one year. The next year, the Italians were invited to the church council meeting for its budget discussion. When the subject of fees and tax payments came up, the Italians, joined by a few of the native Swiss, voiced their preference not to have any. The rest of the members tried to explain this would mean drastic changes in the church service but the money was voted down anyway. With Swiss logic and efficiency, the discussion then turned to planning for a year in which there would be no funerals, no weddings, and an absence of many other things the people were used to. The participants now understood that their actions had consequences and that they were in charge—but regretted what they had done with their authority. The fees and tax assessments were restored and the meeti̇̀ back to its previous track.

Thus community government in Switzerland does not merely operate the philosophy of giving the people what they want. Because a member of a community, one of the people, is not indifferent to the question of whether the people's understanding of what the options are is informed, or corrupt, or misled, or intelligent. It is, rather, a style of leadership that accepts the citizen as sovereign, and therefore looks to the improvement and perfection of the citizen as the best (and ultimately, the only) way to bring about effective solutions. Rather than merely reading about self-government, however, the Swiss learn, as well, by doing.

Bellinzona

My train is chugging North toward Bellinzona. We are not going to make it in time for me to visit the cantonal statistics office, which from the telephone sounds like an information gold mine. At a little before six, on a Friday, they have already closed. Outside in a tiny park area is a kiosk with announcements; there appears to be some kind of discussion meeting at 7:30 on the other side of the train station about the snow removal, or fixing the roads in the spring, or transporting people to some spring event—to me it's a bunch of Italian words and a nice little picture of a truck in snow, one that looks like it was taken off the Internet or from one of those "graphic images."

There is a small news stand by the train station where the lady probably speaks a little English, or can understand even my German. She directs me to a coffee shop pub not far up the street.

Inside there are seven or eight men and women around a table. Most are drinking coffee or some warm beverage; one or two have a soda or a beer. "Is it okay for me to join you who's not from the town?"—those are, roughly, my words to the group, in very poor German.

A woman at the head of the table looks at me for a second. In addition to the natural, human sizing up of the other person, she is giving me the "Swiss Language Look": What is his accent? Where is he from? How do I address him? She frowns slightly in concentration.

"Yes, okay—for the meeting?," the woman answers in English. Like most Swiss, she can tell, even when listening to what is a second or third language for her, what the accent of the speaker is and instantly either shift into English to accommodate me, or respond in German—but with a few English words like "okay" peppered in, apparently to let me know there is a little help available, if needed. A couple of Swiss told me that my dress is a further tip-off, but that was probably not a factor today—although it is true that my efforts to maintain at least a few seconds of national anonymity did much better on the telephone, particularly in conversations with French-speaking Swiss.

a while sir—for the meeting. Would you like any-

please, would be very nice." Only it undoubtedly ; in this translation. "It's okay with you, to work on

;wers in German.

his, your Italian," a younger man from the table The woman laughs too; the young man turns to explain his joke to the others. The guy has scored two or three points: He said something in English, he's made nice banter, and he's loosened up the group.

"You only think I speak Italian because you've heard my German." They chuckle.

An awkward little silence follows, which is my chance to explain why an American has any interest at all in their meeting. My little speech about democracy, Alexis de Tocqueville, and this book follows.

"Are you the town council?" My eyes roam around the table: Five men, three women, mostly older than me, two of the men younger, both in their early thirties. The woman translates briefly for her friends and then answers me.

"No, but I am on it and several of these are. We are a committee that works with the council to try to help some of the older people and others get plowed. They are supposed to get plowed by the town, but the town can't afford to get everyone; we do not want to have to buy more equipment. These people don't need that level of service anyway; they are not asking for it; but they want something more than being left where they are now."

The woman appears to be sort of the head of the group, at least in this functional setting. The other people at the table ask her questions in Italian and she points or answers and more or less leads the conversation.

"In a few minutes we will start," she says.

We are waiting for someone named Marko or Marceau, an auto mechanic who has a snowplow, to show up, as well as for a couple of retired people who want to complain about the roads being closed.

Two old men arrive in hunting-jacket plaid-type shirts; the one bears some resemblance to the "Fred Turbo" character that used to appear on Johnny Carson. The woman announces something to the small group, now at the table. Then she turns to me and says, "I am telling them we had scheduled this for thirty minutes. Marko is not here. We are going to hear from these men and then discuss it and see if we can come up with something."

The two men, speaking politely, appear to be laying out a request—something about Tuesdays and Fridays, or the weekend. One man, with very soft-looking boots—the non-Fred-Turbo fellow—has brought a little map, nothing fancy, but a crisp, hand-drawn map. He has made three copies—enough to pass around the table and let everyone have a look, but not splurging on eight or ten copies to provide everyone with an original.

The woman looks over her shoulder at me, handing me the brown file she has had on her left. Vintage Swiss: running the meeting, solving the problem, translating for the outsider, and briefing the journalist; no fanfare.

"They are here to speak for the people who have various complaints," she explains. "These are the complaints. There aren't that many problems, but we should do a better job on the side road that feeds off into that area. But the canton is always complaining to us if we neglect certain of the other roads."

She looks at the clock; 7:48. The men are still talking at the end of the table. She looks back at me, for another translation McNugget.

"Marko offered to do some plowing for the people, but he charges other people for services—he is using his own machine. He does not mind doing it for free for a few, but then others complain. The town does not want to have to pay him, either. We are trying to work something out."

One of the older men, the Fred Turbo fellow, has a question. A young man at the end of the table answers; Fred Turbo seems satisfied. He looks at the woman and nods. She asks the other gentleman, the one with the soft boots, a question, apparently something like, "Is that all right?," because he looks a little glum, but nods. It appears he is not totally satisfied, but can live with it.

The woman starts to lead a short prayer or statement. The clock says 8:04. She crosses herself at the end; it was definitely a prayer. Some of the others cross themselves, some do not.

"Our granddaughter has a such-and-such tonight," the lady says. She didn't say "such-and-such," but she said some German word that wasn't familiar to me. "I hope you will excuse us for leaving so soon."

"Of course—do you mind telling me what happened?"

"Here?" She gestured with her hand at the table. The two older men were smiling and drinking some warm beverage out of tall cups with the young fellows.

"Yes—if you have a minute."

"Well, when Marko comes, I will tell him he has to plow the roads for the town. And the town won't pay him. But he will get paid. I think some of the people who would like to see that road plowed more often will pay him a little extra to do some other plowing he already does for them—you understand? A little extra, not the full amount. I am not going to tell the older men about this; as far as they are concerned it is the commune, and in a way it is. So they will get their service every so often with respect to the snow. If they want more often, or faster, they will have to pay Marko something extra. I told them that is only fair."

The meeting, and the woman's explanation, reminded me that even in the heart of democracy, a little secrecy and elite leadership are sometimes necessary. Maybe, in fact, there is no real contradiction between them. In a more regimented, top-down system, the woman would have eventually fallen prey to the rules. There would have to be a rationalized, concrete regulation about snowplow usage, who pays, what people's entitlements are, and so on.

In Switzerland, there are rules, to be sure, but there is confidence in whatever can be worked out by the people of the community too. It is not just rules, or just anarchy, nor a kind of 50-50 compromise between the two. The woman was able to work something out partly because she has intimate knowledge of the situation, partly because she has people's trust, partly because she doesn't have the power to merely compel a solution—but a number of parties are looking to her to help them find one.

It is the combination of decentralization and democracy; of economic freedom but also a kind of local communism. "Culture of consensus," the Swiss like to call it, but in their Swiss way, they neglect to leave instructions as to *how* this consensus is achieved. Joe Nye, the Dean at the Kennedy School, calls this the use of "soft power," of leadership by example and craft and persuasion. There are probably whole business school management books written about it. Table 10.1 reviews not only which powers the Swiss allocate certain functions *locally*, but in some cases, *how* the local government handles them. The two factors must be thought of as one, or at any rate, as inextricably linked.

Appenzell and Swiss Commune-ism

The result of this combination of decentralization and democracy is a kind of politico-spiritual mystery, a democracy seánce.[1] The paradox is highlighted by something very astute that one of Carlo Schmid's constituents said about Schmid and about the *Landsgemeinde*. Schmid is the senator from Appenzell Innerhoden, but also the *Landamman*—the mayor or chairman of the cantonal council. He therefore chairs the annual "town meeting" at which the citizens of the whole canton make the laws and approve the program for the state for the coming year—voting on citizens, questioning budgets, demanding more snowplows or fewer. The constituent was a nice lady, about fifty years old, who ran a little news stand near the town hall or cantonal seat—some impressively old building under renovation. She was telling me about the forthcoming Landsgemeinde, and some of the issues, flipping through a notebook of pictures she had. On one page were the men in their uniforms and swords, ceremoniously marching into the great square. On another they were raising hands to vote; another, separating. "This fellow," she told me, "is sort of a heckler. Not really a heckler, but he likes to talk, likes to act up a bit."

"Mr. Schmid really knows how to handle him," she continued. "He keeps the business moving, but everyone feels they have their say; it is fair.

"You know, our system, because of the degree of democracy, places a great importance on effective leadership."

Table 10.1

**Communities in Contrast: Decision-Making Level and
Method for Selected Acts**

	Switzerland	Japan	Britain	Russia	U.S.
Citizenship (conferred by)	*local*—council or *popular vote*	federal—law applied by official	federal—law applied by official	federal—law applied by official	federal—law applied by official
work permit	*canton*, official	federal, official	federal, official	federal	federal
income tax: report income	local, *elected official*	federal, official	federal, official	federal, official	federal, official
income tax: pay tax to ...	*local*	federal	federal	federal	federal
administration of army units	*mixed—canton* *	federal	federal	federal	federal
railroads (run by)	federal	federal	federal	federal.ck	private
welfare benefits (issued by...)	*local*	federal	n.a.	federal	*state*

Source: "Federalisms in Contrast," Research Memorandum, Alexis de Tocqueville Institution, copyright © AdTI 1999, all rights reserved.

Notes: *In practice, much of the army operation is now centralized, but it is still a cantonal responsibility. The Swiss system is far *more* decentralized than any other modern military.

On the surface, of course, nothing could place less importance on leadership than a democracy. Everything is the people, to an extent that some feel the system caters too much to the popular mood or fancy.

Yet, on the other hand, this places the skill of the leader at a higher level. "It takes more skill to deal with people," as François Loeb commented in talking about the direct democracy, "than to deal with chess pieces. People are chess pieces with a mind and will of their own."

Schmid, in putting together and holding a Landsgemeinde with thousands of voters in one place, is in effect holding and planning an American political convention. And unlike the typical presidential nominating convention, the results are not preordained; the decisions taken are real decisions, they could go either way. The "heckler" is a voter and a taxpayer who must be handled with a certain fairness.

The Swiss system is highly dependent on its Schmids—on the lady in Bellinzona nuancing Marko into plowing the old man's street for the city, but not on a city line item. This dependency on citizenship is one of democracy's great strengths in Switzerland, but would make this system awkward or even dangerous if applied uncritically in other countries—countries where the capacity for real self-government, for popular leadership, has grown somewhat weak through lack of use or a lack of real power.

This does not mean the Swiss system, or major parts of it, may not be usefully emulated. It does mean that those who do will have to give some thought to creating the kind of citizens needed to carry out the steps of this sensitive political dance—a system that extols majority rule but is constantly yielding, willingly, to the minority; where laws are clear and simple, yet are there as tools to be handled with flexibility and common sense. George Bernard Shaw once complained of communism that "it takes up too many evenings." The same is true of democracy in Switzerland—or Swiss commune-ism, if you well. It takes up a lot of evenings.

We have looked at the history of Swiss institutions and we have looked at the institutions as such—viewing the parts of the whole somewhat in connection, somewhat in isolation, but always in something of an abstract or static framework.

To understand how democracy in Switzerland really works, however, it is best to take a look at some of the actual problems and conditions it deals with. How do the Swiss organize their schools? Pay their taxes? Defend themselves? What sort of problems have they proven adept at answering, and what sort, if any, does the Swiss system appear ill equipped to deal with?

Note

1. Interestingly, a "seance," or "meeting," is how a typical political gathering is described in the French cantons, a fact that always tickled me when reading the *Tribune de Geneve*: "At its seance last night, the city council of Fribourg voted to compensate victims of last month's flood using the city's capital budget," or, "the federal council will deal with the shortfall in cantonal budgets at a seance next week."

Part 4

Issues

11

Education

Walking down the streets of Bern, the Swiss capital, one sees a country teeming with education. For every grocery store there appears to be perhaps three bookstores. These are generally stocked with serious volumes: reference books and computer software galore; history; and a plethora of how-to-do-it, solve-it-yourself volumes, from home repair to honing your shooting skills. A member of Parliament, Dr. Onken, recognizes me and waves hello; Onken operates a correspondence learning institute in Southeast Switzerland. Newspaper stands are as ubiquitous as in Manhattan, and have more newspapers. At a kiosk near the train station, the usual ads for rock-and-roll bands and small theater productions are sprinkled liberally with cards and flyers of French and Italian tutors, financial management services, and computer courses.

One thing to notice about the examples above is that there is no mention of a strictly "regular" school for children aged five through say eighteen—the K–12 years in the United States. There are many of these, too, of course. But one of the striking aspects of the Swiss passion for education is that it is not locked up in "the classroom." It ambles about the society freely, like the bustling pedestrians on the *Bahnhofstrasse* in Zürich or the cobbled streets along the river in Luzern.

This hunger for learning sprawls out across the society and into every activity in Switzerland, in a way that is hard to quantify or summarize, except by providing some examples that truly seem to be common. At a Swiss factory that builds large weaving and sewing machines in Aargau canton, we encounter a worker on his break. He is sitting by his machine reading a book about electrical engineering, which he is studying at the technical school. Visiting a housewife and member of the cantonal parliament in St. Gallen, my colleague begins the conversation in German—but our hostess replies in fragmented English. Her children, she explains, are keen to learn English, and she wants to practice so she can help and learn along with them.

Swiss students consistently perform close to the top in international standardized tests of math, science, and reading, as Fig. 11.1 suggests.

Figure 11.1

Math Performance by Country

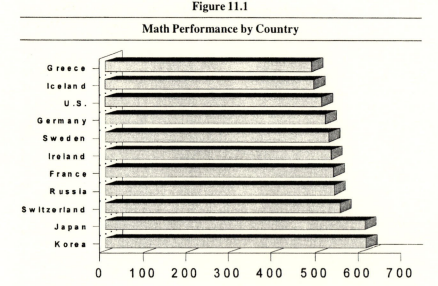

Source: OECD data compiled by the Alexis de Tocqueville Institution.

Indeed, if there were tests for fluency in a second or third language, the Swiss would almost certainly rank first in that category year after year, and their scores on math and other tests, if corrected to reflect the fact that many are taking the tests in a second language, would be close to the levels of more or less monolingual Korea and Japan. People are perhaps more satisfied with the schools than in any country in the world—Sweden, Australia, and Germany, in my experience, would offer significant competition; the United States, Canada, and Britain would not. The Swiss "seem to have great confidence in the country's schools," Robert Schneebeli notes. "Whenever a problem arises, people think it should be made a subject at school."

At the same time, there are interesting features in the system that might even cause one to think they take formal schooling lightly. We speak here of "the system" as an amalgamation of generalizations about the systems of the cantons. Immigrant children are not put into separate bilingual tracks but learn in the local language of instruction, supplemented by special work. Students generally start compulsory schooling at age six or seven and are finished after nine years, a fact that was of great concern to my traveling guide and companion—who resides much of the year in the United States, but remains a Swiss patriot. "How are Swiss children going to *compete*," he kept pressing educators and others, "getting started at this age? The children in the United States start school at five, and they can *already read*." (My colleague lives in Princeton, N.J.)

High school graduates receive no diploma as such. Three out of four go on to vocational school, which is more rigorous than such schools in the U.S. or Britain, but is still "only a vocational school." Some 8.8 percent graduate from a university, one of the lowest rates among all members of the Organization for Economic Cooperation and Development. The state-run universities are impressive, but there are none of the great private institutions one finds in most Western countries. Private education in general is practically nonexistent, covering approximately 3 percent of the K–12 students.

Many of these statistics reflect simple statistical anomalies. For example, the Swiss technical schools are not necessarily less rigorous, and perhaps more, than an American "university" but are not defined as such. On the other hand, critical skills normally imparted at a French, American, or British college might not be even at the Zürich Technical Institute, where students grumbled when they were required to take one or two humanities electives. The Swiss system, like Japan's, is inferior at the liberal arts—though not, in the Swiss case, at languages.

Table 11.1 compares various policy aspects of Swiss schools for primary and secondary children (K–12) to several other developed countries.

Swiss parents and educators believe their education system to be highly decentralized compared to other systems. It is, in fact, decentralized—but perhaps not much more so than many other countries.

The basic policy for education in the public schools is set at the cantonal level. Officials in Zürich set guidelines for the Zürich canton; the cantonal government in Aarau does the same for Aargau canton; and so on. The average size of a canton is approximately 300,000 persons, making this unit of government comparable to a city with the population one-half the size of Oakland, California or Washington, D.C. The median would be larger.

Cantonal policies are then implemented at the local level, as in the U.S., Sweden, Germany, and many other OECD countries. But the Swiss administrative units are not markedly smaller or more local than in the countries mentioned. There is a much greater degree of decentralization of administration than in, say, France, Australia, or Denmark. But these countries have school choice or voucher schemes which in effect decentralizes education down to the individual family: The parents decide which school their child goes to, and government assistance follows their child according to their decision.

None of this means that the Swiss are wrong to think their school system is decentralized. It may be, however, that their system is not as radically decentralized, compared to others, as they sometimes think.

The strongest element of Swiss federalism in education is something they lack: A federal department, above and atop the general administrative apparatus described, to plead for or even impose certain policies on its communities and cantons (or states). In the United States, for example, the federal Department of Education provides only about 10 percent of the funding for

Table 11.1

Swiss Schools Compared

	Switzerland	U.S.	Australia	Germany	Sweden
teachers hired by...	parents, board (varies by canton)	school officials	school officials	school officials	school officials
tenure	no (3-5 year contract)	yes	yes	yes	yes
choice/voucher system	(no)	(no)	yes	(yes)	yes
union pluralism	yes	(no)	(no)	yes	yes
noncompulsory religious classes in public schools	yes	no	(no)	yes	(no)
local control (1 to 10 scale)	9	5	6	7	7

Source: Alexis de Tocqueville, Institution, selected studies, 1996-1999. Copyright © AdTI, all rights reserved.

public education in the U.S. It enacts, however, more than half the volume of regulations imposed on a typical school, and of all the forms and reports local schools are required to fill out, an estimated 80 percent are federal.

In Switzerland, we visited the closest thing to a Department of Education, the intercantonal education directorate in Bern. The modest office next to a public library takes up one floor; it is smaller than the offices of one official, the Secretary of Education, in the United States (counting the secretary's conference room and staff assistants). Of course, the United States population is approximately fifty times that of Switzerland, but even so, its staff of about 2,000 persons dwarfs the office we visited: fifteen persons, of whom ten are full time, or the equivalent of perhaps a dozen staff. The city of New York alone employs administrative staff many times the Swiss "federal depart-ment." A former U.S. Secretary of Education has called this morass of experts and rule makers, who endlessly analyze one another's theories and studies, the "education blob."

In Switzerland, by contrast, "the blob" almost does not exist. If we com-pare the amount of money a country spends on teachers with the amount it spends on nonteaching personnel—administrators, guidance counselors, and others—we arrive at a rough index for the size of this class as a feature in any given country's school system. The measure is inexact, but suggestive. Fig-ure 11.2 shows how various countries rank based on this index. The larger the bar, the more money that country is spending on administration and other personnel compared to actual teachers. Only Belgium ranks very far below the Swiss, and its system includes significantly more private schools than the Swiss do. (Private schools tend to have a high ratio of teacher pay to admin-istrative pay, partly because they have to compete without subsidies in many countries, partly because they often do not have to obey as many rules and regulations as the public schools.)

The more distinctive feature of this system is the selection of teachers directly by the parents and the communes—with little intermediation either from above or from the side (such as a board of experts accountable to the parents, but only at periodic general intervals). In cantons and communities that still have direct democracy, this means at a town meeting. Even in those with less direct means, teachers are hired at meetings generally open to all the

Figure 11.2

Education Bureaucracy Index

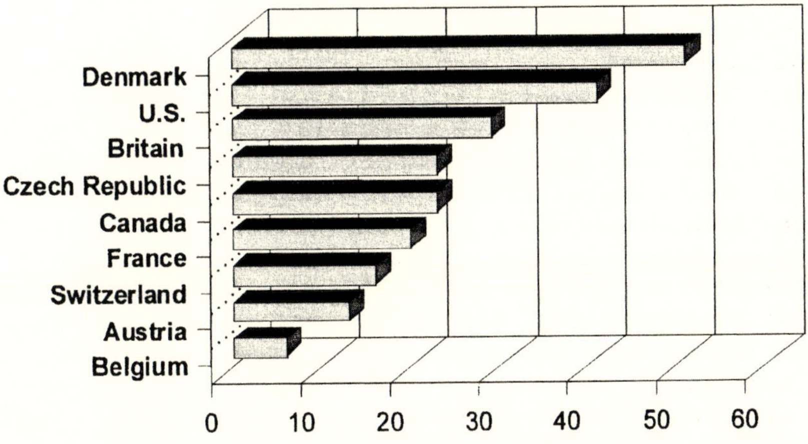

Source: OECD data compiled by the Alexis de Tocqueville Institution.

parents—sometimes by all who care to show up and are qualified voters, sometimes by large commissions that are easy to obtain election to and that seldom vary from any strong sentiment in the community anyway. Teachers are hired for contracts of three, four, or five years as a general rule. No board of experts intervenes; no mandates or regulations from Bern or, generally, even the cantons say who can be hired and who cannot, within the technically qualified pool of applicants. As these are set by the cantons, the "teacher certification" process is less burdensome than in most other countries. The programs for teacher training generally require 10 years of schooling for admission—a little less than a high school diploma in U.S. terms. There follows three to five years of further schooling; Swiss teachers generally enter the marketplace between the ages of twenty-one and twenty-five.

As with many other public positions in Switzerland, the vast majority of teachers who seek reappointment after that time receive it for another three-to five-year contract. It would be wrong, however, to think that this means the system is no different from one in which teachers are tenured, and a similarly tiny minority are fired. The fact that teachers must seek reappointment helps, to put it bluntly, to keep them on their toes. Very seldom will the Swiss capriciously remove someone who is doing even a marginally creditable job; the Swiss people, like all good managers, like to keep people where they are if possible. Yet, the need to respond to the customer is just a little sharper. At the same time, the election of the teacher by the community serves as a kind of affirmation. It is a public act of confidence that the teachers (or anyway, the vast majority) seem to appreciate.

"A minority of people in our group have strong reservations about the hiring of teachers by the communities and commissions," says Irene Hänsenberter of the Dachverband Schweizer Lehrerinnen und Lehrer—the Bern office of the largest teachers union in Switzerland. "The vast majority, however, is satisfied. It's good that the communities are responsible for which teacher their children have. Parents who are not involved then cannot complain, because they 'have their chance.' I think the people who are involved in the schools are happy with them, and this is the majority of people here."

"This system helps keep people involved," agrees Wolf Linder of the Swiss Conference of Cantonal Ministers of Education—the Swiss equivalent of the U.S. Department of Education. "People here have the feeling that they can change things, that the system responds to them. That is a plus. We have our problems in Switzerland, but we do not have a problem with parents being involved in their children's education."

The Swiss level of satisfaction with their schools is very high. They view the schools with perhaps the same patriotism as the army or the political system (which the Swiss also prize).

When one asks the Swiss—teachers, parents, officials—why they are so satisfied, there is nearly always a pause. The Swiss seem slightly taken aback at the notion that, somewhere in the world, people may not be as happy. Then, typically, comes an empirical proof, which is fair enough, given the data. "They seem to do a good job," a woman on the community council in Hittnau comments. "Swiss children do well in their basic subjects."

But what if there is a problem?

"Do you mean for me personally, or with the school in general."

Well, let's take both cases.

"I guess they're both the same, actually. I would take it up with the teacher. And I think that is what most parents do."

Yes, that is what most parents would probably do in the United States, too. In Switzerland, you seem very comfortable with what happens then. Why do you think that is?

"Well, the schools usually respond."

Probably it is that simple—in Switzerland, the public schools seem to be unusually responsive. The parents perceive them that way, which is the same thing. Why are the Swiss schools so responsive? The answer is a mix of cultural and personal traits, policies that have directly to do with education *per se*, and broader institutional and political arrangements.

The Swiss tax code, for example, does little to encourage private education, providing tax deductions for gifts to such institutions only in narrow cases having to do with large corporate or individual trusts. The result, however, has been to focus all attention and interest on the public schools, for compulsory schooling, and even the universities. As there is very little in the way of a safety valve for the frustrated or the alienated, they work for a solution within the political system.

The Swiss polity, of course, makes such action somewhat easier than in other countries. Even if the recourse to teacher elections does not prove effective, "there is," as a public school teacher in Basel told me, "always the ballot box." In the cantons of Bern, Zürich, and Basel, three of the country's largest, there were dozens of referenda and citizen-led ballot initiatives on education policy. In Bern in the 1990s, Ms. Hänsenberter of the teachers union estimates, approximately one-third of all ballot initiatives concerned education policies. "When people are especially frustrated," she adds, "or simply have a strong idea about something, it grows even larger."

Indeed, many of the proposals—perhaps half—emanate from teachers and their unions themselves. "It is one of their major activities," a teacher from the Ticino says. The union proposals do not fare any better, and perhaps do a tad worse, than those proposed by small groups of parents and teachers.

The initiatives that do pass, such as a referendum on parental rights in 1992 in Bern, enable the Swiss education to make constant, rolling improvements in itself over time. Other education systems seem to be more sticky. Precisely because education is so important, the smallest decision over a textbook, the conduct of a school nurse's office, or a song at the winter festival can become a heated controversy. This is not to dismiss the concerns or motives of those who engage in these battles; rather, to empathize with the fact that such matters will be fought out, if they must be, and if not given an outlet that is constructive, they will be fought destructively.

Alexis de Tocqueville noted this during one of the French parliamentary debates over policies allowing parents to use their family's education support from the government to send their child to religious schools. "When men cannot argue about principles, they will argue about interests, and then, personal morals. Soon we will be debating nothing but canals and conflicts of interest." The broader Swiss political system, by allows voters who cannot get the policy they want from the school administration, or the teacher, to appeal directly to parents and teachers as a whole—and, of course, allows teachers and administrators the same privilege.

Over time, of course, the most important impact of this process may, ironically, be pedagogic. By constantly empowering even the smallest voices to set off a legislative debate and making frequent recourse to the jury of the people, the Swiss education system, in combination with the political, leads a constant dialogue. And, unlike an abstract, academic discussion where nothing changes as a result, this is, if one may co-opt a 1970s phrase, a "meaningful dialogue."

Responsiveness may help explain why Switzerland is able to offer religious instruction in its public schools with little rancor or controversy. This is not to say school curricula are theologically based throughout such courses as science and history. But each canton is allowed to encourage religion and even "establish" a particular church. Elementary schools in Geneva, Vaud, the Ticino, Bern, Luzern, Schwyz, and Zürich cantons allowed me to visit for parts of a day to get a flavor for the instruction in different languages, urban and rural settings, and among contrasting confessional preferences.

The younger Swiss students in the rural cantons often dressed uniformly, as if a certain type of dress were the norm, but not as in a parochial school. Those in Zürich and Geneva were less uniform, but still relatively disciplined in appearance and behavior compared to American, French, and British children. On the walls were occasional religious items. They were not sufficiently plentiful to make one think oneself in an American parochial school, but there were enough of them to make it clear one was not in an American public school either. At the school in Zürich, but only there, one noticed several artworks with a star of David or Hannukah menorah, one a beautifully conceived scene rising up over what appeared to be Lake Constance. Otherwise the images were all Christian—usually neither distinctively Protestant or Catholic, though occasionally in the older grades, especially in Schwyz and Bern, one could make out what seemed to be ideas from one branch or the other.

In Hittnau, an outlying suburb of the city of Zürich in Zürich canton, the town minister sits in as some of the other town leaders and the leaders from the school plan out various repairs and events. The meeting is seamless; there are no large transitions between "religion" and "other" civic affairs, and it does not feel awkward to have the subject change from the new pipes that are going in, to next month's church festival. In Schwyz, a Catholic priest strides up the steep hill toward one of the schools. He has classes and coaches soccer in the afternoon, and will probably hear a confession or two on the side as he makes his rounds. The presence is very low key, but widespread. Even in Bern, which is relatively more cosmopolitan and wears no piety on its sleeve, such symbols are common.

When one asks Swiss officials or individuals who are in the majority—that is, who within their canton adhere to the faith that is the cantonal one, Catholic or Protestant—about this mixing of religious and secular affairs, they seem partly to expect the question, partly to have a difficult time grasping it. The Swiss take for granted that this overlap does not constitute an imposition on the minority provided it is bounded. "Remember, there is nothing compulsory about religion in Swiss schools," a member of the Hittnau community council told me. "Freedom of conscience is strictly protected." In many countries, though, even this degree of interaction and in this spirit would be regarded as a grotesque offense against the minority.

The responsiveness of the schools in Switzerland—and, for that matter, of most institutions—explains a portion of the difference. When people feel involved in a process, their day-to-day opinions heard, they are less likely to feel alienated from it even if a particular policy does not suit their preference. If only some aspects of policy—such as the religious element in the schools— were merely transferred from Switzerland to other countries, one might not see the same harmonious result. It is also worth remembering, however, that for hundreds of years, the Swiss were bitterly divided over religious questions, and in particular, between the Catholic and Reformed churches.

The schools, of course, also operate within a cultural context.

"In Switzerland," as a Catholic priest told me in Bern, "sometimes, the minority gives way to the majority." The very formulation, with its deliberate irony, suggests something the Swiss know in their bones, though they have had to work many years to achieve it. In Switzerland, the majority, as scholar Carol Schmid puts it, often "does not behave like a majority."[1] That is to say, there are majorities in Switzerland—Protestants, German-speakers, and others—that abstain from establishing certain practices they might otherwise prefer, out of a deliberate respect for the minority. There are practical and self-interested considerations as well, including the social peace. This deference, however, goes well beyond a narrow pragmatism.

One sees this in the Swiss schools in many practices. In German-speaking Switzerland, students assiduously study French or Italian in order to meet the requirement that they be fluent in one of the national languages other than their own. In the French-speaking portions, German is studied, though with less enthusiasm. The French-speaking Swiss, paradoxically, as Schmid writes, "behave like a majority," in the sense that they are confident in their rights and status, feeling less need to assert them because of the arrangements made to suit them and the respect of the German-speaking majority. Schmid offers an elegant suggestive proof of this by interviewing Swiss students and asking them to estimate how many Swiss speak German as a first language, French, and Italian. The German-speaking students, because of the complex cultural signals they receive about the importance of French, consistently overestimated how many Swiss speak it as a first language, and underestimate the size of their own group, the German speakers. The French-speaking students, confident in their status, likewise underestimate the Germans, and overestimate themselves. And both groups, German and French, overestimate how many Swiss speak Italian as a first language. Italian television, radio, and other cultural affairs all receive a disproportionate share of public funding, for example—the majority deliberately accommodating the minority. In modern times, one even sees this approach extending to the Jewish community, and being felt and appreciated by the Jewish community itself. That it is not more so has largely to do with the fact that Jews are still a tiny (about one percent) share of the Swiss population. The matter of Jewish life and culture in Switzerland is taken up in a separate discussion.

There is a price for this kind of educational system, but the Swiss—teachers, parents, and students—seem willing to pay it. You see it on a late evening in February, walking along the river in Baden. A single light is burning in the elementary school, which looks to hold normally 100 to 150 children. Inside what appear to be one teacher and several parents, several mothers and a father or two, are working on some kind of stand or bleachers for what looks like it will be an historical presentation the next day. Though they are inside, they are wearing medium-weight jackets—it appears the heat is either not working, or turned down to save money.

To teachers in the U.S. or Britain, that kind of volunteer help might sound like a Godsend, but the educators pay a price as well. After all, in many Western countries that kind of volunteer labor by parents, and late-night work by one of the teaching staff, could be construed as a violation of the union work contract.

"We supported the passage of a parental responsibility policy in 1992," Ms. Hänsenberter of the teachers union notes. (The measure also asserts parental rights.) "And it passed. Now sometimes the parents take too much responsibility. Still it is the best thing to have too much civic responsibility than too little."

Note

1.   *Conflict and Consensus in Switzerland*, Berkeley, University of California Press, 1981.

12

Taxes

In no country on earth do the people think taxes are too low or too simple, or the burden imposed by the authorities to enforce them too light. Switzerland is no exception to this rule. "The taxes on capital and investment," says Hans Bär, the former chairman of Julius Bär, a respected investment bank in Zürich, "are too high." Edwin Somm, the former chairman of Asea-Brown-Boveri, the giant Swiss engineering firm, agrees. "There are a number of changes that must be made in the tax code to ensure competitiveness," he argues—and then pulls out a series of charts that detail, Ross-Perot-like, what sectors suffer from the rates that are too high, and which ones have allowances too wide or too narrow. George, affable, six-foot-five porter at the front desk of the Bellevue Hotel in Bern, agrees. "The Swiss tax system is not that great," George offers. He pauses. "What are you comparing it to?"

The question illustrates the fact that if the Swiss are unhappy with their taxes, they are probably less unhappy than in most other countries. Asked if there are things they would like to change about their tax code, most people in Switzerland answer yes. Asked if they would trade their tax laws for the tax laws of Germany, Japan, or the United States, most Swiss quickly answer no.

Certainly a part of the reason for this is the simple fact that Swiss tax rates are somewhat lower than in many Western countries. Their value-added tax is the lowest in Europe, a cause of some friction vis-à-vis the rest of Europe and apprehension among the Swiss, who fear they may have to choose between integration and their low-tax traditions. Swiss income tax rates are among the lowest in the industrial world, as Table 12.1 illustrates.

Similarly, the Swiss value-added tax is about half that of the rest of Europe. (The United States had no value-added tax at the turn of the century, though one was occasionally proposed. The U.S. does, however, have sales taxes; the Swiss do not.) Taxes on corporate and investment income are on the one hand slightly lower than the average for other countries—but the differential for these is much smaller than in the personal income codes.

145

Table 12.1

Personal Income Tax Rates by Country

Country	Highest rate of tax on wage income
Hong Kong	13 %
Bolivia	19 %
Botswana	30 %
Switzerland*	36 %
Mexico	38 %
Chile	44 %
Great Britain	46 %
United States	47 %
Israel	50 %
Japan	62 %
France	64 %
Germany	65 %
Russia	67 %

Source: Author's calculations derived from Coopers and Lybrand annual tax summary and cantonal revenue authorities; Swiss cantonal data from Dr. Nico Burki, Burki-Rechtsanwalte, Zürich.

*—Swiss federal income tax rates do not exceed 11 percent, but as the tax is fundamentally cantonal and even communal in nature, comparisons are difficult. The 36 percent figure is close to the highest one would pay as a combined effective rate in a typical canton, such as Luzern, Glarus, or Fribourg, as the U.S. figure is based on a typical state, such as Illinois or Virginia. Even this is not the highest possible figure: In the cantons of Geneva and Zürich, for example, the combined rate reaches 44–46 percent. It is common in these cantons, however, for high-income taxpayers to establish a residence in neighboring communities, avoiding the highest rates. Note that even at 40 percent, Switzerland would still have among the lowest tax rates in the developed world.

Although these low rates are an important part of the code's relatively high acceptance by the Swiss people, they are by no means the only factor. Another is the relative simplicity of the code and of the reporting of income. In the cantons of Ticino, Geneva, and Aargau, officials allowed me to see the basic forms that taxpayers use to pay their income tax. The resulting documents looked like one of those postcard returns designed by various U.S. politicians to show how easy taxes would be if their "super simple reform tax code" were adopted. The simplicity of the forms becomes a metaphor, not only that the process is not complicated but that there is a rough, simple fairness to it—and that the government, at least by appearance and in the Swiss case in reality, is not itself extravagant. Swiss who have lived abroad in France, Germany, or the United States generally compare the process of paying taxes in Switzerland favorably with that in these other countries.

Another cause of the relative acceptance of taxes in Switzerland is the balance of the code between different types of income. Many national tax codes are built upon the idea, whether stated or not, that certain types of activity are "good," and some bad—or at least, not as good as the favored activity. Accordingly, they may tax various activities at very different levels. This introduces an element of seeming unfairness into taxation, and encourages envy and divisiveness politically, as some groups seek to expand their privileges still farther, while others strive simply to gain equal treatment.

Thus some codes tax foreigners heavily (the Arab states, for instance) while others (Russia, much of the former Soviet Empire) literally tax their own people more.[1] Some codes tax corporate income higher than personal income, feeling that large enterprises need to be controlled or that they have more money and can therefore afford to pay more. Others tax companies (Europe, the United States) at much lower rates than people, in the thought that "investment" is good and creates jobs, while people having those jobs spending money on things is "consumption" and is not as good for the economy. Treatment of income by capital gains also varies widely. Some countries tax such gains more heavily than wages; others, such as the U.S. and Europe, more lightly; others have no capital gains tax at all; while in some countries, capital gains are simply treated the same as rents, wages, profits, or other incomes. Switzerland has no federal capital gains tax as such; the rate is zero. And many of the cantons treat capital gains the same as regular income in applying income tax rates, which are applied locally. Many cantons tax real estate sales, while gains on the disposition of other personal property is tax exempt. Business capital gains and income are all taxed—and at rates as high as 50 percent.

The distortions that result from such differential taxation can appear comical to the outsider. In Britain in the 1970s, for example, the rate of corporate automobile ownership exceeded the rate of personal automobile ownership for a time. The combination of high tax rates and generous write-offs for "business transportation" made it much more economical for companies to provide transportation to many of their employees than to pay them wages, taxed at high rates, so they could buy cars of their own. But to the citizens of a country, such exceptions and imbalances can be infuriating. In the United

States, so-called "flat" tax systems were proposed which in fact taxed wages at rates of 20 percent and more, while taxing capital gains at 0 percent.

The Swiss code has its share of these elements, particularly when it comes to farming activities. On the whole, however, rates are balanced. Wage income, capital gains, and corporate income are all taxed—none at more than 40 percent, few at less than 10 percent. This attribute has been called "longitudinal fairness"—a fairness of taxing not merely the rich and the poor at fair rates, but at taxing different types of activity at a reasonably even rate.

The Swiss tax on total net assets—a wealth tax—broadens the base still further, and enables a somewhat lesser penalty on the production of wealth to be traded off for a low-rate tax on static wealth. This is a tax with many attractive elements (if, of course, it is not simply layered on other high tax rates). Of course, one can argue whether such designs are, in fact, the most fair. The Swiss seem to regard this approach as acceptable. It is worth noting that a tax on wealth, or accumulated riches, may have a very different impact on the incentive to take risks, add value, and create jobs, than a tax on profits, gains, or income.

By other measurements of fairness the code performs reasonably well. The richest Swiss do not appear to pay as high a percentage of the national income tax as in the United States, Japan, or Germany. The actual rate that applies to their income is even lower, comparably, than in those countries: In the United States, the federal tax rate goes from 0 percent to 38.5 percent, and in such populous states as California and New York, from 0 percent to more than 10 percent.

From a redistributive point of view, then, the code is "less fair." This does not appear to bother the Swiss for several reasons, the first of which is they are not especially focused on comparisons of wealth, and in particular, have little desire to achieve economic equality through government redistribution. If a wealthy Swiss were to engage in great displays of wealth, he would be thought rude, and would be shunned by most of the society; but this social "tax" on the rich is thought, in part, to obviate efforts to seize property through the tax code or other means. In Switzerland, even today, one finds relatively lesser extremes of wealth in fact than in the United States, Britain, France, or even Germany. And there is almost no display. Corporate salaries in the multimillions of dollars, as seen in the United States and Europe, are less common, though no longer unheard of.

The Swiss comfort themselves in the fact that if the rich do not face extreme rates of taxation on paper, neither can they arm themselves with an array of loopholes to escape paying any taxation in fact. Nor are the most productive and creative members of society driven overseas by confiscatory schemes. A young police officer who discussed taxes with me at a coffee shop in Zürich commented that "what matters is that everybody pays some fair amount." Unlike many of their European and American counterparts, the Swiss do not have the nagging sense that while, in theory, the rich are paying half or more of their income in taxes, in practice, there are some who pay no taxes at all. Nor do they have much desire to tax others at such rates, even if it could be achieved.

To some extent, the tax code causes and reinforces these attitudes. To some extent, the society's condition of few extremes causes this tax code to be acceptable. In societies with greater disparities of wealth, and greater envy, it might not be.

Switzerland's size and position contribute to the country's determination to keep tax rates under control, indeed low by developed-country standards. Always dependent on trade and economic competitiveness, the Swiss are economic internationalists. They have a keen eye for the importance their own "domestic" tax or monetary policy will in fact have on their position in the world economy. A factory worker in Baden who talked to me at the train station had a relatively extensive knowledge of the different cantonal tax systems, praising Zug for its extremely low personal income tax rates. He had some knowledge, though not as detailed, of foreign systems. For example, while he could not quote personal income tax rates, he knew that they were higher in nearly all the surrounding countries. He also appeared to have a detailed sense of how the different rules for value-added taxes affected his wife's shopping habits when the family goes shopping in Germany.

Even so, there is reason for concern that the combination of various income taxes, social insurance rates, and the assets tax have begun to scare away some of Switzerland's most talented and productive members. This was especially acute in the 1980s when the United States and a number of other countries in the Americas slashed their tax rates while Europe cut rates, but not as much; and the Swiss, while starting from a very low-tax base, endured mild increases, later followed by the imposition of the value-added tax.

Where there is redistribution, the Swiss prefer to carry it out in a positive way than in a punitive one. For example, the educational system has a leveling impact, but does so more by lifting up and empowering the working class than by limiting the rich or the productive. Similarly the social welfare system carries out assistance, and needs no large base of revenue because the number of cases where it must be used is relatively small.

Swiss government spending tends to be concentrated not in transfer payments, such as public assistance, but in education, public works projects such as tunnels and roads, and other investments and value-added activities. These tend to help the middle class, rich, and poor alike, but surely they help the poor the most by expanding the base of potential production, spurring employment opportunities. They also yield a visible result, products and public goods—parks, bridges, buildings—that give the taxpayer some tangible return for his payments.

The result is a sense not so much of equality, as of community. There is a difference between feeling that everyone contributes, and feeling that everyone contributes the same, or contributes enough. The Swiss do not necessarily enjoy the latter sensations, but they are perhaps less focused on these. They do share a sense that for the most part everyone contributes something and everyone enjoys some benefits, from the state and, thus, from the money it collects in taxes. They sense, economically, that their tax code is sufficient, and this in itself is a relative rarity in modern societies.

Politics play a role in the tax code's acceptance in Switzerland. It is remarkable, in fact, that with all the turmoil over taxes in most countries, the interconnection between the tax code and political institutions is seldom considered. In Russia, for example, political corruption and slack tax revenues are discussed in isolation, when by all appearances the country's onerous tax code helps generate black market activity, both economic and political. In the United States, frustration with the tax code is seldom addressed in its political dimension. This is not to say that Switzerland structured its political system with the intent of smoothing over the difficulty of tax collection common to Western societies. The political system does, however, have an impact. There appear to be two political structures in Switzerland that substantially ameliorate the classic tension of taxation.

First, of course, is the system of direct democracy at the federal and still more so the cantonal and communal levels. In one way, the ability to challenge any federal tax increase by means of the facultative referendum has proven a powerful tool for keeping tax rates down. And this is an important element; it is, however, only the most superficial result of the Swiss populism. The voters have the same power, indeed greater power, to limit taxes at the cantonal and local levels—yet they have proven more willing to approve new and higher taxes at those levels than the voters in perhaps any other country in the world.

As Tocqueville observed in the nineteenth century, "it is the cantons and the communes that provide things to the people"—services and goods, schools and roads. Although the Swiss polity is somewhat more centralized today than when he made those remarks (1848), it is nevertheless still one of the most decentralized systems in the world. And local government is highly popular—in large part because of the extreme degree of popular participation in it. Almost no tax may be increased without a popular vote—in many cases, at a direct popular assembly, where the electorate may confront the politicians or other voters who propose the new burdens face to face, "looking them in the eye," as the Swiss like to say.

The phenomenon can perhaps be best understood if we compare the process by which taxes might be raised in Switzerland to that of other countries that have representative—but not direct—democracy. In the United States or Europe, most tax changes or increases are passed by a legislature, typically by narrow margins, and with much political agitation. The agitation must be greater, not lesser, because of the fact that everyone seeking to influence the decision knows there is no ultimate check by the people. The political message of the electorate, everyone realizes, is filtered before it reaches the few dozen elites who will make the decision—and accordingly, all concerned seek to turn up the volume in order to get their message across. Voters, who do not enjoy the privilege of acting as legislators themselves, pay less attention to the merits and details of such issues than they would as quasi-legislators— they must spend a proportionately greater amount of their time contriving ways to make their voice heard by the system. Likewise, their leaders, of whatever party, spend proportionately greater energy and time trying to stir up the passions of voters, and alert them to their direct interest on an issue, than in educating the electorate toward what all know will be the ultimate decision—a vote by the people.

As a result, not only is the process less educational, for leaders and the people alike, but it results in the feeling that the popular wisdom has been cheated. How many of the major tax votes in the United States, for instance— 1981, 1986, 1990, and 1993—were passed by narrow margins, with many of the decisive votes determined by lobbying and other pressures having little to do with the overall merits of the change? How much was the electorate stirred up and urged by both sides to contact their representatives—but, in the end, without any direct voice in the outcome? The elitism of this process renders the legislative process more vulnerable to manipulation at the same time that it creates the appearance of a rigged game and alienates the voter from the result.

As a review of the initiative and referendum process suggests, it is more difficult to raise taxes in Switzerland than in perhaps any other country. Yet, taxes are raised and altered from time to time. And when they are, there is less resentment than elsewhere, because the burdens are self-imposed.

The resulting feeling of self-responsibility and accountability by voters is perhaps analogous to the findings of doctors who have studied medication by patients in U.S. hospitals. For many years, the common practice among doctors was to oversee the administration of painkillers closely. Wise physicians, of course, consulted closely with their patients regarding the amounts and timing of the doses. But it was generally thought that the doctor must make the detailed decisions—their objectivity, and more so their expertise, meant that their judgment would be far superior to that of the patients, who would naturally tend to overdo the doses of such medication in order to relieve their pain.

In studies in the early 1990s, however, doctors decided to give some patients control over the administration of their own painkillers. (The patients were of course monitored to make sure they did not go outside of a certain band of safety; but within that very wide band, they applied the medication to themselves). The result, perhaps not surprising, was that they complained much less about pain than they had when the doctors were administering the medicine—the complaints dropped to less than one-third of the previous level. Perhaps more surprising, the amount of painkiller used by the patients plummeted. On average, use of the medications fell by more than 40 percent. And in only 10 percent of the cases did use of the painkiller exceed what would have been prescribed by the doctor—and then, generally, by only small amounts.

Even if a giant computer or highly sophisticated doctor could have some-how determined what patients would have chosen to take and when, the result would not have been the same. It was the feeling and reality of control that enabled patients to ration use of the painkiller in their own. There was no need to complain to the doctor, because each patient knew that in duress, if he or she felt a need for a sudden increase of dose, it was available. While the Swiss do not have the privilege of setting their own tax rates individually, they do enjoy, as a people, a degree of control over the process seen in few other political systems. As a result, tax rates are lower—but they also arouse less resentment when they go up.

There's a second reason for the relative lack of turmoil over taxes in Swit-zerland: the high degree of variation in tax rates among the cantons. In the U.S. and most of Europe, the fact that income taxes are largely and in some cases wholly the province of the central government leads to a situation in which there is little variety in tax rates. This can best be understood if we compare tax rate variation in Switzerland to that of another country, such as the United States.

In the United States, a person living in New Hampshire, Florida, or Texas—three states with no income tax and thus the lowest possible combined rates in the country—a worker still winds up paying approximately 45 percent of her or his income in taxes.[2] If the same person lived in New York or California, which with personal income tax rates close to 10 percent are among the highest tax states, state tax rates (deductible against the federal tax) might push the combined rate up by five or six points in the highest bracket—for a combined total of a little more or less than 50 percent in the top bracket. All other states fall somewhere in between. Thus, the spectrum of possibility for a high-income earner in the U.S. would be a lowest possible tax rate of 45 percent, and a top possible combined rate of 50 percent. That's not a lot of difference, and it provides little in the way of choice for different people with different preferences. Someone living in New York who really hates high tax rates could move to New Hampshire, but would only be a few percentage points better off. On the other hand, someone living in Texas who misses the high level of social and other services in Massachusetts or California and doesn't mind paying for them can indeed move there. But they may find the milieu less satisfactory than they hoped for, because the uniformity of income tax codes and other revenue sources, a product of both higher federal rates and deductibility of state income taxes has made for a relatively similar picture on the revenue and spending side of most state budgets.

In Switzerland, the combined rate of income tax ranges from as low as 24 percent (Zug) and 26 percent (Schwyz) in some of the older, central cantons to as high as 43 percent (Zürich) and even 46 percent (Geneva) in the largest cities. Not surprisingly, such cantons as Luzern (35 percent), Glarus (35 percent), and Fribourg (36 percent) fall in the middle. The combined spectrum of possible tax rates thus moves up and down by 22 percentage points, or about 90 percent, expressed using the 24 percent lowest top rate as a baseline. (Note: Tax rates mentioned here are rounded off).

This variation contributes, like many other aspects of Swiss federalism, to a subtle and ongoing social peace. Citizens who strongly dislike taxes and prefer the more dynamic but less protective environment of a small local government tend to congregate in the cantons that fit that model. Those who prefer a larger economic role for the state, and don't object to the costs, tend towards Geneva, Zürich, and the cities.

A third important reason for Switzerland's relative calm over taxes is local administrative control of tax payment and enforcement. The Swiss have no equivalent of the U.S. Internal Revenue Service—a federal agency charged with vast powers to gather information and enforce penalties. There is, in fact, no Swiss "IRS" concerning the income tax at all, and the small tax enforcement office that does exist handles mainly customs issues. The Swiss have a handful of officials that help ensure accurate payment of the value-added tax, but this compares to agencies in Japan, France, and Germany that employ agents into the thousands.

Income taxes are paid to the community, which reports and divides income with the canton; the canton in turn reports and directs income to the federal government. Even at the community level, means of enforcement are few. When asked what they would do if someone were not paying their taxes, or how it would even be discovered, the town council members in Hittnau shrugged. "People would not want to do that in their own community," one of the council members speculated. "It doesn't seem to be a problem—people not paying their taxes." Indeed, international surveys of corruption and tax problems generally place Switzerland near the bottom of countries with substantial tax avoidance. By contrast, countries with large and powerful tax enforcement administrations, such as the United States, often report significant tax evasion. This problem appears to be acute in countries such as Russia and Nigeria, which have high rates of taxation.

This does not mean, of course, that if other countries were to eliminate their tax collection agencies, a sudden surge of payments would result. The opposite might be the case, unless other aspects of the system were adopted, not to mention the Swiss political culture of what can only be called a kind of local communism. The Swiss insistence on privacy is such that neither federal nor local authorities have access to banking records, even in cases of suspected tax evasion—which in Switzerland is a civil offense but not a criminal matter, much less a felony. Nor are such matters commonly discussed even in close circles. Asked why such matters do not, for example, get leaked to the press, Ivan Pictet, a respected private investment banker in Geneva, explains that "there is such respect for privacy that one doesn't see that happening." The Swiss appreciate the protections they enjoy, and the fact that their government is constrained—and so, sensing that to abuse these privileges would be to lose them, they respect the system voluntarily. "People do not want to see a system they like challenged by irresponsible behavior," Pictet continues. He was talking not simply about tax privacy, but privacy in general; and yet, to hear a taxpayer from a Western country describing the tax code as a system the people like is somewhat arresting.

Nearly all income tax systems rely to some degree, usually a large one, on voluntary compliance. The Swiss system, unconsciously, is well suited to this. Unlike consumption taxes or customs, the income tax is an unusually intimate tax, one that touches nearly everyone in society. Yet unlike consumption or property or other taxes it does not deal in the realm of tangibles, of purely physical goods more easily seen and rationalized. For this very reason it is perhaps most suited to the kind of sensitive, intimate treatment as in Switzerland is afforded by the fact of strong, generally popular local government.

One does not want to overdo the tired metaphor that government and community are "like a family," but among the Swiss, there is something to this metaphor. This is particularly so since the level of government that is most active and most real in the life of the average Swiss is that which is smallest and most intimate. The Swiss commune is capable, in scale, activity, and psychology, of acting somewhat like a family.

To recreate these results, one would have to recreate not only Switzerland's minimalist enforcement bureaucracy, but much of the whole society. This would include Swiss federalism, with its weak center and (more important) strong communities. It would also include the system of direct democracy—and the feeling of popular empowerment that accompanies all these formal institutions. That the Swiss tax code can even function, given the degree to which it relies on the voluntary patriotism of its people is, however, evidence of the inadvertent genius of Switzerland's political arrangements.

Notes

1.   The statistics and examples that follow are taken from a survey of world tax codes excerpted in Gregory Fossedal, "What the Tax Reformers are Missing," *Wall Street Journal*, 7 November 1997.
2.   This is the top federal rate of 38.5 percent plus Social Security plus zero rate for state and local income. On paper, Social Security taxes are paid half by the employer, half by the employee, but however they are accounted for, they represent a "wedge" between what the employer pays and what the worker receives.

13

Crime

Swiss crime rates are not the lowest in the world, but they are close. Japan suffers fewer murders per capita. Scotland is more free of (reported) cases of rape and other sexual assault.

As in many other fields, then, Switzerland cannot quite claim to be number one. But the country ranks near the top in the effectiveness of its criminal justice system on all measures. And it performs respectably, indeed well, over a number of different crimes and crime measurements, as Figures 13.1 through 13.3 suggest.

The Swiss disagree about what causes these statistics, though the discussion is a happy one. Some stress societal factors. Switzerland enjoys high employment that has exceeded 98 percent for most of the century. The people have an ethic of citizenship and cooperation that all countries strive to instill, but Switzerland seems to succeed in instilling this ethic to an unusual degree.

These factors, though, are to some extent products of the regime and of policy: We see the hand of political institutions, though indirectly. Economic performance is partly a function of tax, monetary, social welfare, and other policies. Swiss citizenship is partly a traditional and historical phenomenon, but also a result of such institutions as the national militia, the schools, strong local government, and direct democracy. The army, with its universal male service, may play a double role. On the one hand, this is a society in which a large share of the population owns and maintains a firearm and knows how to use it responsibly. Guns are taken seriously, but they are a part of life; nearly every Swiss male between twenty and fifty years old has his rifle ready at home and practices regularly. The army also serves to tighten the bonds of citizenship and friendship, of community and shared duties. This will be less so as the services reduce their size and extent in the years to come, but is still a factor. While it is not impossible that people in this relationship would commit crimes against one another, it stands to reason that such individuals would be less prone to crime.

Figure 13.1

Murder Rates by Country.
Intentional homicides reported per 1 million population.

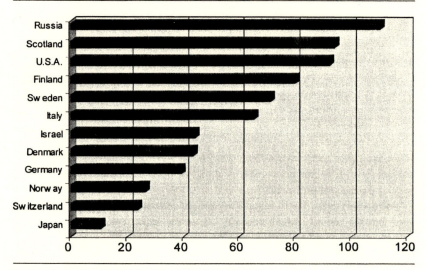

Source: Author's calculations from United Nations' data.

Figure 13.2

Rape Crimes Per 1 Million Persons.
Forcible rapes reported per 1 million population, 1991.

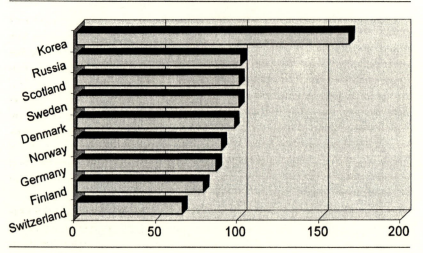

Source: U.N. data from country reports; author's calculations.

Figure 13.3

Total Drug Offense and Drug Trafficking Rates

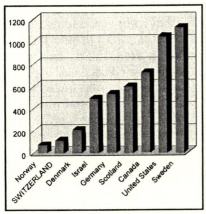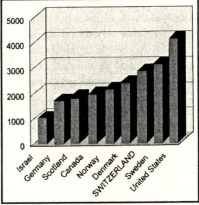

Left, drug offenses (possession or sale) per 1 million persons. Right, drug trafficking offenses alone, also per 1 million persons.

Source: U.N. data, author's calculations.

Likewise, the high degree of racial and religious harmony in Switzerland does not result from lack of diversity, but from the way the country deals with diversity. In the United States, two-thirds of all arrests for violent crime are among blacks, Hispanics, or Asians, whereas they constitute less than a quarter of the population. Indeed, a large share of U.S. violent crime, tragically, involves blacks attacking other blacks. Switzerland offers a nice refutation of the idea that Western European countries have been able to achieve low crime rates, particularly for violent crimes, only because of their ethnic homogeneity. While there are European countries with strong ethnic or language uniformity, Switzerland is not one of them. The Swiss do have a problem with foreigners and crime, particularly in the drug area, where about 60 percent of arrests are of nonnative Swiss. And it has some racial overlap—many arrests and deportations are of Dominicans, or Moslems from various Eurasian countries. But there is no major linkage between crime and race per se. Minorities do not feel the system is stacked against them as minorities, and the white majority, by and large, does not fear that certain racial groups are violent or criminal as such.

Others stress the contribution made by the courts and justice system directly. These must have some importance. Switzerland's court system is not as distinctive in structure and operation as are its executive branch or its legislative processes. There are, however, important differences between the Swiss system and other European countries, and these are somewhat sharper still compared to the United States.

The Swiss, for example, make use of the jury, but not as frequently as the United States and Great Britain. It is one of the few areas in which the Swiss system is markedly less populist than the rest of Europe and America, in the literal sense of relying on the people to render decisions. In most features, however, the Swiss legal system remains highly dependent on the wisdom and initiative of citizens as such, and somewhat less reliant on the expertise of attorneys and magistrates than is common in Europe and the United States. If juries are less frequent, so are appeals from a jury's or judge's decision in the lower courts. A comparison of the Swiss appeal rate for major criminal cases with that of the U.S. illustrates the slightly different spirit that animates the two systems.

In U.S. federal and state courts, felony convictions are appealed some 60 percent of the time. In some states and in serious cases (drug cases and murder in New York and California, for example) the figure approaches 90 percent. About four in five decisions are eventually upheld. But more than 15 percent of convictions are, in fact, sent back or "overturned." And even those that are not sent back are subject to extra delay and expense. The original trials themselves, too, are affected. Judges and attorneys on all sides must take extra steps and put in many hours of work in an effort to avoid having key parts of their case thrown out—or to lay the foundation for later appeals that will undermine the case of their opponents.

In Switzerland, about one-third of convictions for serious crimes are appealed—and generally to the cantonal, not the federal court. This not only removes one layer of likely complication, but also makes the system more intimate. The judges and magistrates of the local courts know the thinking and the tendencies of their cantonal supreme court members personally and well—certainly somewhat better than, say, a typical U.S. judge would be acquainted with his federal circuit court of appeals judge, or still less, a justice on the Supreme Court.

Furthermore, since each canton makes its own rules of procedure, there is more intimacy within each canton among the judges and attorneys. The practice of law is somewhat more local in character, somewhat more specialized by geography and people than by area of expertise. An attorney who wanted to make a career of filing boilerplate lawsuits or criminal appeals on a certain narrow set of issues would find herself or himself needing to study the differing laws of many different regions.

The U.S. and other European court systems, to be sure, have decentralization and diversity of their own, and Switzerland has some uniformity. As a matter of degree, however, the Swiss system is substantially more dispersed than the U.S. This is probably one of the prime causes of the different nature of the appeals process, and the large disparity in the frequency with which it is used. A Swiss lay judge who was on the community insurance court, Fred Isler, told me that his court's decisions were only rarely overturned—"it happened about as often as we have strikes in Switzerland," which is to say, once or twice a year, and in some years, not at all. A justice on the cantonal supreme court for Aargau Canton, Ernst Roduner, did not remember a case in which any of his court's decisions had been appealed to the federal court on grounds of procedure. "They really leave it to us," he said—meaning the cantons. Although the federal supreme court can strike cantonal laws if they contradict the federal constitution, they cannot, as mentioned earlier, do so with federal laws. As a result there is a more humble approach to the cantonal laws as well, an ethos of lawyerly restraint toward the laws the people have made that one sees throughout the court system. "I am familiar with the practices in the United States, France, and some other countries which are more centralized and uniform," continued Justice Roduner, "and there are many advantages to this. It is not our system, however."

The Swiss, in fact, not uncharacteristically, are somewhat concerned that their system may be out of step with Europe and the United States. Some believe it has too many idiosyncrasies and contradictions to function smoothly. There are repeated appeals, as in the education field and among tax authorities, to bring greater uniformity to the code. Judges and lawyers from different cantons meet periodically and have made some strides at bringing greater order to the system, particularly within the three language blocks. Valais, Geneva, and Vaud, for instance, three of the French-speaking cantons, have coordinated their procedure laws, as have Zürich, Aargau, and Luzern, to a lesser extent, in the center-east. Still it remains a highly divided system of unique components. Even the language barrier, while not huge in absolute terms for most Swiss, is a subtle factor in reinforcing the decentralization of the courts. In the end, the dominance and differences of the cantons may be a blessing, though a mixed one.

Thus the Swiss court system places a heavy trust in the people, and relies on them to perform competently. Once a decision is reached, either by a jury, judge, or magistrate chosen directly or by a highly accessible assembly, the system is loathe to overturn it. It is not impossible for a judge to reverse what the people have decided, but it is less likely. When this system is abused, the remedies are themselves, likewise, popular in nature. "We have to be reappointed," Roduner points out. "The laws we implement are subject to the direct democracy." In this way too, the system is highly citizenbased.

The influence of initiative and referendum on the legal profession is also apparent. Because of popular participation directly in the legislative process, the laws have an added aura of legitimacy and invincibility. To go against or ignore or overturn them, judges would be going just a little bit more against the people themselves, the very source of the state's authority. What the people have made, to a greater extent, is more difficult to break. This is not to say that a good judge in the United States or Germany or France will overturn the laws of the representative assemblies for light or capricious reasons. There is, however, somewhat less of a stigma attached to this than there is in Switzerland, and somewhat more of a feeling of independence from the popular check.

Another aspect of the system's populism is its reliance on sheriffs and the courts, much as the Swiss education system relies on teachers, to make decisions and administer laws with little review by higher bureaucratic authorities. Swiss police spend more than half their time on crime prevention, and little of it filling out forms or defending decisions to review panels. In the United States, by contrast, according to the Department of Justice, "police spend one-third of their time on crime prevention," and comparably more responding to other authorities within the system. To my surprise, Swiss attorneys report that the initial trial phase for a serious crime is not significantly shorter than in France, Germany, or the United States, and slightly longer than in Japan. Once a trial is over and sentencing occurs, however, generally a matter of nine to twelve months for major offenses, the process is generally at an end, whereas in many Western countries there would follow a long cycle of appeals.

The value and reliance the Swiss place on police can be measured by the relative salaries and composition of the system. In Zürich, a judge's salary is approximately twice the average salary of a cantonal police officer. In most U.S. and British cities, the judge's salary is more than triple the police officer's. There also appears to be a higher population of police officers compared to judges in the Swiss system, although statistical comparison is rendered difficult by the fact that Switzerland has very little by way of a federal police force, almost none, leaving law and crime matters to the cantons. A typical Swiss judge has far less administrative support staff than a U.S. judge. The cantonal judges who spoke with me typically had a secretary working for them—whose labor they shared with another judge or two in the more austere cantons. In the United States, it is not infrequent for a federal or state appellate judge to have three or four clerks, themselves lawyers or law students, plus administrative staff.

The professional background and demeanor of judges is likewise less formal. In the U.S., one rarely encounters a judge who does not have a law degree. Only one-third of all U.S. judges are "lay judges" as a whole, and even fewer at the federal and state appellate courts. In Switzerland, there are 751 "professional judges" and 1,672 "lay judges." There is significantly more turnover among the Swiss judges, none of whom have life tenure. In a random survey of cantonal and community judges, the Alexis de Tocqueville Institution found that less than 10 percent served in their position for ten years or more. This is very different from the ratio of the United States, where the U.N. reporting methodology for such matters calculates there are 889 professional judges and 467 lay judges.

The Swiss make extensive use of professional arbitrators, and in fact the civil regular courts operate in a manner similar to a U.S. or British arbitrator. Courts that allowed me to visit both in Ticino and Aargau, including a branch of the Aargau cantonal supreme court, had small panels of judges seated around a table. There is a rough resemblance to Japanese practices as described by the U.N.'s international crime reports:

> In Japan, active public cooperation is indispensable to effective functioning of the criminal justice system. In addition to the above mentioned field of police work, there is, in the field of prosecution, a unique system called Inquest of Prosecution which was designed to reflect the opinion of lay citizens in handling public prosecutions. Laymen can also take part in court proceedings. One of the examples is the laymen counsel in criminal cases before the Summary Court, Family Court and the District Court. A defendant can select a person or persons, who are not qualified attorneys, to be their own counsel by permission of the court.

In the Swiss courts we visited, the judges (two men and one woman in Aargau, one man and two women in the Ticino) wore business suits, not robes, and sat on the same level as the attorneys and the defendant. This may seem to have only symbolic importance, but represents an important psychological difference of the British and U.S. practice in which the judge sits up on a kind of throne behind a great podium-like desk. Likewise, the Swiss court buildings are restrained, with no great statues and none of the quotations from great supreme court judges of the kind one sees etched on court buildings in the U.S. or even Germany. The Ticino and Aargau courts had no pillars or such material at all, and even the federal supreme court houses in Lausanne and Luzern (insurance) are understated by Western standards. The building that housed the Aargau court looked more or less like an administration building on a modest U.S. campus or a federal or state regional office building in the U.S. In short, the architecture, dress, protocol, and the other arrangements of the Swiss courts seem to give a quiet message that the courts exist not to house great legal minds or construct brilliant arguments and theories, but to render decisions.

Police, judicial, and related functions are conducted on a more decentralized and local basis in Switzerland than in most other developed countries. Comparisons must be made carefully because of Switzerland's size and population—about one-tenth the population of Germany, one thirty-fifth that of the United States, and an area the size of the state of Connecticut. This means, on the one hand, that all scales are reduced: The Swiss "federal" government is no larger, and no more remote probably, from its people, than that of Cook County, Illinois, or the cities of Berlin, Paris, or New York. It may even be more "local" in character than these. Likewise, such U.S. states as Indiana, Minnesota, and Missouri have larger populations than the entire country of Switzerland, and are many times its physical size. Yet administratively, these

Table 13.1

Criminal Justice Spending by Level of Government

	Switzerland	United States
federal	6 %	14 %
state		32 %
canton	67 %	
county		25 %
municipal		29 %
commune	27 %	

states are the equivalent of the Swiss cantons—standing under the federal government, but above the cities and counties. When comparing the activities of different levels of government, is a U.S. state the equivalent of a Swiss canton, or of the Swiss federal government? Is the Swiss canton of Zürich, with a population of several hundred thousand, closer to the state of Virginia, or to that state's Fairfax County, with similar size and geographic size?

Table 13.1 compares spending on police and the courts by various levels of government in the United States and Switzerland. The layout of the table goes from highest unit of government to lowest, placing the cantons of Switzerland as closer to the federal center than a U.S. county, but somewhat farther and less similar to it than a U.S. state. The result is a kind of graphic top-down effect that gives us a feel for the extent to which criminal justice functions, as measured by spending, are carried out at the top, middle, and bottom of the system.

As a general matter, the U.S. column has more numbers and larger numbers bunched toward the top and middle; the Swiss places most of its chips in the middle and lower portions. If we compare what the federal government of Switzerland spends on police and court functions to what its smallest and most intimate level of government spends, the result is a ratio of somewhat more than six to one. For the United States, the ratio is only two to one—a much stronger federal presence, and weaker local one.

Of course, this leaves the cantons out of the picture, which is a serious problem for comparing Swiss government to other states. If we consider the cantons and communes to be roughly comparable to U.S. counties and municipalities, we see that in Switzerland, the local character of justice administration is 94 percent of the spending, in the U.S., 54 percent. This probably overstates the disparity somewhat—but not much. The state of California is roughly ten times the population and extent of Switzerland; the government in Sacramento is at least as remote and imperial as the government in Bern. One can parse the data, but the general picture remains one of greater federalism in the Swiss system, and this reflects the reality. In their function and level of accessibility, the cantons are much closer to a U.S. county, and the states of the U.S. are not terribly different from the Swiss federal government. Each government has an added layer of administration when making comparisons then—the U.S. federal government is a unit of size and complexity that has no analogy in the Swiss system, and the Swiss communes have an intimacy and level of responsiveness seen only in the smallest U.S. towns.

All this, of course, expresses only the economic relationship. As the Swiss towns and cantons have much greater authority and autonomy vis-à-vis their federal government, the resulting statistical picture if anything understates the decentralized nature of Swiss criminal justice. The states of Europe are generally in between, with France close to the U.S. and perhaps even exceeding it in degree of centralization; Germany and Britain in the middle.

This system would appear to be open to abuse by local judges and sheriffs, who have great discretion compared to a modern-day judge in the U.S. or most of Europe. What is to prevent a judge or sheriff in Eastern Glarus, or along the road leading to the Gotthard pass, from becoming a kind of Macon County kingpin or Mexican patrol officer—abusing his authority to squeeze fines and bribes and worse out of suspects? There are in fact some complaints among the Swiss, and more from foreign visitors, about traffic policing both along the Northern highway system and in the Southeast passages. For the most part, however, the Swiss seem to have avoided any severe conflicts between citizens of the different cantons or the cantons themselves.

There are several reasons for this. First, the Swiss courts do not attract men and women whose ambition is to rise to great power, or acquire riches, through the legal system. The pay for judges remains as low as it did, in relative terms, in the 1920s, when Lord Bryce noted that there were periodic difficulties filling some vacancies on the bench. As well, the presence of so many lay judges and volunteer administrators throughout the commune governments, and of part-time lay persons even at the cantonal level, gives the whole system a broad base of people and economic interests. The insurance judge who in fact is an executive at the local textile company sees his position as a voluntary gift to the community, not a sinecure. He was probably appointed by a cantonal legislature of housewives, part-time professionals, and other citizens, or asked to fill the job by a town council. He works with a group of similar volunteers and underpaid de facto volunteers. Few or none of the actors in this drama want anything so much as to render a fair decision and get home. It would not be impossible for them to favor their own neighbors in a dispute, and, in fact, they would have a natural inclination to do so. But it would be nearly impossible to systematically do so, and very difficult to do so for gain.

Thus, while the Swiss system is open to such abuses of locality, they do not appear to have become a serious problem yet. The courts, though not formally composed of temporary juries as such, tend to function somewhat in the manner of juries. The Swiss courts are a half-way house between juries and legal experts, with a bias toward the popular jury side.

This metaphor may explain how the Swiss are able to mitigate another obvious defect of their legal system—its lack of professional expertise and considered legal opinion. "There is no doubt that Switzerland does not have the practicing lawyers and judges with the knowledge and experience of the U.S., Germany, or other countries," a Swiss attorney concedes. "But the system does draw on expertise from outsiders." For example, lay judges frequently are experts in their own field of cases, which in the cantonal and federal supreme courts are divided by area of knowledge—insurance cases, intergovernment disputes, contract issues, and so on. Of course, there is nothing to stop a judge in Germany or France from soliciting a formal or informal opinion from an expert, in court or as a consultant—and many do. In the Swiss system, this process is more regular. Leaders from very different walks of life are integrated into the legal profession, both directly, when they serve as judges, and indirectly, as their presence leavens the legal community as a whole.

The result still leaves the Swiss short of the kind of broad, deep pool of legal brilliance that one sees in the United States. The system is particularly weak at the top and in the intellectual realm. There are few legal journals, and the writing and research in them does not rise to the level seen in American, French, and German journals. In international legal disputes, where one would think the Swiss would excel by virtue of their multilingualism and cultural adaptiveness, Swiss attorneys have a relatively poor record in representing both their government and their large banking and other commercial firms. If one needed to litigate a case or defend one's self of a murder charge, one would almost certainly want an American attorney, and might hope for a British or German judge. For brilliant reasoning about the theories underpinning the dispute, one might turn to the French or the Americans. If one were able to choose any venue in the world for the case to be tried, however, one could do worse than to select any of the Swiss cantons at random.

A Swiss attorney who practices now in the United States put it this way: "Swiss law does not lend itself to the cutting-edge hairsplitting argumentation and drafting seen in the United States. Swiss law and jurisprudence often take the approach of stating a broad principle and leaving it to the good common sense of legal practitioners to fill in the details. In other words, the law says, "A," ergo the more direct applications of "AA," and "a," and "aa" are covered. A Swiss lawyer trying to argue that "aa" is not covered simply because it was not stated in the explicit language of the "A" statute would be laughed out of court. In the United States, an attorney not arguing that "aa" was left uncovered by the broad principle "A," despite the common-sense application, would probably be vulnerable to a malpractice suit." These observations have special application to contract law, but their spirit applies to criminal law differences between the U.S. and Switzerland as well.

The Swiss, in other words, may have an inferior system, at least at the higher reaches of law. But the Swiss system is able to function as a whole because of the work and the generosity of its citizens; it is a justice system not only for, but of and by, the people. If we consider one of the system's great failings in recent years—the growth of Zürich into a great center of drug trafficking in the 1970s and 1980s—then we see an interesting illustration of the system in action.

Rita Fuhrer does not look like the person who busted up the Zürich drug runners. Her face is soft and round, her eyes sympathetic. Bangs and medium-length hair gently wrap around the side, completing the effect. Frau (Mrs.) Fuhrer, as she prefers to be called, wears a tweed business suit that is neat, but not padded or sharply angular. She smiles and apologizes her English "not very good," which given Swiss standards means she has roughly the fluency (in this, her third tongue) of the median graduate of a U.S. high school.

Fuhrer was elected to her post in 1995. One assumed she had some background as a prosecutor or an attorney, but when asked her profession, she answers, "housewife." Her answer had the feeling, through the slight language barrier, of someone who still considers herself primarily a wife and mother—and wants to be seen as such, in ever-so-slightly a counter-cultural fashion. ("Being a housewife *is* a profession"—she did not say this, but seemed to convey it by her understated manner.)

On further probing, however, it appears the answer was not merely attitudinal, but accurate, and even illustrative. Prior to her election to this post, Mrs. Fuhrer served on the cantonal council, one of the many important but low-paying positions occupied by many women in Switzerland. (Women constituted 23 percent of the cantonal legislatures in 1998.) As well, she worked briefly as a newspaper reporter. But there are no advanced degrees, no years as a litigator or high-profile political activist. Mrs. Fuhrer was an attentive mom who did public service for modest pay and decided she might be able to do something to help the police make Zürich a safer and better place to live.

In her present office, Fuhrer has implemented what amounts to a two-point program. "I was not trained for it," she admits. "But I like to talk to people, different people. I talked and listened." The program she implemented was not original, and not even controversial—it represented the trend in thinking in the city when she took office. But Fuhrer saw the wisdom of it, and put it into practice.

First, she had the cantonal police clamp down on drug dealings at the Zürich airport, the train station, and the nearby park, *Platzspitz,* that became almost synonymous with drug dealing during the 1980s and early 1990s. ("Platzspitz" translates into English as "Poined Square," though it soon became known as "Needle Park.") Dealers of even small amounts were arrested, as were their customers. The federal government shared information and manpower—a rarity in Switzerland, but possible in this case because of the canton's request for such help. With the assistance of the canton, the city police of Zürich implemented essentially the same measures, and the two units cooperated in a way they previously had not. Arrests for drug possession and trafficking shot up for two years as the Polizei cleaned up the streets, then tapered off as the population of criminals shrank. The amounts of heroin and cocaine seized by the police moved in a similar pattern, rising sharply and then falling with the declining incidence of drug use. Figures 13.4 and 13.5 nearby show these statistical trends.

Second, Mrs. Fuhrer worked with the city and canton to increase and upgrade facilities for treating addicts—helping them get off drugs. The canton and city expanded existing facilities and set up new ones. Spending on these programs and their associated capital budgets increased. Addicts were encouraged to sign up for programs voluntarily even when suspected of posses-

Figure 13.4

Total Drug Arrests in Zürich City
Includes arrests by cantonal and city police. Does not include arrests for
importing drugs (generally, 150–200 per year).

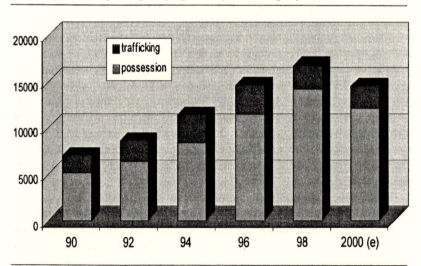

Source: Jahresbericht, Spezialabteilung 3, Kantonspolezei Zürich, 1990–1998 inclusive.

Figure 13.5

Drug Seizures by Zürich Police (cantonal and city, combined)

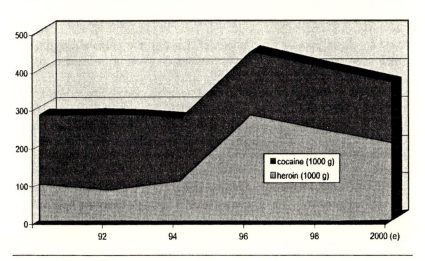

Source: Zürich canton, as cited in Fig. 13.4.

sion and therefore vulnerable to arrest. City and canton district attorneys arrested addicts to avoid prosecution if they entered a detoxification program. Judges in the canton were encouraged to sentence only the most stubborn addicts to jail terms. Swiss judges were already lenient when measured by the length of sentence typically imposed for major crimes, although given the high rate of apprehension and conviction achieved by the Swiss courts, and the low rate of successful appeals, the overall deterrent impact was as high or higher than many other Western countries. [1]

The program appears to have worked. From 1985 as a base year, the number of drug addicts estimated in Zürich tripled. Since 1995, it has fallen by half. Entrants into treatment programs surged, thanks almost entirely to the arrest referrals and sentencing. Of the entrants, "about one third" kick their habit immediately, Fuhrer says. "Another third have some repeating, but are able to give up the drugs after several tries. Another third"—she pauses, looks to the side—"cannot be reached." Overall, the program's office says, 65 percent eventually kick their habit.

These program statistics, of course, suffer from lack of time. The policy has been in place only a few years, making judgments about its long-term effectiveness tenuous. But the tentative figures above are borne out by related measures of drug use and crime. Zürich's rate of such crimes as robbery and burglary fell by more than 10 percent, largely due to the decline in the number of addicts needing to supply an expensive habit. Albeit a grim statistic, a good index of drug usage is simply the number of deaths by overdose or improper use. These fell from a high of 92 such deaths in 1992 to 89 in 1994, 65 in 1996, and 58 in 1998.

Which part of the program was most important—the police crackdown, or the focus on treatment?

Mrs. Fuhrer gives a sincere answer, but also the politically astute one: "You need both. I think we might have made some progress with just the arrests, cleaning out the park, or with just the treatment."

Yes, Mrs. Fuhrer, but many members of your party—she belongs to the SVP, the Socially Conservative Party of Switzerland, roughly equivalent on many issues to a Pat Buchanan or Jesse Helms in the United States, or perhaps an Ariel Sharon in Israel—would like to see the expenditures on treatment cut back, and the police approach toughened even more. Would that be a mistake?

"Let me say—I think both are useful and important. But if I had to keep one, if I had to say one was more important, I think the treatment approach has done more good. There's a very simple reason: The treatment program has reduced the population of people addicted substantially. This helps rob the traffickers of their sales.

"But I would want to keep both parts of the program. They work together. If someone wanted to do away with either one, I would try to persuade them not to, whether it was the treatments or the arrests, and whether they were from my party, or some other."

With this answer, of course, Mrs. Fuhrer establishes a slight distance, perhaps, from her party on a matter of rhetorical emphasis. Yet she defends its core idea that a reduction in drug trafficking, including arrests of users and suppliers, is a public good that should be pursued. And she stubbornly (and intelligently) keeps it bundled into part of a program that has blended the approach of different partisans in the drug issue into a coherent whole—a whole that has worked for Zürich.

Many, perhaps most, professional politicians in the United States or Europe would probably answer the question in roughly the same way. But Mrs. Fuhrer is not a professional politician—she's a professional housewife. The Swiss system makes it possible for the head of one of the country's largest police departments to credibly call herself that. And herein lies one of the sources of its vitality.

Note

1.   For example, of all Swiss men convicted of rape, only 35 percent are sentenced to jail. This is low compared to the United States (more than 80 percent), Sweden (71 percent), and Japan (65 percent.) On the other hand, the Swiss system catches, tries, and convicts a larger percentage of offenders than many countries. Of all reported rapes, a culprit is convicted in Switzerland more than 20 percent of the

time. This is significantly more than in the United States (5 percent) and Sweden (8 percent), though less than Japan's 39 percent rate. About 10,000 persons in Switzerland are sent to a prison each year for all offenses but sentences of several months are the norm, and of more than five years, extremely rare. There is no death penalty. The number of Swiss assigned a life sentence has averaged 1.8 persons per year over the last two decades; now and then a year goes by in which there is no assignment of a life sentence at all. Punishment for crimes in Switzerland is thus less severe per conviction than in many countries, although what punishment there is is swift and certain.

14

Welfare

At a superficial glance, Switzerland has very little experience with welfare as Americans or other Europeans know it. This is true in a double sense. First, Switzerland simply never established (until 1990) an income support system for the poor that compared in scale with those of Europe or the United States.[1] Second, the country enjoyed relatively low unemployment rates and reasonable wages for many years, so that there was less need for transfer payments to help the poor. Some would argue that the relatively low level of transfer payments is a substantial reason for the low level of poverty.

Whatever the cause, the combination of policy and economic condition is such that among the Swiss, welfare was not a matter of great controversy until the last decades of the twentieth century. Then, a combination of somewhat higher unemployment rates, tight national and communal budgets, and the issue of immigrants receiving public assistance combined to make welfare at once a larger factor in the Swiss economy, and more controversial.

The country's prosperity—and the evenness of it—is such legend that it led me to an interesting, if in the end embarrassing, discovery. Riding the train into Zürich from Bern, around the region of the airport and perhaps ten miles West of the center of the city we passed through an industrial belt of what seemed to be warehouses, large factories, and light chemical or pharmaceutical plants. Suddenly, near the tracks and in some cases squeezed in between the tracks and the factories, little clusters of shanty houses began to appear, in clumps of fifty to 200 units by my estimate. As shanty towns go, these were nice. The rows were neat. The houses were made out of what appeared to be cheap wood (better than cardboard) and ribbed fiberglass roofs that looked as if they would, at least, keep out rain and snow. Some of the houses even had Swiss flags or the flags of other nationalities or cantons or organizations flying out in front, and all were laid out in rather neat rows. The places seemed strangely deserted, even for a working-class neighborhood. There were very few moms and small kids, if any. Decently dressed people, usually men or couples and often of obvious non-European ethnicity, occasionally wandered up and down the tidy rows of shacks, sometimes beating thick work gloves together. "*Swiss* ghettos," it struck me—the nicest ghettos in the world. But still ghettos: a mild surprise.

My traveling companion aroused my suspicion further when he responded evasively—it seemed to me—when asked about these obvious little pockets of poverty among the Swiss prosperity.

"What are those, Hans?"

"What are what?," he answered blandly.

"Those—over there." My hand pointed to Northwest.

"The one on the right looks like it is storage for ABB," he answered. "I don't know about the one on the left." But he was looking too far out.

"No, not the factory. The little houses in between us and the factory. There."

"Houses?," he asked.

"Yes, Hans, the little shanty houses right *there*." It felt bad to corner him and make him explain something negative about Switzerland. But these little unpleasant truths, it seems to me, are what give a country's strong points their real merit.

"You mean the *Schrebergärten?*" he asked, keeping it up.

"Well, yes, if that's what they're called. What are those—company houses for temporary *Gastarbeiters* or something?"

"Gregory, those are gardens. People come out and work on them in the evenings and the weekends. Some of them grow a few vegetables or flowers for their home, and some just like the gardening."

"What did you say you thought they were?"

Thus my discovery of shanty towns, so promising for a few minutes, turned out to be another Swiss efficiency, almost an annoying self-parody.

You have to look closely at Switzerland—and do more than look, it turns out—to avoid falling into one of two opposite errors. One error is that Switzerland has no poverty (and little or no welfarism) at all. The other is that the Swiss have huge, complex "hidden" class problems lurking just below the surface, or a developed welfare system along the lines of Sweden, Britain, or France. Neither is really the case, or to be more precise, each is partially true.

Swiss poverty rates place Switzerland near the bottom of the world in terms of social want. Measurement is rendered difficult by the typically federalist Swiss system of social assistance, and its informality and adaptation to individual cases. Surveys, however, suggest that about 5.6 percent of the population had an inadequate income to meet basic physical and health standards. Even this figure does not include some types of payments and assistance, though. And this figure is for the year 1992, which was just after a fairly sharp recession in Europe (coincident with the relatively mild U.S. recession of 1990–91). In fact, then, compared to many affluent countries where such statistical poverty rates often hover close to 10 percent, Switzerland has enjoyed a poverty rate of about half the developed-country rate, and for most of the time, one-third or less.

Little of this poverty, while real in a sense, is hard core. That is to say, few of the people who may be poor one year in Switzerland are poor two or three years later. For example, about one-quarter of all the statistically poor are twenty to twenty-nine years old These are typically years in which young men and women emerge from school, dabble in different part-time jobs, and so on. Many U.S. youngsters are "poor" in the year they graduate from high school or college, since they may then enter the work force, but for only half a year or less. In Switzerland, persons aged forty and above make up about 54 percent of the population, but account for only about 37 percent of all the poor. Divorced men (10 percent) and women (20 percent) make up another significant chunk of the poor. Again, while these people often suffer real hardship, they are also often likely to land on their economic feet within a year or two. They are temporarily, not semipermanently, in need.

The shape of poverty in regional, ethnic, and other terms is happily even. That is, in Switzerland what little want there is does not tend to associate itself strongly with different races or other groups. For instance, of all the statistically poor, about 74 percent are of Swiss birth, and 25 percent are foreign born—roughly their proportion in the work force as a whole. Similarly, 65 percent of the poor live in cities, and 35 percent in the country. About 64 percent live in a German-speaking region, 27 percent French, and 9 percent Italian—again fairly close to the nation as a whole.

This spreading of poverty, where a little poverty there must be, is a great blessing, because it means that economic need does not readily spill over into racial or other frustration. One sees it even in the layout of major cities such as Zürich and Geneva. While any city has high and low rent districts, the ghetto is largely unknown among the Swiss. It is partly the result of Swiss decentralization, and partly makes it especially effective. Another contributing factor is the strength of Swiss education, especially vocational education. And then there is, according to former Zürich Mayor Sigmund Widmer, "the old-fashioned work ethic of Zwingli and Calvin." Widmer recalls a number of instances in which his constituents would keep a job rather than accepting unemployment insurance or public assistance—even though they could have made nearly as much money for a time without having to work. "The Swiss would rather work," Widmer argues.

Welfare programs to respond to these needs, like many other Swiss policies, vary widely by canton and community. For basic family assistance, the federal government contributes only about one-eighth of payments, at 12 percent; the cantons, 34 percent, or about one third; and the communities, close to half with 45 percent.[2]

The result is not merely a uniform, national system administered locally, because the cantons and the communes have adopted distinctive approaches to social payments. The amount of spending per inhabitant on welfare varies widely by canton. As Figure 14.1 shows for selected cantons, the average combination of *Soziale Wohlfart* (social welfare) and *Fürsorge* (assistance) is 2,200 Swiss francs per month. This ranges, however, from a high of 4,500 francs a month in Geneva, and 3,400 in Basel to as little as 1,200 francs in Uri and 1,100 in Schwyz and Appenzell Innerhoden. Part of these differences reflect higher living expenses and poverty rates in the larger cities, but they also reflect a higher affinity for such transfer payments in general in the different regions.

Rates of statistical poverty, especially those that measure poverty before transfer payments are accounted, are also in turn influenced by the subsidies available through social welfare programs.

There is equal or even greater variation between how different individual cases are handled within a given community. Even in Geneva, where the social welfare system is relatively more rationalized and bureaucratized and less personal and flexible, social payments can be significantly adapted. "We try to work with people, find employment, adapt the program to their needs," Monica Tross, a social welfare worker for Geneva canton, explained. This can include increasing payments for families where, say, someone is engaged in a training course, or where medical or other family circumstances have intensified the problem of a job loss. It can also mean decreasing them for people who aren't getting out and aggressively trying to get off the dole. There aren't a large number of such cases—"five or ten percent, somewhere in there"—but the ability to make them has an impact on the way the entire system functions.

In other cantons and communities the flexibility to adjust to different circumstances is even greater. "We have a great deal of ability to decide how to handle the situation of people who need social assistance," a member of the Aarau town council said. "We have certain normal practices, but we can decide what to do by the person or family."

Indeed, family assistance among the Swiss is more family-based than in much of the West. On the one hand, couples struggling to make ends meet, but who have not divorced, do not necessarily lose benefits they might need. On the other hand, the Swiss look to the extended family—parents, brothers and sisters, in some cases even aunts or uncles—to provide help too. In bureaucratic systems, the need to reduce such factors to formal codes often leads to a labyrinth of rules with little flexibility. Under the local, pliable system of the Swiss, such subtleties are incorporated into the program, but not necessarily the written law.

"We had a situation with a young man in my community," Giancarlo Dillena, a newspaper editor in the Ticino, recalls. "A young man with a problem," perhaps drugs or alcohol. "The village made a job for him, gardening and doing other chores. These were things that needed to get done, and it was better for him and the town than his having to continue on assistance."

Figure 14.1

Average Combination of Social Welfare and Assistance by Cantons

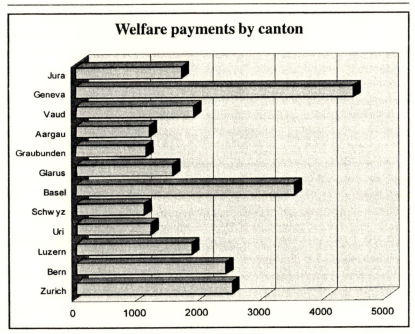

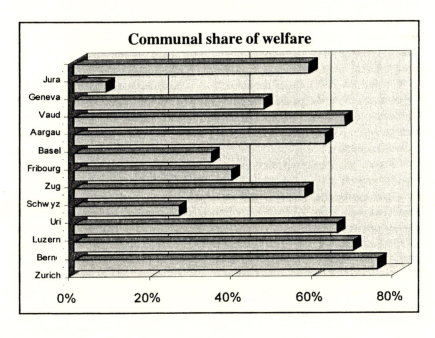

Of course, this is the kind of flexibility many social welfare advocates in other countries plead for. In most cases, their publics would like such common-sense adaptability as well. Such flexibility, though, does not come without a price. Sometimes programs don't work, and in Switzerland, when they don't there are fewer regulations to hide behind. Where there is human discretion, human mistakes are more clearly visible as such. During my stay in Southern Switzerland, a case in the canton of Valais appeared in the local newspapers about a man who was drawing assistance from three different cantons, amounting to a tidy sum in total.

Likewise, allowing officials to reduce or increase payments within reason would be less feasible in countries without the tradition of honesty and self-government of the Swiss. Larger amounts could be used as small payoffs or other corruption. Smaller amounts would bring lawsuits from persons arguing they were entitled to full payments. The position tailored for the young man in the Ticino, in some countries, couldn't be offered legally—it would violate a union contract or other agreements. A young woman for whom a similar setup was established in Bern, running a part-time day care center while receiving some assistance, would probably have run afoul of child care laws and much other red tape in the United States, France, or Canada. These kinds of human arrangements, if they were allowed, would inevitably lead to occasional abuses, followed by a scandal in the press, and corrective legislation and regulations.

Thus at least a part of Swiss welfare system's functionality rests on factors outside the system. If it encourages citizenship, as it surely does, it is also enabled by citizenship. Swiss welfare policy, like the Swiss topography, is thus characterized by sharp changes and extremes—not a smooth, flat, equal plane. It can be very generous, almost extravagant, in one case, and frugal, almost harsh, in another.

Viewing the evolution of social welfare in Switzerland over time, we can learn much about the economic philosophy of Swiss voters—and about the tendencies of the Swiss political system and its interaction with trends in Europe and the United States.

Welfarism began in Europe in the nineteenth century, with Germany, France, and Britain all expanding their programs into the early twentieth century. The Swiss were relative laggards. Some attributed this to the country's lack of affluence. At the time, Switzerland was still emerging from centuries as a medium- to low-income country in the European context. As well, the country's politics resisted change at the same time as Swiss traditional beliefs resisted anything outside the Calvinistic framework of work, thrift, and personal responsibility. "People not only dislike Bismarck's military system," observed an 1874 *Neue Zürcher Zeitung* editorial, "but his economic methods," referring to the German's use of social welfare programs to buy off potential opposition to his empire-building militarism on behalf of the Kaiser. A similar round of social-service growth hit the United States after World War I and in the Great Depression, but was relatively unknown in Switzerland.

For nearly a century, the Swiss didn't seem to need social welfare either. Unemployment topped 1 percent only twice in the twentieth century—first during the Great Depression, when it never rose above 5 percent, and the second time during the 1990s, by which time the Swiss had constructed a relatively extensive social welfare program. Of course, many social scientists would argue that there was a connection—that the lack of significant transfer payment programs helped keep employment high, and the Swiss emphasis on productivity generated sufficient goods and services to keep the economy functioning through the engine of private-sector growth. As reviewed earlier, economic initiatives that aimed at social spending fared poorly throughout the century and into the postwar 1950s and 1960s. There were two major exceptions from 1900 to 1975. The first was a gradual acceptance of government-assisted pension schemes from the 1920s onward. The second was the establishment of a labor concordat after World War II that raised wages and established further unemployment benefits—but at the same time, established an almost strike-free continuation of many years of labor peace through the end of the century.

For whatever reason, the Swiss resisted the formation of the modern welfare state for many years. Social democrats in Switzerland and outside saw this as evidence of backwardness by the voters, or the system, and there is certainly a stubbornness in the Swiss character. On the other hand, when one looks at a chart of Swiss unemployment for the century and sees the long strings of "0.4 %, 0.3 %, 0.3 %, 0.2%" year after year, one sees a case for the Swiss resistance.

From 1974 to 1981, Swiss voters approved some national initiatives establishing funding for greater unemployment insurance and family assistance programs—and many more cantonal referenda along the same lines. By the time these systems were becoming established there was a general economic boom in the West and in Swiss export industries in particular. Swiss expenditures on social welfare remained tiny, fueled by high rates of employment through the 1980s.

In 1990, Switzerland finally suffered an economic slump while having significant welfare programs as backdrop. Clearly the cause was not simply the fact of such benefits, because they had now been in place for some years without producing falling employment or a recession. They may, however, have exacerbated the troubles once they were set off by other events.

The collapse of the Soviet Empire in 1989 brought a flood of immigrants and asylum seekers not only to Germany but to the rest of Europe. Other countries, other than West Germany with its fellow Germans, were less welcoming than the Swiss with their tradition of hospitality to the foreigner. Not long afterward, the beginning of ethnic and religious unrest in former Yugoslavia created a new wave of humanity. While all this was going on, a mild recession hit the U.S. in 1990 through 1991—a recession that was felt more severely in Europe with its greater dependency on foreign oil. Perhaps most unfortunately, the Swiss chose this time to permit a crackdown on immigration in the most perverse way. Fearful that immigrants were "taking jobs" from skilled Swiss or dragging wages down for the less skilled, the confederation passed tighter restrictions on work permits for foreigners, and many cantons increased enforcement of the same regulations. The result was that many asylum seekers could not work—but did receive social welfare assistance. Paradoxically the Swiss were making it difficult to work, and easier to be on the dole.

Finally, the taxes needed to pay for all these programs had climbed gradually in the 1980s—and were raised significantly in 1990 through 1991. The higher tax rates were a drag on private sector activity and employment, driving more Swiss into the arms of public assistance.

The combination of these forces and policies was a deep recession indeed in Swiss terms. Unemployment topped 4 percent nationally for the second time in a century, and in some cantons exceeded 6 percent. Geneva, Vaud, Basel, and even Zürich went into an associated fiscal crisis from which they had still not fully recovered at the end of the decade. From 1989 to 1994, in each of those cantons, social welfare expenditures more than tripled. Swiss expenditures on unemployment benefits surged to more than 5.8 billion francs in both 1993 and 1994 from 500 million in 1990.

The nature of the Swiss system, however, put the Swiss in a good position to adapt to this new experience. For one thing, social welfare as a significant economic factor was a new thing to the Swiss. Switzerland hadn't had these programs long enough, in 1990, for social welfare to have settled into a hardened series of coalitions and expectations, resentments, and set battles. The politics of welfare, in short, were fluid. Furthermore, given Switzerland's still relatively strong economic position, it was possible to make adjustments to programs without touching off an economic crisis. Four percent unemployment isn't as good as 1 percent, but it's still relatively low compared to most of the developed world—indeed, a 4 percent jobless rate would be a thirty-year record for the United States or most of Europe.

Perhaps most important, the federalist nature of the Swiss system allowed and even encouraged experimentation with different changes. Some cantons and communities simply cut payments under fiscal pressure, as Peter Frey reported in the *Aargauer Zeitung*. An intercantonal commission that some hoped would standardize social welfare payments instead helped spur a competitive series of downsizing and program reform in 1994 and 1995. Some cantons cut benefits; others asked for (and received) a greater contribution from the confederation; still others established limits that make it more difficult to continue receiving social welfare payments beyond a period of several months.

The net impact was to make welfare easy to get on, but hard to stay on—resembling the reforms enacted in the United States, Germany, and elsewhere in the 1990s after a much longer experience with welfarism. Looked at from one point of view, it took the Swiss eighty or ninety years to catch up with the U.S. and Europe. On the other hand, it took the Swiss only five years to reform their system in much the same way that Europe and America were only able to enact after tortuous decades of rancorous debate.

This pace—now maddeningly slow, now breathtaking in its methodical quickness—is vintage Swiss. For instance, it took some Swiss banks decades to fully grapple with the problem of dormant accounts left over from World War II. Yet it took the Swiss only a few months after the rise to power of Adolf Hitler to gear up a major rearmament effort. By 1935, a major anti-German cultural and ideological resistance was underway at a time when most of the West was still appeasing the German dictator. In any case, it is wrong to think of the Swiss system as always being slothful, any more than it fits the image of democratic impulsiveness feared by political philosophers. Rather, democracy in Switzerland is capable of moving fast—but often, it seems, chooses to deliberate, and move slowly.

During a visit to the *Schrebergärten* a few days after my investigation from the train window, a man of about fifty-five accosted me. He said he heard there was an American making a study of Swiss democracy and as a newcomer or outsider himself he had something to say. Dark-skinned, fluent in neither German nor French, he appeared to be of Middle Eastern descent, Yugoslavian or Iraqi, perhaps.

"Switzerland is the most—democracy," he paused. "More in the democracy—," he continued, looking, it seemed to me, for the adjective. His English wasn't bad.

"The most demo-cratic, you may want to say," a young man, apparently his son, added.

"Yes, the most demo-cratic. I do not say anything bad about America, which is a great country. But Switzerland has the best democracy, even better than yours. It is good that someone studies it." He was under the impression, it seemed to me, that this was some kind of official mission.

The young man knew about my interest in immigrants and the working class generally, and offered that the older one, named Karl or Karlo, was working occasionally, but also receiving some assistance.

"No, no," Karl corrected, perhaps not getting the full gist of what the younger man had said. "I am working this week," he said, dusting some dirt off his hands. He was evidently maintaining some of the gardens for people too busy to tend them on their own. "There are not payments."

"But next week, if you do not—then you will get some help."

"Well, yes, if I need that I will go see the woman who handles that in our town, and I will be back on again—for a week or two. I hope it would just be for a couple of weeks."

There was a lot going on in that situation, it seemed to me. On the one hand was a social welfare program sufficiently free from red tape—sufficiently human—to fit itself into a family's situation in that way, like a glove rather than a one-size-fits-all mitten. At the same time, there was the man, more of a citizen (though he almost certainly was not one yet) than many people in many countries of their birth. And there was his sweet, simple disposition, his propensity to accept what was his from the system, but not advance claims of entitlement when assistance is not needed.

Those *Schrebergärten* became an apt metaphor—in Switzerland even the shanties are symbols if not of affluence, certainly of a mentality that views dirt as a place to grow something, and a layoff as an opportunity to do some other kind of work.

Notes

1. This is a reference to "welfare" programs for the poor and unemployed. This does not include state and private pension plans, private insurance, and other forms of income support and charity.
2. Again we must keep in mind that while these levels of government correspond administratively with those of the United States or Europe, each level is significantly more intimate than its U.S. or European counterpart. A welfare recipient dealing with a U.S. state government is dealing with a unit, on average, of some 5 million persons; the average population of a Swiss canton is about 300,000. The source for these and other general statistics that follow include interviews with cantonal and community officials, popular press, and the Swiss Federal Statistics Office, *Statistisches Jahrbuch der Schweiz/Annuaire statistique de la Suisse*, published by *Neue Zürcher Zeitung*, Zürich, 1998, pp. 340–80.

15

Press

Thomas Jefferson is often quoted as saying he would rather live in a country without elections than in a country without newspapers. Jefferson said this to emphasize his belief in the importance of the free exchange of information and ideas. In fact, the two, far from constituting a kind of either-or choice, tend to go together.

Newspapers in and of themselves provide a kind of freedom by enabling the people to keep track of what their leaders are doing and, knowing this, to keep those leaders in check. A free press helps make elections meaningful by enabling people to cast an informed vote, intelligently directed toward the ends they want. In this sense, they have a similar effect to that of direct democracy. And newspapers help ensure the fact of elections in any case, as those who read them insist on having that voice in the way their country is governed. Newspapers and elections thus are each vital by themselves and they support one another.

Switzerland has plenty of both. The typical Swiss surely casts more votes every year than the citizen of any other country. And the people read more newspapers per capita than in any other country in the world. (With a respectful nod to Norway, first by some measures.) In fact, if we may suppose that the Jefferson relationship applies incrementally—if an improvement in degree in the free press equals and causes an improvement in democracy, while a decline in the state of the free press weakens that democracy—then Switzerland must have an excellent press corps. After all, its democracy is in a refined, balanced, and advanced state. It is hard to believe this would be the case if the press in Switzerland were not highly effective at informing people. This is, in fact, the case, whether one judges by the quantity or the quality of the Swiss journals.

One reason for this strength and diversity is structural. The political division of the country into small but important units creates a demand for local news. Thus there are at least two strong newspapers in the capital of Bern, two in Zürich, and two (again) in Geneva, as well as important papers serving

Basel, canton Aargau, Vaud, Luzern, and three major Italian-language papers in the Ticino.

Yet because of Switzerland's size, such papers can be available almost anywhere in the densely populated Northern tier of Switzerland within roughly two hours. Switzerland's language groups, which are concentrated regionally but also cut across the cantons, also help provide a national market for these largest urban papers. The French-speaking Swiss of Zürich may well take the *Tribune de Geneve*—not out of necessity but from a natural affinity for his first tongue. Likewise the German-speaking resident in Geneva may subscribe to *Tages Anzeiger* or the *Neue Zürcher Zeitung*. It appeared to me that many Swiss elites take newspapers in more than one language, both to achieve a balance of subjects and coverage and to keep their first two or three languages polished.

The *Neue Zürcher Zeitung*, the newspaper of record as *The New York Times* is in the United States, appeared to be more widely available and read in French-speaking Switzerland than the leading French papers in German-speaking Switzerland. If this is so, it probably reflects somewhat the size of Zürich, as well as the tendency for a national newspaper of record to form, much as the world seems to gravitate toward a main currency and one main language of international business. Although the *NZZ* isn't the first or second leading newspaper in terms of raw circulation, it is read widely by political and business elites. Even so, if accurate, this appears to be a rare exception to the tendency to emphasize the French portion of Swiss culture. Figure 15.1 shows this graphically by comparing the number of newspapers, radio stations, and television stations by language. There is a preponderance of French and Italian radio stations over German, and an even stronger one among television stations—of which there are more in Italian than either French or German. This progression may reflect the fact that television has a strong entertainment component, while newspapers are more information based, and radio lies somewhere in between.

As well, the Swiss culture of openness to foreign ideas and persons opens Swiss newspapers up to significant foreign exposure and competition. Since the Swiss newspapers are of a high and serious quality, there is remarkably little penetration by the major French and German dailies, but there is some. English newspapers, on the other hand, are highly popular, considering the language is not an official one. London's *Financial Times*, the "pink sheet," is widely available, and one sees it being read on the train between Zürich and Geneva; less so as one ventures South of the main, and highly cosmopolitan Northern line. Naturally *The Wall Street Journal*, being both a serious English language paper and the newspaper of financial record for the world-dominant U.S. markets and dollar, is widespread. *The New York Times* is not nearly as visible as one might expect, but this is partly because of the availability of the *Herald-Tribune*, which offers copy not only from the *Times* but

Figure 15.1

Comparison of the Number of Newspapers, Radio Stations, and Television Stations by Language

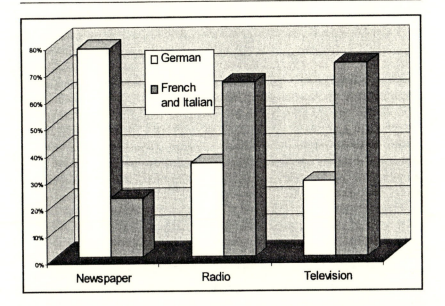

from other newspapers and wire services. The *Washington Post*, a powerful but somewhat less global paper, is virtually invisible in Switzerland. By contrast, one does see the London, Manchester, and other major dailies from England, on occasion.

Compare two reporters of international news—or of merely "economic" news, which all recognize is increasingly global in nature. One reporter is fluent in French, German, and English, or at least two of the three, and can perhaps stumble by in Italian as well. The other is fluent in one of these, and may have studied another in college, or even reported from a foreign-language country for a time, but is not integrated from the day she or he is born right up through the present in that other language. Swiss newspapers, from the *Blick* tabloid up to and including *Neue Zürcher Zeitung*, generally contain significantly more international news than one would find in a U.S. paper. It is obvious that the multilingual reporter would have certain advantages in keeping up with daily events and trends. More than this, however, the Swiss reporter has a certain multicultural advantage, a facility for seeing certain events through the eyes of a different language and an alertness to developments or ideas that may, for a time, be present only in some culture different from his own. Both American and British reporters have enjoyed a portion of this advantage over the last fifty to one-hundred years, and this in part may account for why English-language journalism is relatively distinguished, even considering the "size" of the English language in world culture.

A portion of this is natural and somewhat misleading, considering Switzerland's size and position. A news story in the *Chicago Tribune* about events in Cleveland, some six hours away, would be a domestic story. In Switzerland, events comparably distant are usually foreign. As well, the Swiss, being European, are affected by the rulings of the federal government of Brussels, and the central bank in Bonn, as the people of the U.S. are influenced strongly by events in Washington, D.C.

Domestic news is most noticeable not for its difference in quantity from the American press, but for its different focus and tone nature. News about the culture outside of politics and business is roughly equal in volume, but different in character. The typical Swiss newspaper has somewhat more news about cultural events, such as operas or even movies, and somewhat fewer pieces about personalities or "megatrends." Within the Swiss press, the Romance language newspapers place more emphasis on the arts, and treat them more seriously than do the Swiss German papers. If one wanted to follow fashion trends, or read a serious essay about Fellini's technique or the latest American action films, one would be more likely to find it in *Corriere del Ticino* than in the German papers. The German papers, especially *Neue Zürcher Zeitung*, treat movies, ballet, and literature somewhat in the manner of the *Financial Times*—more space and broader coverage than in, say, *The Wall Street Journal*, but far less than one would find in *The New York Times* or *Le Monde*. Since Switzerland is fully integrated into three major language cultures (Italian, French, and German) and at the same time is as or more fluent in English, its analysis of cultural matters, as with politics, is often revealing and sophisticated. It is surprising, in a sense, that Swiss scholars and journalists have not established themselves as a more dominating presence in European literary culture.

Switzerland has fewer crime stories both in print and in the press, and the stories there have a less sensational tone and photographic coverage. Of course, Swiss crime rates, particularly murder, are lower than in the United States and even much of Europe, so part of this difference reflects a difference in social conditions. One gets the sense, however, that for similar incidents, there is a greater restraint in the Swiss press.

During one of my visits, a story broke in the *Aargauer Zeitung* about an ugly child custody battle between a husband and wife involving outright seizure and what could be called kidnapping of the children, international rescue and extradition attempts, and allegations of violence and abuse. One of the parents was a well-known and respected official in the Aargau government. Yet the paper had declined to report the story for more than two years because of possible repercussions for the children, allowing the legal battle over their status to be concluded without adding to it a media circus to add to the confusion and heighten the bitterness.

Konrad Stamm, editor of *der Bund*, the venerable Bern daily, notes that Swiss newspapers make more than 95 percent of their sales to subscribers. This is a much higher proportion than one sees in most of Europe or in comparable parts of the United States—namely, large cities. "There is less pressure to sell a paper every day by having the most glaring photograph or headline, under this system," he notes.

Swiss political news contains relatively fewer stories about maneuverings in parliament or the administration. This reflects partly the fact that these institutions have less concentrated power than in the United States or Europe. There is also, however, a visible tendency in the press to be somewhat less confrontational. In 1999, the Alexis de Tocqueville Institution surveyed more than 150 news stories on the issue of Swiss participation in the European union that appeared in major Swiss newspapers in February and March. A majority of these articles referred to one or another leading participant in the debate. Among these were Christoph Blocher, a leading opponent of Swiss entry, and Ruth Dreifuss or Flavio Cotti—both supporters of European union entry and the country's presidents in 1999 and 1998, respectively; Cotti was also foreign minister for several years in the 1990s. But in only seven of the articles, or about 4 percent of the sample, was there a strong element of personal confrontation described. The Swiss stories portrayed the European debate as a substantive debate, more than a clash between special interests. Here again, it is difficult to isolate completely which differences in coverage occur because the Swiss press does its job differently, and which differences simply reflect the fact that their society is different. For instance, money appears to play a significantly lesser and different role in Swiss elections than in other democracies; the parliament and the administration are of a completely different character. The Swiss capital, being that of a country not as "great" as others in terms of sheer might and economic size and weight, does not attract as many ambitious and venal fortune seekers as one might expect to find in Washington, Moscow, or Berlin. But there are clues that the Swiss press, if it could somehow be transplanted into the major cities of the United States, would probably cover the same events much differently. When Switzerland did have a major scandal involving one of its federal council members in the 1980s, the result was a flurry of stories for several days and a resignation. The index of the *Neue Zürcher Zeitung*, the year of her resignation, contained more entries having to do with guest-workers and asylum-seekers than it did about the greatest scandal in the history of the Swiss presidency.

This is not to say that Swiss people are somehow never confrontational, competitive, greedy, or unethical in politics as in other spheres. As a matter of emphasis, however, the culture tends to muffle rather than amplify these traits— the political system in part, but the press as well. The Swiss journalist seems to be, if one may use a word that has almost become pejorative at times, rather patriotic compared to his counterpart in many other Western countries.

"It's our system," Giancarlo Dillena, the editor of *Corriere del Ticino* told me, smiling. "We have to like it." One used to hear this more often among citizens and journalists of the representative democracies, and still does at times. One hears it, however, less often than among the Swiss, and it has less personal feeling or immediacy to it. If a reporter from some advanced country made a comment like that, he would feel somewhat trite, and speak of the "system" being "ours" more in the manner of an absent landlord discussing a property he does not tend or even often visit. In Switzerland, even among a highly cynical group of professional scoffers, a sophisticated journalist such as Dillena says such things unself-consciously, in a matter-of-fact tone.

In contrast to the lesser emphasis on elite maneuverings, Swiss political journalism, as might be expected, places somewhat more emphasis on popular trends. The initiative and referendum tools makes the people themselves an integrated part of the legislative process, and thus, a natural and indeed inevitable part of the story. Thus, for example, the lead story about a law passing or a treaty agreement being reached will frequently refer prominently to the prospects for its being challenged by a facultative referendum—especially, of course, if the change was in any way controversial. In October of 1999, for example, parliament wrestled with the issue of medical insurance premiums, which late in the decade began to rise at un-Swiss-like rates exceeding 5 percent a year in many cantons. The president at that time, Ruth Dreifuss, proposed a measure to enact progressive rates—charging the rich more money for their insurance. In announcing the government's annual adjustment in rates, Madame Dreifuss made front-page news across the country. The stories covering this event in *Aargauer Zeitung, Corriere del Ticino, Le Temps, Neue Zürcher Zeitung*, and *Tages Anzeiger* all made mention of the likely referendum battle within the first four paragraphs.

It is tempting to attribute all of these differences to the difference in political structure—popular access, a restrained federal center, and others—and its important and pervasive cultural impacts. The emphasis on popular wisdom, however, and the tone of respect for it by editors and reporters goes beyond what these structural political factors can account for. There is a subtly different spirit in the Swiss news room and in the Swiss journals. It is a feeling of citizens communicating with other citizens—who, if not precisely equal in economic or educational terms, are nevertheless of a rough sort of equality or level of judgment.

In the summer and fall of 1999, for example, *Le Temps* ran a number of articles that either focused on Blocher or that discussed him at length in the course of some broader discussion of an issue such as taxes or European integration. Blocher is not reflective of the paper's editorial policy, which is centrist and internationalist. Still less is he a natural favorite of the Geneva voters, who tend to be liberal and, if not anti-German, certainly suspicious of a cultural conservative German Swiss such as Blocher. Yet *Le Temps* made it a frequent point to mention Blocher's intellectual seriousness and contrasted him favorably with other politicians who were less forthright in advancing their beliefs. One article solicited a brief summary of the Blocher phenomenon from Uli Windisch, a Geneva sociology professor. Windisch obviously didn't agree with most of Blocher's policy positions. Yet the professor warned of the tendency to demonize Blocher, and spoke of the need to "detoxify" him.

The result of this approach, and of the relatively objective approach taken to reporting on Blocher's party in news stories in *Le Temps*, was not only to arm Genevans against dismissing Blocher lightly but also to provide valuable insight to domestic and foreign observers. Blocher's efforts to strengthen his party in Western (French-speaking) Switzerland was one of the more important stories in Switzerland in 1999. Without such support, he and his party's ideas were reaching natural limits of growth in Zürich and the East. With inroads into Vaud, Fribourg, Geneva, and the Ticino, by contrast, Blocher's party, the "SVP," seemed likely to continue its growth and eventually overtake one or more of the three established parties with two seats on the executive council. By treating Blocher seriously, even respectfully, *Le Temps* provided more fodder to both his opponents and supporters alike—because it was supplying important information about him.

Oddly enough, the political parties as such seem to receive substantially more political coverage in Switzerland than in other democracies. After all, in many political theaters, such as the operations of the parliament and the voting for seats, partisan considerations appear to be less important than in the rest of Europe and North America. The coverage, however, treats the parties primarily as vessels for ideas. A typical story in *Le Temps* in the fall of 1999 tracked how the social conservative parties were trying to attract voters through tax cuts and other such measures, while Mrs. Dreifuss and others on the center left were offering social benefits. But since many of the organs of representation are proportional in nature, the result was not the series of bitter fights to the death in district after district, but a *relatively* civil debate about ideas. Every politician naturally wants to see his or her party and their ideas do well, but few politicians need to defeat some personal rival in order to survive. Here again the line between what reflects the press's choice in coverage and what reflects its mere reflection of a different style of politics, is blurry. But there is at least a strong element of press choice.

There was little of class-war coverage in these stories, treating news and policy changes as if the main job was to determine who was "hurt more"—the rich, the poor, owners of automobiles, renters of apartments, or any other group. Instead, policy debates were described and conducted in the press, relatively, as if most members of society were blindfolded from such considerations or could see them or wanted to see them only dimly. During interviews, journalists showed little interest or inclination to pursue issues like this very hard. As one example, when asked which groups of people entry into the European Union would tend to help or hurt, editors and reporters at *CASH*, the financial weekly, and at *Tages Anzeiger, Le Temps*, and *Corriere del Ticino* all reacted blandly.

"I don't think we've done anything on that," former *CASH* editor Markus Gisler said. "And I don't think it's been a major issue.... It's probably true that there is more support for integration among higher-income and well-educated people, and less support lower down. But most people are for or against the EU because they think it will be good or bad for the country, not because it will be good or bad for them." Gisler now heads one of Switzerland's first, and largest, online news and trading sites, "Moneycab." In the United States, by contrast, an economic treaty with much narrower ramifications for America's vast economy—the 1993 trade pact with Mexico—was debated largely in class or special-interest terms. Moreover, the press in the U.S.—and, one might add, in Britain as well—appears to be keenly alert to such matters. In Switzerland, while there are some class conflicts, journalists tend to amplify them only slightly, or even muffle them.

One obvious difference is a kind of populist optimism among Swiss journalists. Hugo Bütler, editor of the *Neue Zürcher Zeitung*, traces much of this to the evolution of the Swiss press itself in the early nineteenth century. Although many conservative forces opposed the establishment of referendum, first in the cantons in the 1830s and 1840s and then nationally, Bütler's paper favored many such revisions and, in fact, added *Neue* (or, "new") to its name after the revision of 1830. Like many Swiss, he refers to the culture of consensus as an important explanation for the press's nonhostile tone and lack of "gotcha"-style reporting.

"Most of the important forces in society have a role in government," he notes, thanks to such institutions as the executive, proportional voting in parliament, and the direct democracy. "Therefore the opposition equals the people, and all are a direct participant in the state." Again we see how the somewhat mystical "culture of consensus," far from being an inexplicable force of nature or a function of climate or genetics, results in large part from the institutions of the Swiss.

The Swiss system, unlike many democracies, empowers the people continuously and particularly, as opposed to sporadically and indirectly. The Swiss voters may veto laws and initiate new ones in an ongoing and item-by-item process. In most other democracies, the voters make policies only by means of an election every few years, with candidates running on the basis of hundreds of votes they've cast. This difference leaves the Swiss citizen somewhat more relaxed about his or her own voice in the process; there is less need to fight or make noise to be heard. As well, because particular officials and institutions have less power, "there is less need for institutions other than the people" to hold them in check, as Bütler put it.

Naturally, the press reflects many of these attitudes and response to them as well. This feeling of greater affinity with the people's institutions, Konrad Stamm of *Der Bund* argues, probably has something to do with the relative degree of respect that the press shows for the executive council's deliberations.[1]

"Our readers are very intelligent," echoes Esther Girsberger. "They need information, not a tutor." Girsberger, now at *Weltwoche*, but the editor of *Tages Anzeiger* at the time of our interview, explains her paper's handling of the European integration issue to me. Likewise, Girsberger treats her editors and reporters with a greater measure of decentralization than one is used to seeing in the American press. "We have people with many different views on the abortion issue, for example," she notes. "People at *Tages Anzeiger* differ." The paper, she says, is "flexible" in style and substance about the issue, allowing somewhat different approaches to flourish. This would be highly unusual at an American newspaper, many of which have issued instructions on whether various groups may be called "pro-life," other "pro-choice," and so on. (Girsberger's tenure at *Tages Anzeiger* ended, however, partly due to this flexibility. Upper management wanted more sensational stories to compete with Swiss and European tabloids. Girsberger declined.)

If we look at matters the press covers outside of politics, it becomes clear that this nonconfrontational culture does not merely extend to the government itself. Accordingly, it is not just a function of the Swiss political system, although the system helps to inculcate these attitudes of mutual respect. Swiss banking secrecy, or "banking privacy" as the Swiss prefer, is a good example. Despite the vast wealth of the country's institutions, which would seem to offer a temptation, the details of personal or corporate banking are seldom revealed in the press. This is true even in the case of foreigners, whom the Swiss would obviously have less reason to favor or protect.

"One factor is, people don't want to go to jail," as Markus Gisler of Moneycab points out. This is certainly an element: the Swiss banking laws are strict. Still, one senses a different attitude among Swiss journalists. Among American journalists, and to a large extent the French and British, the fact of any secret is almost a standing insult to the press. Among the Swiss, there is greater acceptance of such privacy. Swiss journalists view themselves as part of "the system"—not because they have been coopted by special interests or other elites, but because the entire system is accessible.

This does not mean that Swiss newspapers do not perform investigative reporting, and with some impressive scoops. Jean Ziegler, the social critic and author of several books about the role of Swiss banks and politicians in World War II and in the present too, credits the press with a "significant change" over the last ten years. Ziegler notes that after years of what he considered a too-reticent approach to the controversy, the Swiss press began breaking stories about private accounts, government archival material, and more recent activities by the Swiss military. Ziegler believes a major factor is simply the competition with Swiss tabloid papers, such as *Blick. Blick*, although not highly respected by other Swiss press, has broken a number of stories, and put the heat on more traditional papers to follow suit. Not all Swiss, of course, consider these trends wholesome.

Even the investigative reporting, though, has a more substantive edge to it. When *Tages-Anzeiger* broke the story of Elisabeth Kopp's involvement in her husband's financial woes in the late 1980s, the story concerned her actions as a government official—not petty financial activities she was unaware of, or a politician's bedroom paramours. Kopp was federal councilor and the head of Switzerland's Justice Department, in charge of leading an investigation into a firm—and then telephoned her husband to give him a head's up on the gathering storm.

Likewise, Swiss media, led by Urs Paul Engeler of *Weltwoche*, played a key role in breaking the story of Switzerland's P26 and P27 brigades. These were secret Swiss armies that had been organized, trained, and operated without the public's knowledge.

Reports like the above have, in the words of *Tages-Anzeiger*'s Markus Somm, "established new strength in the Swiss press." They have also made some political and journalistic careers. The parliamentary investigation of surreptitious surveillance, for example, was headed by Moritz Leuenberger, later a federal councilor and president of Switzerland. The investigation lifted him to prominence.

Swiss radio and television, like the newspapers, have a serious tone. This reflects the general preferences of Swiss audiences for solid content. In the case of the broadcast media, however, structural and economic factors play a role as well. Even today, Swiss public television and radio enjoy an audience share of roughly 50 percent—a figure unheard of in developed countries.

Part of this has to do with the high quality of both the services. Part is due to Switzerland's small audience, divided further by four national languages, which makes private stations less tenable. A French radio service in Switzerland, for example, appeals to only about a third of the country's 7 million people—and must compete with nearby broadcasts from France which enjoy a large domestic base to begin with. There are also numerous natural barriers to effective broadcasting—Switzerland's mountains break up signals as well or better than a drive through West Virginia. The largest factor, however, is simply legal. Paradoxically, in this generally pro-market country that values competition and diversity, private TV and radio were essentially outlawed until a few pilot programs were launched in 1981, followed by licensing of private stations in 1984.

The man who brought private radio and television to the country, more than any other, is Roger Schawinski. A maverick and rebel in the mode of Bill

McGowan (or maybe William Tell), Schawinski began his career as a consumer journalist. In the late 1970s, he began broadcasting from the mountains of Italy, near the Swiss frontier in the Ticino, beyond the reach of Swiss authorities, aiming his message at the lucrative Zürich audience. In the battle to keep him off the airwaves, Swiss authorities seized more then 200 retransmitters in and around Switzerland, which were needed to provide a clean signal. Undeterred, the self-styled "Radio Pirate" kept broadcasting. Within a few years, Schawinski had won a political and economic following, as the Swiss began to wonder why they shouldn't benefit from some media diversity. "He broke the monopoly," as Marco Färber, chief editor of Swiss Radio's German news broadcasts, nods in credit. Today Schawinski's Radio 24 and Tele 24 in Zürich are still struggling to catch up with the public services, but are already making their presence felt in both markets.

Thus, to understand Swiss radio and television news and news-related talk and programming, you have to imagine an entire country where half the people listen to NPR or watch the News Hour with Jim Lehrer. "We're not in NPR's league as far as what we can produce; we're a level, maybe two, below," Färber concedes, athough from my observation, the Swiss radio and television news are, in fact, quite close in quality to their larger American counterparts. There are, to be sure, differences of scale and funding that give other national media services an advantage. On the other hand, the Swiss public television and radio services are so respected that they do not face such a great competitive disadvantage in gathering news against private news sources.

Perhaps the most popular news broadcast in Switzerland, in fact, is a 12:30 radio news broadcast. Radio listenership actually spikes up over the lunch hour to its highest levels of the day, in contrast to the "drive time" spike and low rates of listenership during mid-day in the United States. The Swiss used to go home for lunch, at which time the family listened to the noontime (12:30) broadcast. But even with changing family and work patterns, the broadcast remains huge. Many Swiss tune into the broadcast during their lunch break or at their desk. From noon to 1 p.m., an average of about 17.5 percent of all Swiss over age fifteen are listening to their radios, exceeding 20 percent at 12:30. More than half are tuned into the news. The main evening radio news, anchored by Casper Selg, a former correspondent in the United States, in German at 6 p.m. and repeated at 7 p.m., draws fewer listeners as the audience for radio declines in the evening. But it may be as or even slightly more influential than the noon-time broadcast in content and impact, since there is more time for reporting and features. "Selg in the evening is something of an institution," comments Hans Bärenbold, of the German-language television news service. "He's one of the most respected broadcast journalists in Switzerland."

Television lacks the broad selection of U.S. or European offerings, even in the news and news-related programming areas. There are, however, interesting selections. The evening news show, "10 vor 10," which comes on at 9:50, is a kind of info-tainment hybrid combining the news reporting of "20-20" with electronic magazine-tabloid material. "Arena" is a cross between debate shows like "Crossfire" on CNN, and the kind of electronic town hall popularized by Ross Perot, ABC's "Nightline," and others. An "Arena" debate, aired just before a June 2001 referendum on the military, enjoyed a huge audience, pitting Blocher and a leader of the pacifist Gruppe für eine Schweiz ohne Armee against the federal councilor Samuel Schmid, minster of defense. The notable feature of Arena is the co-participants, several dozen of them, who are both well-informed and well-mannered enough to take meaningful part in the discussion without the show dissolving into a shouting match.

Like its broader political culture, then, the Swiss press and broadcast media are highly serious, but non-confrontational, and investigative in some sense, but not highly invasive of personal privacy. Critics of the regime question its actions, but not, in general, its fundamental legitimacy.

"People are basically satisfied, and we are part of the people," as *Weltwoche*'s Girsberger notes. The journalism of Switzerland reflects the country's ongoing search to refine and perfect itself, but it is not bitter or on a search for powerful figures—Robert Bork, Bill Clinton, Ronald Reagan, Bill Gates—to cut down to size. It is creative, even aggressive, but not deconstructionist. One has the feeling that this is what Thomas Jefferson was talking about.

Note

1.   Despite having a seven-member executive composed of representatives of different parties with disparate ideologies, the Swiss executive's deliberations, and even who votes how on major decisions, is only leaked on rare occasions. See Chap. 6, "Executives."

16

Family

Swiss families are not radically different from their counterparts in the United States or Europe, affirming the truism that "all happy families are alike." They are, however, slightly more stable and close. The laws of the state, likewise, are somewhat more pro-family, or family based, than in most other highly developed countries. There is, moreover, a somewhat greater modesty in manners and dress, and in statutes governing such matters as decency in the mass media. Policies like those of social welfare treat the family, rather than the individual, as the fundamental unit of society, and thus, reinforce family structure. Switzerland has divorce, child abuse and neglect, deadbeat dads, and many of the other ills seen in the West. It has them, though, with marginally less frequency. And it responds differently, legally and socially, when these maladies appear.

The net result, for an American, is a feeling that one is somehow visiting with a group of American families from the 1950s who have been transplanted into modern Western society. It is not an artificial, time-warp sort of feeling, and the culture does not in any way feel restrictive. On the contrary, the time appears to be the present, but the family structure somewhat transplanted. The modesty of the Swiss, if you will, is modest—a quiet preference for stable, family-based life and a disciplined and responsible commitment to it. One probably hears appeals to "family values" and the like far less in Switzerland than in the United States, or even much of Europe.

One of the first social impressions likely to strike someone visiting Switzerland, second only perhaps to their facility with languages, is that of the large number of couples still married to their original spouse. My own sample in visiting was admittedly biased, at first, toward meetings with affluent professionals. It felt unusual, nevertheless, to meet one high-income man after another who was with his wife of twenty, thirty, and even forty years. Of course, this impression built up only cumulatively, until after many weeks it struck me that very few divorces seemed to take place. A little resolution formed, made both to test my own powers of observation and to keep such observations fresh from any sociological preconceptions, to make sure not to look at any statistics about Swiss family life. Similar, but even more subtle, was the impression formed by meeting young people in large numbers whose parents were still together. Time after time, these youngsters did not describe, for example, plans to spend the week before Christmas with their fathers and the week after with their mothers, and the like. Mothers and fathers most commonly lived in the same place, or so it seemed. After a time, a social relaxation takes place in Switzerland. There are not quite as many dual locations to keep track of; there are fewer Doreen Smiths no longer married to Jasper Smith, and vice-versa; in Switzerland, one worries just a little bit less that the Hendersons will disagree about what restaurant to go to, or whether their daughter should study architecture.

Swiss couples exhibit a natural ease, a fitting-togetherness one encounters in America and Europe as well, but perhaps not as often. When Mr. and Mrs. Fred Isler entertained me and a friend, for example, it became clear just how seamlessly their two lives intertwined. Mr. Isler was going over a kind of bar chart of his various charitable and community service activities over the years, telling little vignettes about each bar or answering my questions—"yes, being a civilian in the appeals court, I would be involved in several cases a month. We shared the workload depending on the types of cases and who was particularly busy at a certain time." Now and then, however, Isler would be uncertain about who had attended a particular event, or what had been the resolution of a particular event or activity. At such times, Mrs. Isler would sometimes interject with words such as, "I think this was even three years," rather than two. Mr. Isler, on the other hand, frequently used the word "we" to describe a particular activity or commitment—even if nominally it had been "his" position. In an unobtrusive, unpretentious way, they seemed to agree that such tasks had been joint. In fact, of course, they had. "I went to the meetings," Isler said of the town council (or some similar task), for instance. "But when we got into a real disagreement, I would bring everyone here, and she always knew how to smooth it over."

Similarly, when Dr. Paul Jolles, the former Swiss State Secretary and Chairman of Nestlé, would review his decisions and involvements in government, he would rely on Mrs. Jolles to fill in blanks—and at times, correct him—regarding important events or details. It is natural for many couples to settle into a routine of mutual skepticism. Such raillery between the Jolleses, however, seemed largely to consist of her insisting that his actions had been much more wise or incisive than he would admit—and his countering that it was Mrs. Jolles who had encouraged him to do this or that. When some of Switzerland's differences with the United States and Europe in recent years came up for discussion, for example, Dr. Jolles was inclined to sympathize with Swiss officials. He said they had made mistakes, but that some of these were a heritage from years of neglect by other governments. Mrs. Jolles agreed but added a simpler explanation, which was, "They don't listen to you or people like you. In fact," she added, looking at me, "they don't even really ask for his advice or opinion at all." Dr. Jolles smiled, "which means they also don't get hers—a real mistake."

It is difficult, of course, to paint a portrait of this ordinary family life that works without seeming wide-eyed and, indeed, a bit sappy. The fact is, though, that the Swiss have retained a degree of family solidarity that many would envy, whether or not it has an element of Ozzie and Harriet. Indeed, an honest search of my memory of interviews with more than 500 Swiss brings to mind only a few divorced men or women. Of course, many of these conversations were too short to be likely to have obtained such information. And undoubtedly, some of these people were divorced, some even remarried. It is perhaps revealing, though, that even in cases where there have been divorces, the subject is less apt to come up among the Swiss. There is just a little more of the melancholy that used to attend the matter, socially, still present among the Swiss.

In addition, the relative reserve of the Swiss generally explains much. In the United States and Europe, one sometimes encounters the corporate giant who rides a bicycle to work, or flies coach even on long trips.[1] In Switzerland, such behavior, if not the mathematical norm, is certainly frequent. The chairman of ABB for many years rode a bicycle to work through the streets of Baden. François Loeb, head of one of the largest retail chains in Switzerland, drives a two-seat car, apparently spun off from the Yugo and achieving something like 70 miles per gallon of gasoline in the city. It is difficult enough to imagine a Swiss living in the imperial manner of some American or British corporate chieftans. To picture a Swiss executive bouncing between several wives, or dating young women twenty to forty years his junior, is difficult. It must happen in Switzerland, but it happens infrequently, and when it does, it is less the object of snickering admiration or newspaper headlines than of quiet embarrassment.

The Swiss man is close to family without being a house husband or highly sensitive child coddler. Swiss men with young children seemed less familiar with their day-to-day affairs than their mothers. But when the children reach age ten or older, the fathers become more highly engaged in their schooling and later, their professional life or family life. In conversations about women, Swiss men are less coarse than is the Western norm, and far less coarse than the American norm. There is less of an obsession with sex in normal conversation—whether there is less interest in sex, is impossible to say, but certainly it is less obvious.

The statistics, it turns out, do more or less bear out the impressionistic picture of the Swiss as enjoying a closeness of family life rare in developed societies, as Table 16.1 suggests.

Table 16-1

The Families of Nations
(selected comparative statistics)

	Divorces per 100 marriages	Percent of families with one parent	Divorces per 1000 population	Married (% of population over 16 years)
Germany	39	18	n.a.	55
United States	48	24	4.5	53
Switzerland	29	14	4.3	62

Source: U.S. Census Bureau; René Levy, *The Social Structure of Switzerland*, Helvetica; Swiss Statistical Abstract, and author's calculations based on data.

In addition to all the factors mentioned above, Swiss family law probably plays a role in the relatively high rate of family stability. Divorce laws, of course, vary by the canton, but as a general matter the advance of no-fault divorce has not been as great as in many Western countries. Even in such cantons as Geneva and Vaud, requirements are higher than the P.O.-box divorce systems of some U.S. states. And in the *Waldstätte*, or the central Forest Cantons with large numbers of orthodox Catholics, rules are more demanding substantively and procedures more rigorous.

As well, the social implications of divorce are more serious than in America. Swiss attitudes and laws, and the familiar character of most communities, make it very difficult for fathers to default on supporting their children both financially and emotionally, and for mothers to neglect a child who needs attention, support, or discipline. There are thus somewhat firmer supports for marriage and less of a "ticket to freedom" from marital breakup than in many developed countries.

Children in Switzerland are neither as revered as in Germany, treated as informally as in America, nor shunted aside as in England, Spain, or France. The Swiss take their children seriously and systematically. There is less emphasis than in the United States on early formal instruction, but perhaps more parent-to-child discipline and self-responsibility taught. An American four or five years of age is more likely to read than a Swiss child of that age, or to make a precocious comment, but is also more likely to wander off into the house and scribble all over one of the walls with a pen or waddle out into a busy parking lot where drivers are maneuvering aggressively for a choice spot or a fast exit.

From figures on women in the workplace, and my own anecdotal observations, a larger share of Swiss children aged zero through five are taken care of by their own mothers the bulk of the day, and a smaller proportion sent to day care or pre-school so their mothers can work part or full time, or manage the rest of the children. Although this could not be verified directly from international statistics, it seems supported by estimates of the number of Swiss mothers in the labor force—about one-third of mothers with children at home, and perhaps a fifth or less of mothers with children younger than age six, work outside the home. The same conclusion would also seem to be supported by the complaint of many Swiss that young children do not receive enough formal schooling. From the performance of its economy, the Swiss do not appear to have suffered significantly from this. And there may be benefits in the greater socialization and feelings of greater security of Swiss youngsters.

Sheer geography may even lend a hand to Swiss marriages. Americans with a large number of children often bemoan the great distances that extended families find between parents and grandparents, brothers, and other relatives. Of course, there is little to stop individual Swiss families from living 2,000 miles apart, but if they do so, they will find their relatives in Israel, Turkey, Bulgaria, or even Western Russia. Since emigration is a large step, the vast majority of persons in any country, barring dire circumstances, are bound to remain in the country of their birth. For the Swiss, remaining in the country means living no more than a few hours from any other relatives still in Switzerland. Even relatives who move to Germany or France, two of the most common destinations, are relatively close compared to the distances that often separate members of an extended family in the United States.

As in other countries, the Swiss encounter some problems with their children in the adolescent years. Swiss suicide rates, in fact, are among the highest in the world. Surely one factor in these is the absence of some Swiss fathers in the more sexually divided work roles of dad at the office, mom at home. Others attribute these rates to mere density of population (a la Japan), particularly when one factors in the consideration that two-thirds of the Swiss nation is nearly uninhabitable mountains. Still another factor, according to some Swiss, is the high pressure placed on Swiss youth in the teenage years and early twenties to perform in school and other areas of life.

Among all Swiss, the fact of a seeming permanent affluence has led to a search for meaning. As the suicide rates indicated, not all are successful in finding it. Religion has withered, particularly among Protestants and among Catholics outside the highly Orthodox churches of Schwyz and the surrounding cantons. Even much religious life is quasi-secular. Church services in the major cities, and even to some extent the more fervent countryside, are not highly sacramental or theological. The religion of many Swiss has become almost the civic, Godless religion of Rousseau, though this trend is not as advanced as in France, Italy, or the United States.

A more happy picture, for the Swiss, emerges when one considers other social indices of adolescent adjustment. Perhaps the turmoil that seems evident in teen suicides, for example, is driven largely by accidental factors. Rates of violent crimes, which are normally committed by persons under thirty, are low. Teen pregnancy, abortion both by juveniles and as an overall rate, and similar unhappy statistics are relatively low, as Table 16.2 shows.

Public laws on abortion are characteristically Swiss—federalist and nuanced. A national law prohibits certain kinds of abortion restrictions and guards a right to abortion—but the latter does not cover all cases, and the former allows for exceptions for cases involving the mental or physical health of the mother. In some cantons, these rules are interpreted quite liberally so that there is little practical restriction on abortion at all. In others, especially the Central and Eastern *Waldstätte,* women must visit a doctor, confer with a cantonal or community health official, and so on—a series of three, four, or more steps. According to a 1996 article in the *Swiss Medical Bulletin,*[2] rates

Table 16.2

Teen Pregnancy, Birth, and Abortion Rates

	Adolescent abortion rate	Adolescent pregnancy rate	Adolescent birth rate
Canada	15.5	45.4	24.2
France	12.4	51.2	10.0
Finland	10.0	52.9	9.8
Germany	7.6	23.0	12.5
Ireland	5.9	21.9	15.0
Israel	14.2	35.3	18.0
Japan	13.8	61.9	3.9
Sweden	18.7	69.6	7.7
United States	22.9	83.6	54.4
Switzerland	8.4	21.1	5.7

Notes: "Abortion rate" is legal abortions per 1,000 residents aged 15-19. "Pregnancy rate" equals pregnancies per 1,000 women aged 15-19. "Birth rate" equals births per 1,000 women aged 15-19.

Source: Alan Guttmacher Institute, from country data. Swiss data on adolescent pregnancy calculated by author from Swiss data.

of abortion varied by a factor of three and more from canton to canton. Some of this disparity, of course, may reflect women seeking out abortion services in the cantons where laws are more relaxed, but of course this is frowned on, and often entails a lack of health insurance coverage.

Few people in Switzerland are entirely happy with this cluttered situation, especially those who crave a clear-cut decision either to allow or to abolish abortion. The degree of unhappiness, however, is much less than in many Western countries where one side or the other has achieved a winner-take-all victory. Abortion rights advocates have achieved no national decision—but can take solace that there is some liberty to obtain an abortion for most Swiss women, especially in the major cities. Opponents enjoy less than total ban, but neither have they had to endure, in the manner of the U.S., a sweeping decision by judicial elites to wipe out the action of democratic legislatures. Federalism allows Swiss families to seek out a community where the existing laws on abortion and other social matters comport with their sense of propriety and morality, while letting other cantons and cells establish the order that seems best to them. Where there is lobbying, it is by its nature decentralized, focused in two dozen cantonal parliaments and in thousands of communities overseeing the implementation of local standards by doctors and other professionals.

Periodic initiatives and referenda, at the national and cantonal levels, have the effect of giving voters a feeling of fine motor control, and the voters have generally opted to make compromises in the middle of the abortion debate, preferring not to enact the program of either the committed restrictionists nor the advocates of abortion rights. Whereas in other countries vast campaigns must be launched merely to achieve a vote on public financing, or third-trimester restrictions, before the appropriate congressional committee, in the Swiss system there is always access. This access—the fact of its availability, even if it is not always used—has a soothing impact on the nerves of both the passionate advocates of both sides of the spectrum and of voters in between. The net result is, perhaps, a messy compromise, but one that works for the Swiss. Ironically, given their reticence toward controversy, the Swiss feel that the abortion question is a sensitive one and the controversy hot. This may so be in Swiss terms, but one has the impression that the abortion question and like issues are in fact less agitated in Switzerland than in most Western countries, and far less so than in countries with significant ethnic and religious differences underlying the disputes.

Women at Work

Some Swiss women felt, until recently, stranded "not in the 1950s but in the nineteenth century," as a Swiss feminist leader proclaimed in 1981. Pay for the same work by similarly qualified women runs about a quarter to a third less than for the same work done by a man, according to sociologist René Levy, although like most such statistics, these measurements appear not to account for the greater likelihood that a woman's career will be interrupted by children. Women occupy almost no CEO or COO positions among the top one-hundred Swiss corporations. The highest-ranking woman among major Swiss companies appears to be one of eighty division vice presidents at Nestlé, who oversees the company's operations in Poland.

Swiss executives are so sensitive about the topic that when a high-ranking Nestlé official was told his company has been praised by some as encouraging a more rapid rise by female executives, he preferred not to discuss the matter.[3] "This is an area where all Swiss companies, including ours, would like to do more, and need to do more," he said.

What is true at the top is less true, but somewhat, throughout the work force. Swiss women make up about 44 percent of the work force; in the United States, 47 percent. On this macroeconomic level, the picture for working women in Switzerland is not radically better or worse than in most Western countries. Salaries in the banking, service, and professional sectors are 30 percent higher for men than women, with a lower gap among Swiss age thirty-nine or younger. This is similar to U.S. and European levels. In government service, average salaries are within 20 percent for men and women as a whole, and for men and women under forty the gap is less than 10 percent. All these figures suggest a work equation in which there are differences of opportunity, some of which can be explained by home care and other social choices made by women and men, some of which cannot.

If we start from 1940 as a base year, women's wages have been outpacing men's in Switzerland ever since. In absolute terms, this only means they have been catching up. The years of the most dramatic improvement were from 1960 to 1980, when general economic growth and the decline of large families encouraged women to seek work outside the home in greater numbers. In the 1990s, the rate of closure slowed, partly due to an influx of foreign women (more likely to raise children at home), partly due to the economic slowdown.

Swiss women do not appear to feel marginalized, and the vast majority do not consider themselves the object of any systematic or conscious antifeminine bias by employers. "Many women prefer to work part time, or be away from work for some period to be with their families," comments Beatrice Gyssler, who works with a Swiss investment firm in Zürich. To that extent, some women are choosing to forego some earnings and professional opportunities in order to care for their children and be in the home more. Surveys indicate that for most Swiss married women who continue to work, the decisive reason is the belief that the husband's earnings alone are insufficient. The flip side is that many women, given the choice, would prefer to remain part of one-earner families. Even after the bumpy recession of 1990–96,

Figure 16.1

Swiss Women's Wages, 1940-2000

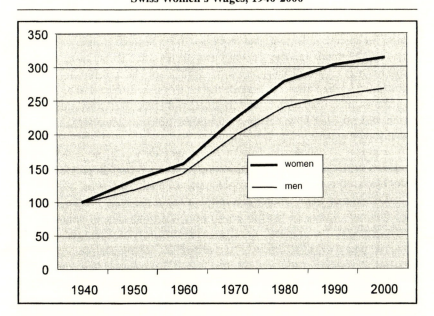

Switzerland's economy still generates sufficient high-paying jobs for men to permit many families to prosper with only one worker outside the home.

In Swiss families with one or more children under the age of fifteen, there are 700,000 fathers working outside the home, and 450,000 mothers. (This figure includes foreign-born residents.) In Swiss families with no children under the age of fifteen, there are 1.4 million fathers working outside the home, and 1.2 million mothers—a much closer ratio.

"The more the husband earns, the less likely the wife is to go out to work," as René Levy, a sociologist at the University of Lausanne, writes. "Many Swiss women prefer a role in the home over work, and if they must work, they prefer the maximum role in the home," observes Esther Girsberger, former editor of the Zürich daily *Tages Anzeiger*. "The statistics on women's pay and employment overstate the problem if you look at them expecting a statistical equality. Women's expectations and their preferences differ from that of Swiss men." Girsberger is an example of a field that has proven a natural entry point for women, journalism. Women are also making rapid strides in such professions as the law, computer software and service functions, and politics, to name just a few.

Small business has proven to be a natural venue for women in Switzerland as it has in a number of other developed countries. Home-based and small businesses often offer flexibility in hours that is highly valuable to women with children. In 1970, less than 20 percent of self-employed Swiss were women. In 1996, 34 percent were. (This excludes farm wives and family workers.) This figure compares favorably to the absolute levels of small-business ownership by women in other Western countries—39 percent in the United States, 30 percent in Britain, and less than 30 percent in Germany, Sweden, Italy, and Finland—and is growing at a faster rate. To be sure, some of these businesses are of marginal profitability, and have difficulty obtaining capital for expansion if they desire it. But they offer another alternative for women who want some income, and some activities outside the home, but may not have the time for uninterrupted employment in a traditional 9-to-5 pattern.

For many, of course, the role of Swiss women was symbolized by the country's decision, in 1971, to allow women to vote—a right previously not recognized. The long delay was not quite as backward as it might have sounded. Women were neither that militant about the right to vote, nor had men (the only voters allowed to act on previous proposals, of course) been firmly opposed. The proposal, needing a supermajority of voters and cantons, however, had always fared poorly in a few of the central cantons—some for substantive reasons, some because they feared that cantonal and community *Landsgemeinde*, literally overfilled by too many people, would become unworkable if the voting population suddenly doubled. Women mostly wanted the vote, understandably, not merely because they might occasionally make the difference in a specific decision on policy, but because they wanted to be heard and to have the institutional respect granted them in all the other democracies.

Ironically, although gaining the vote at a much later date, Swiss women have made great advances in elective politics in Switzerland. Well-educated and articulate, and experienced in thinking about issues as are all Swiss, the Swiss woman brings much to the profession of politics. Given the nature of Swiss government, however, politics is still something of a part-time profession. The cantonal legislatures and even federal parliament are paid little, have no dedicated staff, and are in session less than ten weeks a year. "There is a good fit between the Swiss militia system," meaning citizen government, "and the immense talent offered by Swiss women," as the late investor and publisher David dePury observed.

Indeed, the Swiss have a higher percentage of women in their parliament, more than 20 percent of the combined chambers, than the United States or most European countries. (In the lower house of the federal parliament, more than 23 percent are women, and of the combined membership of the cantonal parliaments, more then 25 percent.) Switzerland has now had one woman president, and following the election of another woman to the federal council in 1998, will have two more terms by women presidents by 2010, under the country's rotating presidency.

Swiss families feel the same strains as families throughout the West, tugged between economic forces outside and the job of raising children inside. It cannot be said that the Swiss have invented any unique answers to these modern tensions, but their institutions have coped with them in interesting and different ways. The Swiss family has proven flexible and, in some ways— such as the rapid movement of women into positions in the country's citizen-government—innovative.

Notes

1. There is a German joke about Swiss frugality that the Swiss enjoy telling, which goes: "Why did the Swiss executive fly third class? Because there was no fourth class."
2. M. Dondénaz, et al., "Interruptions de grossese en Suisse 1991-1994," *Bulletin de medicins suisses*, 1996, vol. 77, pp. 308–14.
3. Asked for the names of prominent women chief executive officers of Swiss corporations, editor Markus Gisler of CASH, the Zürich-based financial weekly, said, "There really aren't any. I think Nestlé has a woman running its Poland division, and possibly one or two others. They are known as one of the companies where women have been encouraged." Gisler's staff helped me track down several other female executives, mostly at much smaller companies.

17

Army

Switzerland's army cannot be fully understood except in combination with Swiss neutrality, and Swiss neutrality likewise cannot be understood in isolation from the Swiss army. Even as the country prepares to enact significant changes in the size and structure of the army in the early twenty-first century, it remains a uniquely universalist institution, and a force for social integration. Whatever adjustments are made to it in the coming years, the Swiss army is likely to remain such a force for the foreseeable future.

Unlike most other neutrals throughout history Swiss forces, while small, have been tenacious fighters and even, for several centuries, one of the most powerful armies in the world. Twice in two thousand years have the ferocious peasant Helvetii of the Alpine redoubt been defeated and occupied. The first time was by Julius Caesar, who, in 58 B.C., stopped the Helvetii when they tried to migrate en masse to what is now Western France. Caesar carefully co-opted the beaten adversary into the Roman security system, the Helvetii guarding the Rhine against Germanic invasions and enjoying a measure of self-rule in their internal affairs in exchange. Napoleon Bonaparte, in 1796-97, consciously imitating Caesar, conquered upper Italy for France and wanted to assure himself of the Swiss alpine passes. The Swiss resisted in 1798, but not as strenuously as could be expected. Part of this was due to initial sympathy to the values of the French Revolution. Part was due to the fear of confiscation on the part of Swiss elites—dividing a society whose poorer members mainly wanted to resist. The French left and returned twice, but continued to enjoy predominant influence in Switzerland until 1813. Napoleon, like many French emperors before him, found the soldiers of Switzerland to be a formidable addition to his armies. "The best troops—those in whom you can have the most confidence," Napoleon advised one of his generals, "are the Swiss." In this he mirrored the assessment of Machiavelli, who considered them, "the new Romans."

Unlike the other nations of great bravery, meanwhile—such small but tenacious powers such as Israel, Britain, Mongolia, Vietnam, or Afghanistan—

the Swiss have been able to maintain a policy of honest neutrality, and a state of peace and freedom from external invasion, for centuries. The Swiss felt tempted to engage themselves in the conflicts swirling around them more than once. In 1914, there was significant popular sentiment for Germany. More than one Swiss official had to be removed for actions contrary to neutrality. Nevertheless, the country has maintained a strict neutrality for nearly five centuries, all the while remaining sufficiently armed to scare away all but a handful of attempts at invasion.

Its toughness gives Swiss neutrality teeth. Meanwhile Swiss neutrality and equality temper and discipline the toughness to be ready to die, but only for defense of the country. "The Swiss have not fought a war for nearly five hundred years," John McPhee writes, "and are determined to know how so as not to."[1]

Today, Switzerland is no longer one of the most feared military establishments in the world. Yet it is not inconsiderable. Some 2,000 or 3,000 airstrips dot the country like Band-Aids, ready to help repel enemy air power and conduct Swiss defensive operations. Mountains, caves, hills, and forest cellars the size of a Home Depot Store are loaded with ammunition, explosives, food, trucks, and other military equipment. People's barns, garages, and even tool sheds are available for use for storage, hiding troop movements, housing troops overnight—and are all mapped out and accounted for in elaborate mobilization plans. Bridges and other transportation chokepoints are mined to be blown up at a moment's notice. While the Northern strip of Switzerland—a lowland of gently rolling hills and dense population—is highly vulnerable to assault, the Southern "redoubt" would be an attacker's nightmare. "You could defend the Gotthard highway with ten men," a Swiss officer estimates.

At the battle of Morgarten, the fourteenth-century Swiss triumphed shortly after the signing of the *Bundesbrief.* Austrian knights trapped in a narrow pass were attacked by peasants rolling logs, boulders, and other falling objects. There was a sensation, according to one later perhaps mythologized report, that "the rocks themselves" were rising up to take arms against the attacker. "Thorn and rose, there is scarcely a scene in Switzerland that would not sell a calendar, and—valley after valley, mountain after mountain—there is scarcely a scene in Switzerland that is not ready to erupt in fire to repel an invasive war," McPhee writes.

The real story of Switzerland's military bite, however, lies not in hardware, but people. With a population of only six million, the Swiss can place 400,000 trained, armed, highly skilled troops in the field within forty-eight hours. On any given day, considering this, the Swiss might have the third- or fourth-largest fighting force in the world.

There is only one way, of course, for such a small country to man a force of this size. Every male Swiss from the age of twenty until approximately age forty-two is a soldier. The enlisted men serve a total of 300 days over that twenty-year period; officers, sometimes more than 1,000, continuing on to age fifty-two. Women are allowed to join, and do, though not in combat roles, but they are not obligated to do so. Men and women are paid by their regular employer while they are on training, and the employer is reimbursed by the government—though only for 70 percent, not 100 percent, of the lost time. Given the number of hours put in informally by the Swiss on army matters, especially by officers, this amounts to a significant subsidy of the military by the private sector. Some companies are happy about this, some acquiesce, some grumble.

After an initial "basic training" course of some 120 days, the Swiss soldier will drill approximately fifteen days a year, and probably commit some hours every month to filling out paperwork, keeping his equipment in repair, practicing his shooting. The Swiss must pass a shooting test every year, and take remedial practice if they fail the test. Gun clubs and shops dot the city of Bern the way used bookstores dot a college campus in the United States. More than 500,000 assault rifles are kept at home by Swiss men, in part so that their sons can get used to having a gun around.

One cannot but notice, even in peacetime, the signs of a nation the whole population of which is involved in active defense. On a Friday afternoon you see the young men in their early twenties boarding trains in Bern, Zürich, or Luzern in military uniform. Businessmen in a coffee shop in Geneva pull out their small military service book to make notations or do paperwork on their lunch break. Walking down a country road you hear regular gun bursts in the distance—too many for a hunter—and know that someone is practicing. On a porch is an old man, probably by now limited to one of the auxiliary services, cleaning a pair of army boots.

The Swiss not only enjoy widespread volunteer involvement in the army; they rely to an unusual degree on individual citizens to take personal responsibility for their own perfection in military technique. Simulator rooms, which help infantry and artillery forces practice in battle, are open for training during off-duty hours and are used heavily, according to an officer with the army's skeletal full-time staff. Rifle training, of course, is everywhere.

On a Saturday, touring a 600-year-old castle ruin on the heights above Baden, my solitude was broken by the sound of a gentle but high-pitched hiss coming down the road. All of a sudden, three young men in camouflage fatigues and white helmets—hiss, zip, hissss—whizzed by me, guns on their shoulder. It appeared to me at the time as if they were on their way to a training session somewhere, perhaps a bit late. But a few hours later the same three young men were at the Banhof, enjoying a bratwurst and bottles of beer at stand-up tables. One of them struck up a conversation with me, during which he explained that the men were not on their way to on-duty training, nor even taking part in a formal training session itself. They were practicing reconnaissance runs and moving about while keeping in electronic contact over the hills, crags, and electronic interference of Baden—on their own time.

The Swiss, it turns out, use not only mountains and barns in their defense, but until recently common passenger bicycles. "The bicycle is fast, quiet, cheap, and flexible," a staff officer later told me with a ninja-master-like tone. "We use anything that contributes to the defense of the country." The man or woman at work is always a citizen—and the citizen does not leave his private skills and ideals at the door, but brings them with him to the collective enterprise of managing and defending the state. There is, in short, a great trust in people. This trust tells much about Swiss assumptions regarding people and the society. It is a sign, surely, of one of the most developed and capable societies in the world.

Universal service thus works on many levels. It generates numbers. If a comparable number of U.S. citizens were members of our army or naval reserve, America would have some twenty-five million men at arms. It also establishes a presence in society. The fact of citizens doing their duty, universally, is too ubiquitous to be unseen. Military activity is legitimized, and linked into practically every home and family in the country. The people's consciousness is raised of the sacrifices that are being made for the national safety. There are even certain practical benefits to promoting an informed citizenry, and one with a strong immediate interest in sound management of the military. Nearly every male voter is also a military man—and, with a full-time military establishment of only about 1,000 officials or less, nearly every military man earns his living in the civilian economy. No doubt this is one reason there have been relatively few of the military scandals in Switzerland, either as to over-priced procurement items, what weapons to purchase, or other matters.

The militia system is egalitarian in imposing its burden. There are a few ways to get an exemption from military service, but only a few, and none is advanced by social standing. Absolute mental or physical inability will get you out. Policemen can sometimes earn a waiver since they might be needed in two places at once. A 1977 ballot initiative sought to allow men to fill their service obligation outside the armed forces—cleaning parks, teaching reading, and so on. It was rejected by more than 60 percent of the voters. A decade later, a smaller proposed exception passed, but is still socially frowned upon.

Importantly, all Swiss men start off as privates. The son or daughter of a Swiss president, member of parliament, or captain of industry is a grunt. The earliest promotion to officer generally takes place after several years of service. Thus there is no separate officer class as in most countries, even the democracies. Most of these officers (roughly 98 percent or more) are part-time or "reservist" soldiers with regular employment. A small, full-time force of less than 1,000 staff constitutes Switzerland's entire professional military.

There is, to be sure, a tendency for military and professional advancement to correlate—but both are based on merit. Generally, many of those who are advancing in their career often thrive in their military service, and vice-versa. "The colonel and the barrister, the banker and the captain, the major and the businessman are one," McPhee writes. And while there are many cases of parallel advancement, there are others of social criss-crossing—of nonprofessionals in daily life advancing in the military, or of high-ranking business executives continuing to serve as privates or sergeants. "There are at least two bank presidents who march with the rank and file. An army captain has told me that he once leaped to his feet because the soldier serving him food was an executive vice-president of the company he worked for in Basel. To be high in business and low in the army is less unusual than the reverse."

Perhaps the most important impact of the militia is the way it integrates the military and the society as a whole. In most developed societies there is alienation between the people and the military class, one of the reasons the American Founding Fathers, rightly, feared such a class. The citizen-based force of the Swiss, by contrast, is practical and efficient in military terms, and wholesome for the society.

Can there be any higher function of the state than the preservation and protection of the state and the people from external violence? As in other walks of Swiss political life—making laws, altering the constitution, defending the nation—we see supreme acts of sovereignty being carried out, for the most part, by ordinary citizens.

In perhaps every fourth or fifth meeting with a Swiss of any length, army contacts and experiences are likely to come up. Christian Kuoni, the president of one of the largest privately owned manufacturing companies in Switzerland, Jakob Müller, asks about my meetings later in the day. One is with Carlo Schmid, an attorney, Landamann of Canton Appenzell, and a member of the federal senate. "Carlo Schmid?" he asks. "We drilled in the army together for years." And Kuoni whips out his little service book, proceeding to tick through some of his assignments with various other corporate officers, workers from his own factory and others, journalists, a union leader from Geneva, the fellow who runs the local post office. As he ticks along, it strikes me that the Swiss have their confessional and other differences, but there is one church they all attend: the army. There is, of course, no even remotely comparable experience in the United States and most of Europe. The Swiss Army slashes across all walks of life, institutions, interest groups, and people and brings every citizen of the state—or rather, every male citizen, but through them, involves a majority of the women as well—together for an act of regular communion.

It is important to note that early in the twenty-first century the Swiss began a reduction in the size and universality of their military service. This reduction, of about one-third, was hard to argue against in terms of the relative military peace in Europe, but the change will have social impacts. The reduction especially of the principle of broad, almost universal service, will change the psychology and role of army service. Switzerland's rate of military service will still far exceed that of nearly any other country in the world with the exception of Israel. For this reason, the Swiss Army, albeit smaller, will continue to play a significant social and economic role in the country.

As the Swiss army makes Swiss neutrality muscular, so Swiss neutrality gives the army—and the society—both a strong moral *raison d'etre* in foreign affairs and, to a degree, an ethos not only for the nation as a whole but for the individual.

Swiss neutrality's roots are as deep as the oath on the Rütli, but the decisive event in its development came with the Swiss defeat of 1515 at the hands of the French army at Marignano. "I have conquered those whom only Caesar managed to conquer before me," boasted King François I. Actually, he had not conquered the Swiss; he had defeated them in battle. The impact, however, was still great. Switzerland was a poor country, and, indeed, still only a country in the most generous sense of the term—a loose confederation of thirteen cantons, linked by a small, impermanent court that floated from one capital city to another every year like Gulliver's island of Laputa. They decided, quite prudently, that this was no core from which to build a vast empire through military conquest. Nicholaus von der Flue, the respected friar and political-religious activist, added powerful moral arguments to these practical ones, and the policy took root.

For centuries, of course, neutrality as a policy of the confederation was really something of a statement of impotence by that rather thin body of government. The cantons aligned themselves with competing princes all over Europe—usually renting the services of their highly sought armies or units of them as mercenaries. For hundreds of years, as one military historian has written, arms of this sort were "Switzerland's leading export."

This practice indeed helped enrich the region, while at the same time maintaining what De Gaulle called "the edge of the sword"—and thus, while Switzerland was neutral, the Swiss were fighting all the time: hard, sharp. This practice, however, led to its own absurdities. It helped keep Switzerland divided and even encouraged foreign meddling, since it was well known that for the right price most cantons could be swayed to shift alliances. It also led to the repeated comedy—a sad comedy at that—of Swiss troops from different cantons facing one another in battle. With grim logic, the Swiss fought bravely in such struggles, killing many of themselves.

On the more glorious side of the ledger, Swiss soldiers participated in (and played a key role) in some of the most important battles of the sixteenth through the eighteenth centuries. The French kings saw the Swiss in action and hired them to guard the royal person. While many French guards deserted during the seizure of Louis and Antoinette during the Revolution, the Swiss fought to the death, and were thereby honored and respected even by the revolutionaries for performing an honest duty so bravely. Centuries before, the Popes, having seen the Swiss bodyguards in action, decided to retain their own units for protection of the Vatican. The brave Swiss guards of canton Fribourg remained in this service at the dawn of the twenty-first century.

As a practical benefit most foreign powers, even the great empires, while they certainly looked to the cantons for troops, generally thought of any occupation or absorption of Switzerland as a high-cost enterprise with few likely benefits. Thus the policy of neutrality, while viewed with an understandable skepticism by some modern-day critics, grew and evolved over time into something solid.

Franz Muheim, a typically Swiss Swiss—former industry leader, military officer, senator, author, intellectual—explains some of the deep roots and wide branches of that broad concept, Swiss neutrality.

"There is a basic point of view that you could call Swiss," he tells me in English—his third or fourth language—at the Hotel Metropol in Luzern, over a pleasant luncheon. "It is not predetermined by the mountains and the geography, but certainly, these make it very natural.

"The Swiss, you see, are not so much a mountain people, as a valley people—separated by mountains. Farmers, small manufacturers, gate keepers. The land makes it not inevitable, but certainly very easy, for small, independent communities to form.

"If one of these communities even wanted to conquer and enslave one of their neighbors, it would not be an easy task," he continued. A picture of Jean-Jacques Rousseau flashed into my mind, with his classic commentary on the impossibility of slavery in the state of nature, from the essay on the origins of inequality to the Academy at Dijon. "Of course, you could not do it, nor did the Swiss ever want to do it.

"The Swiss wants primarily to be left alone by the next village, and to cooperate with his friends and neighbors while retaining a certain autonomy and independence even within this intimate cell. He does not want to be involved in fights against or between his neighbors, both because he knows how hard it is to intervene usefully, and because he recognizes the limited ability his small village would have to influence matters anyway."

"This way of thinking applies from the individual Swiss of those villages, hundreds of years ago, up to the state—and today, as well, from the state down to and through the individual."

Neutrality, thus, is a state of mind and personal philosophy, a broadened version of that very wise beginning of the doctor's Hippocratic Oath: "First do no harm." It is policy, but it is more than that.

Likewise the Swiss military-industrial complex is an arm of the government—but not just an arm of the government. It is, like many Swiss institutions, inextricably linked with the society—achieving something akin to the Maoist dictum that the guerrilla must be as a fish is to the sea.

"You must understand," as Swiss Divisionnaire Adrien Tschumy, told the journalist McPhee, "there is no difference between the Swiss people and the Swiss Army."

Note

1.   *La Place de la Concorde Suisse*, Farrar, Straus, Giroux, 1984. McPhee's book is a quiet classic for Americans, but among the Swiss, it is almost at the level of a cult. McPhee, a *New Yorker* editor, drilled with several Swiss units and described his conversations and experience in some detail. It is a bragging point among the Swiss not merely to have been mentioned in the book, or to have had some contact with McPhee, but to know someone who has. "I once drilled with someone who had previously drilled in that unit, though he was not there at the time McPhee was," a Swiss businessman, who heads a Fortune 500 company, told me proudly.

18

Switzerland Accused

Hans Bär was not ready for my question. It was not on the list of topics faxed before our talk and, in fact, wasn't even in my mind until we were about half-way through. He wasn't angry about it—to my relief. But he was surprised. It surprised me, too; my voice seemed to come from someone else.

"How do you feel about Switzerland and the Holocaust?"

Simple words, but that last one evokes strong emotions. Hans Bär, the head of an old and respected investment bank in Zürich, didn't know me except as a writer interested in Switzerland. It would have been understandable if he were taken aback, even offended.

At the same time, even before Bär answered, it felt right. The question of the Nazi reign of terror and the country's response to it is one that troubles the Swiss deeply. And the international grilling of Switzerland in the late 1990s was a blow to the national pride and a cause of deep hurt. Here was a man who felt all these emotions strongly and personally—an informed man of some sensitivity. The question had to be asked.

"I *feel*...," Bär said, and paused. He seemed to be thinking about his *feelings* on this, improbable as it sounds, for the first time. "I feel very proud and very ashamed of my country. I am a Swiss, and a Jew. I am both."

"Switzerland made mistakes—was guilty of horrible political stupidity after the war. There should have been an active effort to recompense the owners and the descendants of the dormant accounts." (Bär is speaking of accounts opened by foreign Jews in Swiss banks before the war, but which lapsed afterward. In some cases, the account holders died. In others, they simply forgot the accounts, or allowed them to sit fallow. In some cases, money was paid out.) "At the same time, Switzerland resisted the Nazis for years when she was completely surrounded." Indeed, even before the war, Switzerland was the first country to launch a significant armament program to defend against the Nazi threat.

"It is even more complicated than this, because, for example, there were *elements* of anti-Semitism here, too. They were not nearly as strong as in

213

Germany or elsewhere. But there was some. We would see banners in Zürich occasionally, read newspaper articles, hear threats."

Bär's natural conflictedness was well captured when his preparatory school in the United States, the Horace Mann School, asked him to accept an award in 1998.[1] Bär was flattered. He would have liked to receive the honor. "But I could not accept an award in the United States, while my country was being treated as it was by the U.S. government and in the U.S. press—and in the very circles of people whom I would be receiving this award from. I told them, as a Swiss, I could not accept."

A year passed. The U.S. government, while not explicitly apologizing for its allegation that Swiss actions had "helped prolong" World War II, issued a second report qualifying some of the more extreme claims of the first one. Vice President Gore appeared in Davos, Switzerland, to tell the Swiss President, Mrs. Dreifuss, that his government hoped the controversy would wind down and planned no further actions designed to bring pressure or opprobrium on the Swiss. The school offered the award again. Bär accepted, using his speech as an opportunity to put the Swiss record in context—and encourage his American audience to consider our own sins of omission in the Nazi Holocaust and other such events, before lecturing others. The crisis seemed to be defusing itself, the wounds starting to heal. "There is little doubt in my mind," Bär told the Horace Mann School, "that the declared end of the very serious bickering between the United States and Switzerland over its role during and after the Second World War, as it was solemnly declared in Davos only a couple of weeks ago, really marks the end of that episode."

Even if so, however, some painful historical questions remain—not only for the Swiss but for other countries that, unlike Switzerland, have not begun to come to terms with their wartime and postwar banking transactions. Furthermore, it was far from clear, as Bär commented a year later, that the Davos "ceasefire" represented anything more than a temporary lull by some U.S. officials in a long and inexplicable vendetta against the Swiss.

For the Swiss democracy, regardless of U.S. attitudes, there are institutional questions raised by the Holocaust issue. These events raise questions that the Swiss will have to address. The future is bound to bring moral-political issues of this type, issues over the Swiss banking system and issues that arise out of Swiss neutrality—a policy that is always vulnerable to misinterpretation and, at times, abuses. How will Switzerland handle them?

"The controversy," as the Swiss refer to it, was latent in the practices of Swiss banks going back to the early postwar years, and, indeed, to before the war itself. During the war and in the years afterward, some 50,000 to 100,000 accounts fell dormant, or were closed. It is doubtful that a majority of these belonged to Holocaust victims or other Jews. In fact, according to studies of the Swiss accounts, it is all but certain that a third or less were. It is equally certain, however, that some finite percentage of these accounts did belong to

Jews. According to the Swiss Bankers Association, nearly 20,000 persons have registered claims for dormant accounts. (Many of these, of course, are duplicate claims from relatives of the same prospective account holder.) The Volcker Committee, headed by former U.S. Federal Reserve Board Chairman Paul Volcker, studied the matter of dormant accounts and other unclaimed assets in Swiss banks deposited by victims of the Nazis. It concluded, in an interim report, that when interest and inflation over the years are added to the initial principal, perhaps $1 billion to $2 billion in such assets exist. This committee was established by the Swiss Bankers Association in cooperation with the World Jewish Relief Organization and the World Jewish Congress.

These matters remained closed and generally uncontroversial for several decades due to two factors. One was the renowned sacredness of Swiss banking privacy. This policy has always been somewhat misunderstood. For instance, the provisions provide no shield against domestic or international criminal prosecutions. Nevertheless, the policy did make it hard for relatives, journalists, and others both from obtaining specific account information and from compiling a broad profile of the scope and magnitude of the accounts. Often such accounts were opened under fictitious names, or using passwords or numeric codes. If the person who opened the account died, relatives might have no idea where the money was. Relatives coming back after the war, or even decades later, lacking the needed account information might ask the Swiss banks for help, but the banks declined to give out the needed information. The reputation of Swiss secrecy discouraged many from even trying.

The second factor was a certain smugness, or at the least indifference, on the part of Swiss bankers and politicians when inquiries and appeals were made. In the case of some business and political elites, in fact, more than indifference was involved. The Swiss people, in plain terms, were sometimes lied to about the activities of the government and the banks. Individual requests for access to dormant accounts by Holocaust victims were treated no worse than if they involved an account in no way linked to a Holocaust victim, but they were treated no better. Group appeals (from Jewish organizations, corporations, or governments) were politely referred to the banks. This policy might be defensible from a narrow legal standpoint, but it took little account of the special circumstances of this group of people. To keep these matters in perspective, of course, Americans and Europeans outside Switzerland must remember the indifference of some of their own financial and political institutions before, during, and after the war. Researchers have argued that Deutsche Bank, Ford Motor Company, Allianz, and General Motors all benefited from unsavory relations with the Nazi regime before or after the war. "New York State," as Bär points out, "was the beneficiary of most of the Holocaust funds transferred to the U.S. under your escheatment laws—and never returned a penny."

What was underneath the surface became a heated debate when a group representing the families of Holocaust victims filed a class action suit against a number of Swiss banks in 1996. The suit called for the return of what the plaintiffs said was some $20 billion owed in principal and interest to the survivors and their families. The case was ultimately settled for about $1.5 billion, more than the amount estimated by the Volcker Commission as due on dormant accounts to Holocaust victims, and much less than the original suit. As the press, foreign governments, and others began to comment on the specific situation with the accounts, however, they catalyzed a discussion of several broader issues, including:

- gold and other transactions by the Swiss National Bank with the Germans;

- the broader Swiss economic relationship with Germany and the other Axis powers;

- Swiss military efforts to resist potential Nazi aggression; and

- the meaning, benefits, and (if any) harms of Swiss neutrality policy.

That the Swiss carried out large gold transactions with Nazi Germany can not be denied, and never was. As a neutral nation, Switzerland naturally kept up some economic and political relations with her largest trading power. A secret British report late in the war concluded that Swiss neutrality had been highly beneficial to the allies, as did such American officials as William Clayton, Dean Acheson, and John Foster Dulles. As well, as a practical matter, Switzerland was physically surrounded for much of the war by Axis troops. Dependent on other countries for energy and food imports, Switzerland built machinery and other exports for trade, and carried out that trade in the international medium of exchange at the time: gold.

Given the volume of gold being transacted by the German central bank, it is impossible to believe that the Swiss did not purchase some amount of gold from Holocaust victims including but not limited to the particular purchases identified in recent investigations that the Swiss either conducted themselves, or cooperated with. In all, the Swiss purchased some 1.5 billion Swiss francs worth of gold from the German central bank from 1938 until 1945, most of it concentrated in the peak war years of 1941 through 1943.

The supposition that the Swiss traded significantly in the gold stolen and in some cases physically removed from Jewish victims, however, is highly doubtful. Once the issue of gold transactions became a serious issue and the Swiss were aroused to act—too late, but not too little—the Swiss attacked the problem. The Confederation appointed a commission to consider the gold transactions and other issues of policy during the war. Working from shattered records and moldy microfilms spread from Missouri to Moscow, the commission managed to locate at least three specific bars of gold that clearly originated in a shipment from SS Captain Bruno Melmer.

"Specifically," the commission reported, "these were bars from the seventh Melmer shipment" to the German Reichsbank on 27 November 1942, "bearing the numbers 36903, 36904, and 36905 and having a total weight of 37.5411 kfg. They were sent by the Reichsbank to the SNB [Swiss National Bank] in Bern on 5 January 1943." As well, "gold bars with the numbers 36783 and 36784," as well as "numbers 36902 and 36907," were "delivered to the Prussian Mint on 25 February 1943." These four bars were in turn re-smelted and sold to the Swiss and to German commercial banks.

There is a distinction between gold stolen from Jews when they were rounded up, and gold literally taken from their bodies in the Nazi death camps. That the latter was taking place was not known until the final days of the war. The former phenomenon—the theft of gold from people as they were rounded up for what were presumed to be horrible work camps, but not genocide—was understood by the Swiss from their own intelligence reports and indeed press accounts from Germany, Italy, and elsewhere. "For those who want to know," an article in the *Neve Zürcher Zeitung* on August 16, 1942, argued, "there can be no more illusions concerning the real situation of gold trade with Germany." The article went on to detail the looting of gold from foreign central banks and from individuals. "It is known that assets held by private individuals were also confiscated in the occupied territories," the director of the Swiss National Bank's legal department commented on December 2, 1943. "For example, from deported Jews or from persons affected by sanctions, etc."

Nevertheless, Switzerland was not the only country to receive gold the Nazis stole from Holocaust victims, or looted from foreign central banks. From 1935 to 1945, some $20 billion flowed out of Europe to the United States. Much of it, albeit indirectly, was Nazi gold. Swiss purchases of gold from Germany, Italy, and Japan ($319 million) were barely half that from the allies ($688 million), most of it coming from the United States ($518 million). The U.S. was also the leading purchaser of gold from the Swiss, at $165 million, numbers which imply there was some victim gold involved.

The Swiss encirclement was exacerbated by the American economic embargo of the Axis powers, which was a *de facto* quarantine on all of Western Europe. In December, 1941, Washington froze Swiss assets in the United States, including substantial gold reserves. The ironic result was to drive Switzerland, needing gold reserves to conduct trade and defend its currency, into the arms of Germany, a needy supplier of gold and the one country that could unilaterally engage in actual transfers of the metal. Figure 18.1 shows the pattern of Swiss gold purchases from Germany, spiking in the first quarter of 1942, and returning to normal after the third quarter of 1944, when the allies opened a small transit corridor to Switzerland through France.

Figure 18.1

Swiss National Bank Gold Purchases from German Reichsbank, Expressed as a Three-Quarter Moving Average

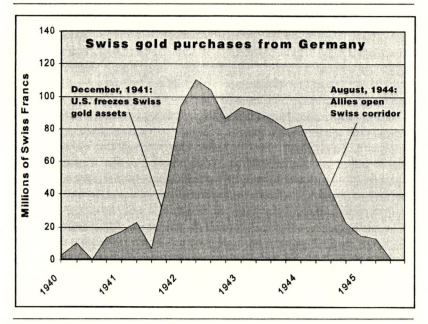

Source: Alexis de Tocqueville Institution from data supplied by SNB, the Swiss Task Force on World War II, and the German Bundesbank.

Especially painful to the Swiss is the accusation that their country was "neutral for Hitler." The accusation takes various forms. Some argue that the Swiss, by selling specific equipment and armaments to the Germans, or trading with them at all, were aiding the German war effort. (The Swiss, despite their position, traded nearly as much with the allies and smuggled out precision instruments vital to the allied effort in the critical air war.) Others suggest that merely by trading with Germany in any extensive way, the Swiss must have been helping the Nazis, and therefore, are culpable.

An official U.S. document, the first Eisenstadt report, argues that Swiss actions even helped "prolong the war." Still others convict the Swiss of a kind of cultural affinity. "They're basically German," as a staff aide who contributed to the Eisenstadt report commented. "You have to keep that in mind." (Report author Stuart Eisenstadt later said he regretted some of the report's conclusions, but critics noted that this retraction took place only after Eisenstadt allegedly went on the payroll of a major Swiss bank.)

These notions of an insufficient disdain for Hitler, and a kind of tacit, cultural self-Anschluss, are highly insidious—nearly impossible to combat.

Once motives are impugned, much objective evidence becomes meaningless, even usable against itself. Any wartime action that advanced Switzerland's own interests, no matter how legitimately, can be added to the tally as another sign of shrewd Swiss venality. Selling paper clips to the Germans? There they go again, providing valuable supplies. Selling paper clips to the Americans? The Swiss are always out to make a profit at our expense. At various points in the war, both the allies and the Germans were furious with the Swiss for what they perceived as a tilt toward the other. America, in a much stronger position to chart its own course than Switzerland, continued a substantial trade with Germany even after the attack on France. We justified our policy as part of a needed effort to rebuild American production capacity for armaments. Later, in order to expedite the war against Nazism, the U.S. formed an alliance with Stalinist Russia.

Finally, the Swiss have no tradition of self-apologetics, and their system is designed against it. America has had great power for a century now, and, accordingly, attracted a long stream of insults and denunciations. The U.S. is inured to being assaulted as corrupt, aggressive, or insensitive. It has calluses for these attacks, and experience at wooing and battering world opinion against them. Switzerland, a small nation that has not threatened its neighbors militarily for centuries, has not often been engaged in defending itself from this kind of attack. The Swiss have faced and repelled armies. The international press, Western politicians, and university researchers are a different matter, and to the Swiss, in some ways more threatening.

For the Swiss, World War II, as an economic phenomenon, began a few weeks after the German leadership appointed Adolf Hitler Chancellor in January, 1933. In the Swiss tradition, the political leaders in Bern, and newspaper readers around the country, had read Hitler's statements before and after coming to power. Unlike most in the West, the Swiss took them seriously. "Our people will never allow itself to be brought into line according to the German pattern," Federal Councilor Rudolf Minger, head of the military department, declared in March, 1933, justifying his proposal for increased Swiss defense preparedness. That October, as Hitler announced Germany's intention to withdraw from the League of Nations, Minger drew up a plan to increase Swiss military spending by 15 million francs in 1934, a 20 percent increase, as part of a four-year addition of 100 million francs—a near doubling of Swiss defense spending by 1938. The *Neue Zürcher Zeitung*, in an October 12 editorial, approved, adding that the country not only needed such armaments, but a vigorous "spiritual defense" as well—a term that became a Swiss rallying cry. On December 10, *The New York Times* published an article alleging that Germany had drawn up plans for the invasion of France through Switzerland. The account may have been spurious, but the Swiss could not assume that it was. On December 14, the federal council approved more than 80 million francs in additional defense spending. Among the items was the start of construction of a vast series of hidden mountain fortifications and guns. This fortress Switzerland program became a $15 billion project in today's dollars—not much less than what Ronald Reagan and the United States spent on his Star Wars defense program during his entire term in office. At the same time, the Swiss decided to build a new museum to house the *Bundesbrief* and other documents of national independence—exemplifying the Swiss political and sentimental separation from Austria and Germany, or what one writer later called "pan-this and pan-that." This is where Swiss policy toward Germany stood in 1933, before Hitler had spent a full year in office.

The war measures continued and expanded through Hitler's abrogation of the Versaille treaty (August, 1935), occupation of the Rhineland (March, 1936), absorption of Austria (March, 1938), the Kristallnacht assault on Jews (November, 1938), the annexation of Czechoslovakia (1939), and the invasion of Poland (April, 1940), Denmark and Norway (April, 1940), and France (May, 1941). In the spring of 1934, Nazi textbook writers drew maps of showing Switzerland as part of a conceived "Greater Germany" based on language and ethnic lines. "Quite naturally, we count you Swiss as offshoots of the German nation," Nazi historian Ewald Banse, author of one of the textbooks, commented. Swiss newspapers and officials attacked his conception. Theodore Fischer, the leader of Switzerland's tiny pro-German faction, promised the country would be liberated from its status as a "vassal state of France under Jewish control."

Federal Councillor Jean Marie Musy, the Swiss finance minister, spoke for most of the country when he promised that Switzerland would "remain a democracy or cease to be Switzerland." The "racial ideal," he said, "can never be the basis of Swiss nationality." Defense Minister Minger echoed: "Events abroad have reawoken Switzerland's ancient defiance and the feelings for justice and liberty have been renewed."

In the following twelve months the Swiss banned the wearing of uniforms by political parties; expanded the period for basic military training by twenty days; increased the defense budget by more than 30 percent; enacted additional protections for the press against German threats and complaints; expelled German agents who were trolling through Zürich and Basel hoping to identify private bank transfers made by Jews; and rejected an initiative, supported by the small national socialist group, calling for greater centralized economic planning such as enacted in Germany, Italy, and the United States.

The Swiss people signaled their support for these measures whenever tested. In some ways they were more anti-German than their leaders. In 1935, the Communist Party and others challenged the near doubling of defense expenditures in a national vote—a "facultative" referendum. They lost, 54 percent to 46 percent. This was the height of the Great Depression in Switzerland. It was the only significant facultative referendum between 1929 and

1946 that passed. And it was the only one between 1916 and 1946 that passed while calling for significant government expenditures.

From 1933 to 1937, land cultivation in Switzerland doubled. While there were government incentive programs, a large portion of the increase was the result of appeals to the Swiss people to increase the country's food supply voluntarily. On the eve of the war, the government asked for volunteers for extra military home defense units. The council hoped to find 20,000 to 30,000 able boys and old men who could shuttle ammunition to key points, aid in communications, and perform similar duties. Within three months, more than 200,000 had volunteered.

Popular war preparations accelerated in the spring of 1938, as Hitler swallowed Austria. This made Switzerland, as *The New York Times* noted, "a democratic peninsula in a politically autocratic and economically autarchic league." A few days later, the Socialist Party of Basel, the city with the closest ties to Germany, collected signatures for an initiative to criminalize membership in the Nazi Party. The initiative achieved the highest number of signatures ever seen in the city. The national parliament, meanwhile, had also approved a significant revision of the penal code. Among other things, it allowed persons charged with treason and other collaboration with the enemy—including civilians—to be tried by military courts. This change was challenged in a facultative referendum, but the new law was approved in July, 1938, with 54 percent support.

In December, 1940, the leading Nazi group was banned and its leaders arrested. In the United States, by contrast, Nazi groups, though small, were still active. America completed its second consecutive year of more than $100 million in trade with the Nazis as Henry Luce and others tried (with little initial success) to rally popular support for aid to Britain and other Nazi foes. The Swiss, of course, faced a much greater threat than the Americans did in the 1930s, and indeed throughout the war; they had more reason to prepare for the Nazis.

Figure 18.2 compares Swiss military expenditures with those of other European countries in dollars per capita for 1937. These figures understate the relative Swiss resistance to Nazism, because of the popular nature of the Swiss Army, which incorporated 400,000 members, expanding to more than 750,000 during an actual attack. The former figure meant that Switzerland, in 1938, had approximately 10 percent of the population under arms. Only Finland (8 percent) and Belgium (8 percent) compare favorably and even these are significantly below the lower Swiss figure. The Netherlands (5 percent), Norway (4 percent), Denmark (4 percent), and France (3 percent) were even lower.

The Swiss looked not only to physical measures, but also to psychological and even metaphysical ones as well. In 1937, Federal Councillor Philipp Etter published a book entitled *Geistige Landesverteidigung*—roughly, *Spiritual Defense*. The book was a Swiss best seller and reportedly was distributed

Table 18.1

Meeting the Nazi Threat Military Spending per Capita, 1935	
Finland	24.9
Switzerland	**22.6**
Belgium	19.7
Norway	17.9
The Netherlands	16.5
Denmark	14.3
Austria	11.9
(in 1935 Swiss francs)	

Source: Alexis de Tocqueville Institution research memorandum, 1999, from national data and population figures.

widely in Czechoslovakia, Austria, and other soon-to-be "possessions of the German Reich," as Hitler termed them.

"The German people will never forget the attitude of the Swiss during this war," growled the *Frankfurter Zeitung* on December 2, 1940. "A nation of 80,000,000, while fighting for bare existence, finds itself almost uninterruptedly attacked, insulted, and slandered by the newspapers of a minuscule country whose government claims to be neutral."

The pages above place a lot of emphasis on Swiss actions prior to the German *Blitzkrieg* of France in the spring of 1940 and in the immediate months that followed. There's a good reason. We learn a lot about Swiss hopes and intentions during the period when Nazism was reaching its zenith. This was the time when Denmark, Belgium, and Austria were either giving up without a fight, or fighting but offering only a few days or weeks (France) of resistance.

On June 14, a Friday in 1940, Paris fell. The Swiss, neutral to the teeth, were already aggressively engaged in the defense of their national territory against "all potential aggressors"—i.e., Hitler. American entry into the war was still more than 500 days away, awaiting Pearl Harbor and the gratuitous German declaration of war hours later. The following Monday, June 17, General Henri Guisan—elected to head the Swiss war effort shortly after the German invasion of Poland—called together the Swiss general staff to discuss preparations for the defense of Switzerland against a possible occupation by the Nazis. Late in June, as the German-French truce became effective, German Captain Otto Wilhelm von Menges submitted a plan for an attack on Switzerland to the German general staff. On July 25, Guisan and the Swiss general staff gathered in Luzern to boat down the lake to the banks of the Rütli, where they renewed the sacred oath of their ancestors from 1291 and the Bundesbrief. Author Stephen Halbrook paints the scene:

On a beautiful day, Guisan faced the senior officers of the army standing in a semicircle on the Rütli Meadow, facing the lake. Canton Uri's flag of the Battalion 87 flew above. Addressing the measures taken "for the resistance in the reduit," Guisan ordered "resistance to all aggression." He continued: "Here, soldiers of 1940, we will inspire ourselves with the lessons and spirit of the past to envisage resolution of the present and future of the country, to hear the mysterious call that pervades this meadow."

Swiss elite troops had already been on active duty for almost a year—they were called up on August 25, 1939. "The country has one tenth of its population under arms; more than any other in the world," William Shirer diarized. "They're ready to defend their way of life."

Switzerland's orders for organization of "the entire army for resistance" promised the Germans that Switzerland as a nation would never capitulate— even if its government did. The order was posted all over the country both to reassure the people and to warn the Germans. In the event of attack, it said, the Swiss would be notified "through poster, radio, courier, town crier, storm bells, and the dropping of leaflets from airplanes." The response would not be limited to formal military groups acting as official units. "All soldiers and those with them are to attack with ruthlessness parachutists, airborne infantry, and saboteurs. Where no officers and noncommissioned officers are present, each soldier acts under exertion of all powers of his own initiative." Bearing in mind the case of other countries which had been intimidated into surrendering because of the capitulation of the national leadership, the order continued:

If by radio, leaflets, or other media any information is transmitted doubting the will of the Federal Council or of the Army High Command to resist an attacker, this information must be regarded as lies of enemy propaganda. Our country will resist the aggression with all means in its power and to the bitter end.

In effect, the government was committing itself and the people to what Etter had called "total spiritual warfare." They deprived themselves of the ability to surrender even if they later wanted too: Swiss army units and citizens were under orders to ignore reports of such a decision and continue fighting.

All this makes it easy to understand the Swiss frustration at accusations that their country was in complicity with the Nazis during World War II. In fact, the Swiss people put up stiffer resistance, against greater odds, to the Germans than those of any other country. As Walter Lippmann, responding to an article in a U.S. magazine implying Switzerland was "occupied" by the Germans, wrote in January, 1943:

The Swiss nation is entirely surrounded by Axis armies, beyond reach of any help from the democracies.... Switzerland, which cannot live without trading with the surrounding Axis countries, still is an independent democracy....

That is the remarkable thing about Switzerland. The real news is not that her factories make munitions for Germany but that the Swiss have an army which stands guard against invasion, that their frontiers are defended, that their free institutions continue to exist, and that there has been no Swiss Quisling, and no Swiss Laval. The Swiss remained true to themselves even in the darkest days of 1940 and 1941, when it seemed that nothing but the valor of the British and the blind faith of free men elsewhere stood between Hitler and the creation of a totalitarian new order in Europe.

Surely, if ever the honor of a people was put to the test, the honor of the Swiss was tested and proved then and there....They have demonstrated that the traditions of freedom can be stronger than the ties of race and of language and economic interest.

"Switzerland stands today as an island in a Nazi ocean," *The New York Times* echoed in a January 28 editorial. Referring to German publications that continually described Switzerland as a country harboring, and dominated by, Jews, the *Times* added, "perhaps the Swiss didn't mind being called a 'medley of criminals, particularly Jews.' To be called a criminal by a Nazi is to receive a high compliment. To be called a Jew by a Nazi is to be classed with those who have suffered martyrdom for freedom's sake."

Over the nine years of Swiss vulnerability, the Germans developed more than a dozen attack plans for Switzerland which were discussed at the highest military levels. These included deliberations by Hitler himself in 1934, 1936, 1938, 1939, 1940, 1942, 1943, 1944, and 1945. Except for a respite in 1941–42 while the German army was occupied with the assault on Russia—which ended as the Nazi retreat from Russia raised interest in grabbing Switzerland as a final redoubt—the Swiss were under near-constant peril.

"We woke up every morning and looked over the Rhein," a Jewish woman who lived in Basel comments, "and wondered whether the Germans would be invading that day." The woman, who asked that her name be withheld, said that her family attempted several times to emigrate to the United States. This was not because they were ill-treated in Switzerland—she lives near Davos where her husband is in a nursing home—but because they knew that if the Nazis did invade, they would be primary targets. They were, however, turned down, as were most appeals for asylum by European Jews to the U.S. State Department.

Why didn't the Germans actually seize Switzerland? The answer does not lie in any especially beneficial economic relationship. Swiss supplies of machinery to the Germans never totaled more than 3 percent of industrial production for a month, and averaged less than 2 percent over the war. Invasion would not have jeopardized much of this total because the Germans could seize most of the factories in the flat, Northern strip of the country that is most easily occupied.

The answer lies in German estimates that concluded that it would take anywhere from 300,000 to 500,000 men to subdue the country, followed by a smaller but still substantial occupation presence. Had they done this as well, the Germans were assured, the Swiss would destroy the tunnel and bridges through the Alps, depriving the Nazis of the most direct connection to their Italian allies. Such a move, in combination with German occupation of the Northern plain, would also have effectively destroyed the Swiss economy. It would have meant death for many Swiss and internees (including Jews) who lived there; the rest would have been, like other occupied populations, Nazi hostages. But the Swiss repeatedly assured the Germans that they would take this step and they mined key transportation points so as to be able to carry that threat out almost the instant Nazi troops crossed the frontier.

A retired Swiss official who was part of the economic planning team during the war told me that in regular meetings the Germans repeatedly threatened both occupation and personal violence against the Swiss officials who were standing up to the German demands. "We were never belligerent back," he said, "but we did calmly and repeatedly refer them to our government's policies for dealing with those eventualities, which were published and repeated often to make sure they understood that our government and our people intended to carry them out."

In the context of all the country's actions, the Swiss threat to commit suicide—but pull Germany down as they went; a reciprocating Mosada—apparently struck the Germans as credible. "The Swiss are just the people," as *The New York Times* observed, "if pushed a mite too far, who would prefer to starve or die fighting rather than give in. Because they are that kind of people, they may not have to prove it in action."

Hitler seemed to sense this determination in the Swiss, and, as a result, had a loathing for them as a nation that rivaled his hatred of Winston Churchill as an individual and the Jews as a people.

At a war-planning conference with Mussolini in 1940, Hitler and the Italian dictator discussed what Hitler saw as the need to occupy Switzerland, to put an end to its "insolent defiance" of the New Europe and "collaboration with and harboring of the Jews." Later that year, Hitler learned of the delivery of precision engineering products from Switzerland to England, and flew into a tantrum. He immediately ordered his generals to draw up fresh invasion plans and described Bern—accurately—as the "center of international spying against Germany." Again in 1941, Hitler and the Italian dictator traded insulting characterizations of Switzerland, discussing the matter for more than half an hour. "The Führer characterized Switzerland as the most despicable and wretched people," recalled an aide who attended the meeting—the Swiss were, he later said, a "bastard" nation because of the intermingling of German blood with those of inferior races. "They frankly opposed the Reich," Hitler said, "hoping that by parting from the common destiny of the German people, they would be better off." Discussing his plans for the post-war economic order, Hitler said: "As for the Swiss, we can use them, at the best, as hotel-keepers."

The Swiss press was a constant irritant to Hitler. It was not just what it said about him, but the very fact of its freedom. In July of 1942, Hitler encountered Swiss press reports about the military strength of Soviet Russia. "Not only in England and America," Hitler groaned, but in Switzerland, "the population believes in Jewish claptrap." The Jews, he told an aide, must have special influence with the Swiss, because they cared about little other than grain prices, cows, and clocks. That August, impatient with the estimates of his generals that the Germans would need perhaps 500,000 men to subdue Switzerland—many times the relative troop strength used to conquer France—the Führer launched into another tirade about the Swiss.

"A state like Switzerland," Hitler told his staff, "which is nothing but a pimple on the face of Europe, cannot be allowed to continue." The wording is revealing: The Swiss state, for Hitler, must not be suffered even to continue. To the Reich, Switzerland's *existence* was an offense.

It was no accident that Hitler linked the Jews with the Swiss in many of his eruptions. Although many Jewish refugees were turned away at the Swiss border, thousands, particularly children and families with children, were accepted. (More by far than were welcomed by any other country in per capita terms.) The resulting Swiss ratio of rejection to acceptance was not nearly high enough to please the Führer. "The Jew must get out of Europe," he exploded at a meeting a few days after the infamous Wannsee Conference, where the plan to annihilate the Jews was drawn into a grisly blueprint. "Out of Switzerland and out of Sweden, they must be driven out."

Like the Finns and the Poles, the Swiss had the special honor of confronting both the German and Russian dictators, and exciting their special contempt. At the Yalta conference in 1944, Stalin proposed the invasion and occupation of Switzerland—ostensibly to foreclose the German option of using it to stage a final defense. The allies refused, and that night, in a conversation with Molotov, Stalin denounced the Swiss as a "contemptible little nation of bankers and farmers," and somewhere, Lenin, Bismarck, and Metternich smiled in agreement. Several months later, Churchill commented on the discussion in a memorandum to his foreign secretary:

> I put this down for the record. Of all the neutrals, Switzerland has the greatest right to distinction. She has been the sole international force linking the hideously surrendered nations and ourselves. What does it matter whether she has been able to give us the commercial advantages we desire or has given too many to the Germans, to keep herself alive?

Swiss today, particularly those who remember the war, are proud of Hitler's special disdain. They are, accordingly, hurt and angry at accusations that their country was complicit in any way with the Nazi regime. For all the superficial similarities of race and language, one can argue that there is not a country in the world that less resembles Nazi Germany than Switzerland.

It is impossible to evaluate Switzerland's total moral position, if you will, in World War II without mentioning the country's positive contribution to the escape of thousands of Jews and other refugees from the Nazis. Figure 18.3 compares the per capita number of refugees accepted by the Swiss to those taken in by the United States, Great Britain, and France.

These figures understate the contribution the Swiss made to the protection of Jews and other refugees from Hitler's destruction, as the country was economically isolated for most of the period. The relative sacrifice made by the Swiss to care for several hundred thousand total refugees, interned prisoners, and others was even larger than the graphic suggests.

Statistics, moreover, omit the human face of Switzerland's humanitarian mission. One such flesh-and-blood contribution was made by Mr. and Mrs. Carl Lutz.

Carl Lutz was born in 1895 in Appenzell, the second youngest of ten children. He emigrated to the United States at age eighteen to work in a factory in Granite City, Illinois, not far from East St. Louis. For most of the 1920s he worked in assorted Swiss diplomatic offices in the U.S. Eventually, the Swiss Foreign Office appointed Lutz as a consular official in Jaffa, Palestine, where he served from 1935 to 1939, an eyewitness to the Arab-Jewish conflicts. While there, he also helped some 2,500 Jewish emigrants from Germany to escape deportation by the British as illegal aliens.

From 1942 to 1944, Lutz worked closely with the Jewish Agency of Palestine, headed by Moshe Krausz, to document and transport an estimated 10,000 Jewish children and young adults to (what would soon become) Israel. Some were orphans, others had parents who had been deported. Most had been smuggled to Hungary from other countries (Poland, Czechoslovakia,

Table 18.2

Havens from the Holocast
Jewish Refugees from Germany Accepted per 1 Million Persons in Country's 1930 Population

	1933-38	1933-45
United States	650	900
Great Britain	1,400	1,600
Sweden	550	1,500
France	850	1,100
Holland	1,000	n.a.
Denmark	750	850
Belgium	1,700	1,900
Switzerland	**2,200**	**8,100**

Source: Alexis de Tocqueville Institution from figures from the U.N. High Commission on Refugees, Yad Vashem, and the Statistical Yearbook of the National Immigration and Naturalization Service.

even Germany itself) by *Chalutzim*, Jewish pioneers. To evade the authorities, Lutz used British-approved Palestine Certificates, which he countersigned and supplemented with Swiss Schutzbriefe, protective "letters of transit."

In March of 1944, the Nazis, who had dominated the country but refrained from blatant interference, occupied all of Hungary, imposing a hand-picked government. On March 21, the Nazi regent closed the borders to all further emigration. This blocked some 8,000 Jews who should have been free to leave. Lutz demanded their immediate, unconditional release. But soon the problem was much greater than a matter of 8,000 emigrants waiting to leave. Though Lutz did not yet know it, SS Chief Adolf Eichmann, aided by the puppet government, had already made plans to deport all 762,000 Jews in Hungary to the Auschwitz concentration camp. The situation grew even more acute in October when the Arrow-Cross Party, the most extreme of the pro-German factions, came to power. The Nazis, feeling the circle closing around them, decided to slaughter as many Jews as they could through low-technology methods: the infamous death march of November 1944, when more than 70,000 Jews were scourged towards the Austrian border.

Working against the Nazis and the clock, Lutz and his wife used every legal method they could think of to bring Jews under his protection. They used many illegal methods as well. When the Germans promised to respect the protection of the 8,000 visas he had issued, but only provided he issue no more, Lutz agreed in order to gain time. In the meantime he continued to print visas, perhaps 30,000 or 40,000—but always numbering them between 1 and 8,000, so that if individuals were stopped and produced their papers, it might appear there had been no duplication of visas. "This idea," the *Encyclopedia of the Houlocaust* reports, "served as a model for various types of protective letters issued by other neutral countries and by the International Red Cross."

When the Germans caught on to this device, Lutz transferred his mission's emigration department to the now-famous Glass House on Vadasz Street, placing the building under his diplomatic immunity. He assembled several dozen leaders of the Jewish Community to act as liaisons, and collected thousands of photographs and signatures in a few days. Lutz then issued a series of "collective passports," covering some 40,000 persons in chunks of 1,000 and more apiece. Again the Nazis eventually penetrated the legal ruse, but it took time, and with the help of some of the Hungarians, Lutz had stalled the game out still further.

The Lutzes formed a circle of sympathetic diplomats from the other neutrals, such as papal nuncio Angelo Rotta, to build a network of safe houses throughout the city where Jews could be placed under his protection. He bought apartment buildings with help from sympathetic officials in the government and transferred several thousand Jews to them. When Eichmann and the SS demanded that the Jews of Budapest be concentrated in one spot to facilitate deportation, Lutz persuaded Hungarian officials to provide him with more than seventy protective houses within the ghetto, in the Szent-Istvan area of Budapest. This bought precious weeks for the more than 30,000 *Schutzbrief* holders that Lutz placed there. Lutz also acted as a mentor to other diplomats, such as Raoul Wallenberg of Sweden, recruiting them to the cause and sharing his methods. By the end of the war these men and women formed a wide network.

At times, the task was truly grim. Several times in the fall of 1944 and winter of 1945, Lutz and his wife were hauled out late at night to the Obuda brickyard. On those occasions, the Nazis would line up Jews holding authentic and forged *Schutzbriefe* with identical numbers, demanding that Lutz decide which documents were legitimate and which were not. If he did not so indicate, the SS guards were under orders to simply deport all the assembled Jews. In effect, Lutz was being asked to determine which people should live and which were sentenced to death. After one such session, Lutz feared he was near a breakdown, and his wife asked if they should consider leaving the country. The next day, there was an attempt on Lutz's life, one of several apparent efforts by the SS officers on hand.

Like the border guards and Swiss families who regularly allowed Jews across the Swiss border, Lutz did not have the support of his government— nor of the British and American governments he represented. More than one exchange between Bern and London indicates that the two states contemplated recalling Lutz—London because it did not want so many Jews sent to Palestine, Bern because it worried Lutz's methods would compromise Swiss neutrality.

Lutz worked to make sure Western governments and eventually Western publics understood what was at stake. When two prisoners escaped from Auschwitz and related the grisly reality of what was taking place there, he immediately dispatched an urgent report to his superiors in Bern and London. When these official channels failed to act, he scurried copies of key documents to a friend who had taken an assignment as a representative of El Salvador. The news of Auschwitz broke in the Swiss press and soon produced an outcry in Paris, London, and New York. Lutz, of course, was risking his job and his life with each such maneuver.

The reward came in the frantic spring of 1945, as Russian troops closed in and the Nazis moved to slaughter as many Jews as possible before having to retreat. As the Soviet artillery neared, Lutz and his wife had to take cover in an isolated part of the city and were trapped for some weeks, out of contact with the world and unable to determine whether their efforts had even succeeded. Not long before the actual surrender of Germany, Lutz himself was liberated from his cellar in Pest.

The letters, the safe houses, the bribes, and the leaks had saved, by a conservative calculation, some 62,000 lives. It measures the magnitude of the Holocaust to consider that this total was less than 1 percent of the number put to death by Hitler's Germany. On the other hand, this was the work of one Swiss citizen.

Though Lutz was in a position to render aid on a large scale, there were many Swiss who helped save others from the Hitler death camps one victim at a time. Official Swiss policy was to turn away all would-be entrants without passports, Jewish (whose passports carried a stigmatizing "J") and otherwise. But the feelings of the Swiss people were considerably more liberal, and families, sometimes whole communities, were willing to defy their own government.

Leopold Koss, now a doctor in New York City, was a beneficiary of this quiet heroism as he sought to escape the German occupation of France in 1942:

> On August 24 or 25, 1942—I no longer remember the exact date—I crossed the French-Swiss border illegally on foot....The odds of being arrested in France as a Polish Jew and former soldier, and sent to a German concentration camp, were extremely high.
> On the way to my destination, I heard that although the official policies of the Swiss government were against acceptance of refugees and that many (including some friends of mine) were returned to France or into the hands of the Gestapo, there was a recent swell of public opinion to open the border. In fact, a woman on the train, perhaps guessing my destination, handed me an article in the *Journal de Geneve*, published some days before, openly exhorting the government to open the borders to the victims of Nazi persecution. Apparently similar articles appeared in August 1942 in the German-speaking press, notably the *Neue Zürcher Zeitung*.
>
> I entered Switzerland without difficulty and was soon several kilometers inland, not having been molested by anyone. Rather exhausted, hungry and thirsty, I voluntarily entered the barracks of a military unit... I was fed and offered a cot. The soldiers, simple Swiss citizens, couldn't have been nicer.
> The next day... I was interrogated by a police officer who promptly informed me that I was to be sent back to France as an illegal alien. However, he consented to listen to my story, told through tears, and offered to inquire of the authorities in Bern what should be done with me. I discovered shortly thereafter that there was a group of at least 30 men in the same predicament.... We were all treated with great consideration by the police and the guards. A few days later we were apparently accepted and sent to a camp for political refugees—Belchasse. I spent several months in Belchasse, followed by several months in a labor camp in Aesch-bei-Birmensdorf, near Zürich. It was hardly luxury—but it was *safe*. I only wish my parents and my sister, who stayed in Poland, could have been with me. They all perished.
> In September 1943, I was allowed to resume my studies of medicine in Bern. During the three and a half years that I spent at the University of Bern, I never had to pay any tuition.... The federal police, to whom I had to report on a weekly and then a monthly basis, were increasingly friendly.... In fact, as I was leaving Switzerland for the United States in 1947 to start a new life, they addressed their last communications to me with the title, "doctor," better than the previous "refugee."

Dr. Koss remains grateful to the Swiss—and takes issue with the "dreary image" of wartime Switzerland presented by some Western governments and press reports. "There was another wartime Switzerland," he says—one "very remote" from the portrait of "greed and collusion with the Nazis" that some present. Indeed, Koss writes:

> The Swiss have not only saved my life and that of many thousands of other refugees, but also gave me an outstanding education that has allowed me to forge a successful scientific career in the United States. I am now 76 years old and eternally grateful to the Swiss people for what they have done for me.

The question is not whether Switzerland or countries such as Britain and the U.S. did enough to stop the Holocaust. None did. The question, rather, is whether any countries did more to liberate Jews and other potential victims of the Nazi death camps, or began a firm (and unwavering) resistance to Hitler earlier than the Swiss. If there are any, they are few.

Note

1. Like many Jews, Bär's family left Europe in 1941 because of the threat from Nazi Germany. Whole companies—Julius Bär, Credit Suisse, Nestlé, and others— moved their headquarters overseas. Most went to the U.S., some to Latin America.

19

Diversity

*"In Switzerland, minorities are not tolerated.
They are favored." A. Togni*

As the country eases into social peace and unity, it is easy to forget that, for most of its life, Switzerland was gripped by Europe's grudges. Alexis de Tocqueville summed up the Swiss situation in 1835 as follows:

One people, composed of several races, speaking several languages; with several religious beliefs, various dissident sects, two churches both equally established and privileged; all religious questions turning into political ones, and all political questions turning quickly into religious ones—in short, two societies, one very old and the other very young, joined in marriage in spite of the age difference. That is a fair sketch of Switzerland.

Even today, Switzerland suffers from natural divisions any one of which would severely strain national solidarity in most countries. The Swiss have three major languages, each of which is the home language to a powerful nation and culture on the Swiss frontier. Those national cultures along the Swiss border—in many cases less separated by natural boundaries from their affinity group than the three major Swiss language populations are from one another—have been an entropic magnet, always urging the country apart. "Nature has hindered movement and exchange within the country," as American sociologist Carol Schmid observes, "more than with the neighboring countries of the same language group."[1]

Ethnic Italians, Germans, French, Jews, and Arabs—groups that haven't been able to get along anywhere else for centuries—swirl together within a work force more than one-fifth foreign born. The country has long been home to two of the sternest Protestant sects in the world, the followers of Calvin and Zwingli, and to a highly orthodox Roman Catholic population in the Forest Cantons. For hundreds of years these sects have held sway in various cantons and communities not merely as the religion of preference, but as state-spon-

233

sored churches. Scholars and historians comparing Switzerland to such multilingual nations as Belgium, Canada, India, Nigeria, and South Africa are intrigued at the degree to which the Swiss have managed to form a bona fide nation.

It is tempting to call the result a melting pot. Yet this would not be accurate. The Swiss system is held together by something, but it does not homogenize its members. In the United States, ethnic groups tend—when not burdened by perverse incentives—to learn English, adopt American customs, and thus, gradually, become one people in many practices. The Swiss blend together on some customs, but tend to retain their mother tongue. They learn to cooperate with others who speak a different language, and, to an extent seen in few other countries, tend to learn one or more tongues outside their first.

Visiting Switzerland today, one remarks at the smoothness with which the Swiss handle their three-way language barrier. At first you notice it everywhere. And then, after a while, you hardly notice it at all.

Riding from Bern to Geneva, the train crosses over an invisible cantonal border—and the conductor shifts effortlessly from German to French. The P.A. announcements continue to be in both languages, but now French is first, and is spoken by the same voice with a nearly perfect accent.

In a court room, one of the more formal and tense of situations, the participants deal in their language of choice—with a translator if necessary, though it seldom is if the languages are German, French, Italian, or even English. In some cases, a listener simply followed along in his second or third language where possible, then asked for a translation if needed. What struck me in several different courts was the matter-of-fact way in which language was simply dealt with. In some ways, there seemed an advantage in the occasional pause for translation. The hiatuses cut against any buildup of emotion of the type one often sees even in an American traffic court. It never caused, in my experience, significant friction. In general, as one might expect, in dealings with the government poly-lingualism is visible and its costs seem high. In almost any settings where government documents are on display, one will see four or five stacks of everything—always German and French, and frequently in Italian, English, or Romansch. Even small public buildings or services often seem to have a second or third official around who appears to be there in large part to communicate with the occasional Italian, English, or Romansch speaker.

Restaurant menus are normally printed in the language of the district, though in the larger and more cosmopolitan cities there are invariably French or German subtexts; occasionally Italian and English ones as well. In German-speaking Switzerland, even in relatively remote parts of Schwyz, Uri, Glarus, or Appenzell, my informal survey found that more than 90 percent of the people could hold a basic conversation outside of German—either in French or English. An American asking for directions in Switzerland would, in many regions, have less difficulty than if he or she were to visit a convenience store or a gas station in the U.S. These statistics far exceed the levels one obtains from more formal surveys, but the problem with the formal studies is that they seek a higher level of competence than my informal test. The level at which a Swiss calls himself or another Swiss competent in a language is higher than the level at which a taxicab driver or office security guard might be able to communicate, with a few added hand signs or occasional German word, with another.

Language, for the Swiss, is the object of a whole invisible superstructure of conventions and assumptions and social devices. When a group of three Swiss, already conversing in German, is joined by a Swiss they know to be much more comfortable in French—and if they do not know at first, the Swiss are adept at finding out, so well-tuned is their ear—then the existing line of conversation will shift into French. On the other hand, an Italian-speaking Swiss, joining a larger group, will resist being spoken to in Italian—feeling that surely some of those present will not be comfortable in that language. He will attempt to steer the conversation back to German—or the whole group will ease into French, which as the second language of choice for both German-speaking and Italian-speaking Swiss, is a handy unit of exchange. In this way, everyone in the room is making some slight adjustment, but no one feels patronized or patronizing.

Interestingly, even "German-speaking" Swiss do not speak true German—but rather one of more than a dozen highly particularized local dialects. "High German," as is used in Germany and Austria more broadly, is virtually always used in Swiss written documents, even unimportant ones. This sets off a whole further set of practices and distinctions. One important effect of these dialects is to make all German Swiss into quasi-minorities. As German speakers they add up to a majority, but no dialect is anything more than a tiny minority. The dialects also reinforce a certain Swiss pride in separation from Germany and Austria. If one wants to insult a German-speaking Swiss on a number of levels, one need only tell him that his German sounds like the German spoken in Bonn or Berlin.

The Swiss linguistic codes are subtle, unwritten, seldom even articulated. Probably for this reason they even vary occasionally from one Swiss to another.[2] But they exist—and are part of a whole ethos of adaptivity and businesslike consideration that is the essence of Swiss culture and society.

In almost any social setting where a group of Swiss who didn't know me (or my origins) came into contact with me, they made a tangible effort to determine as quickly as possible what my primary language was, and to use it. Generally this took place within thirty seconds—though my later practice of speaking French in German-speaking cantons, and German in the French-speaking ones often achieved a delay of up to several minutes before my Americanism was ferreted out.

Watching the Swiss in these situations is like watching a beautiful waltz or minuet danced by a couple emphasizing grace and simplicity, not flair. There are few excesses, no gaudy shows, only an easy agility. In America, the non-English speaker is met with a kind of benign arrogance—the lovable but ugly American at home, who will raise his voice and say to the Japanese tourist very slowly "It's next to the World Trade Center." Germans now exert at least a friendly helpless cultural smile, "nein, kann kein Englisch," in situations where in Switzerland, there would be a prompt turn to a colleague and a resolution. In France, there is an active contempt; even the Frenchman who can speak English will often abstain from doing so, as if exacting some petty revenge. Even in Belgium (Flemish and French) or Canada (French and English) the determination of one party or another to assert his linguistic heritage sometimes makes one feel he is in a battle zone. The quiet dance of the tongues is one of the most endearing elements of Swiss society, and this facility for dancing, developed in one sphere, contributes to balance and grace in a host of others.

How have the Swiss achieved this facility at languages—and more broadly, a national facility, almost an article of patriotism, for listening and adapting to other languages, practices, and cultures? The answer is a mixture of history, special factors, deliberate policy, and predictable (but not necessarily intended) aspects of policy—a tapestry of causes and effects. And yet, behind the picture, or abstracting from it, are strong unifying themes, such as the *Willensnation* concept of a people determined to be a people, adhering by free choice to a credo of democratic ideals.

We can divide the causes of Switzerland's adaptation to diversity into three general groups. The first group consists of historical factors and accidents: some of them purely random—true "accidents"—and others a mixture of luck and institutions. The second group consists of deliberate acts of policy, such as intensive instruction in second and even third languages in Swiss schools. The third group is composed of deliberate policies or institutions that do not have assimilation as their primary aim, but which nevertheless contribute to it. In this group are a whole range of Swiss institutions from the army to the people's strong patriotism and its basis in a set of shared ideals.

Facts, Tendencies, and Happy Accidents

Perhaps the most important fact about Switzerland's various groups is that there are a number of them, and they tend to criss-cross and overlap. There's a sufficient diversity of different societal groupings (race, language, religion) and of different levels of government and other institutions so that most Swiss are in some important minority and some majority groups—particularly if one considers more than one unit of society. Meanwhile the highly fluid, nonpartisan, multiparty structure of Swiss politics brings these groups into regular coalitions and cooperative enterprises. Much as Madison counted on a multiplicity of special interests to act as a check on one another in *The Federalist*, so Swiss society defuses some of the rigid rivalries that have formed in other countries divided into groups.

Religion and language cross-cuts offer one good illustration. In Switzerland as a whole, Roman Catholics are a minority in the population and a minority in the population of most cantons, albeit a growing one. And, of course, the majority of Swiss people and of cantons are primarily German-speaking. Yet there are many German-speaking Catholics in Switzerland, as well as French-speaking Protestants. Anyone who belongs to one of these groups is in one national minority already.

The picture gets more subtle and interesting when we look at the cantonal level. A German-speaking Swiss Catholic who now lives in the Ticino, the Southern, Italian-speaking portion of the country, is in a national majority as to language and a cantonal majority as to religion, but is in a cantonal minority as to language and a national minority as to religion. A French Protestant in Geneva is in the cantonal minority but the national majority in his religion; but his is in the cantonal majority and national minority as to his primary language.

"It is one of the fortunate accidents of Swiss history," Carol Schmid writes, "that the linguistic and religious boundaries do not coincide. Language conflict was moderated, since both religions had their adherents in every language area." The Swiss have learned to respect one another's rights as minorities—and, at the same time, the right of local majorities to run schools, churches, and other institutions by the language and faith of their heritage.

These dynamics become more powerful, not less, when we broaden our scope and look at other group characteristics and interests. Sociologist Jürg Steiner writes: "There is usually a cross-cutting rather than a cumulative separation between political parties, economic interest groups, voluntary associations, and newspapers."

Zürich, for instance, is considered a center of German culture, wealth, and Protestantism. Yet it ranks behind French Geneva and Catholic Zug in per capita income. In economic matters, the French cantons have tended to vote for social democratic programs—higher spending, higher taxes, greater federal powers. On cultural matters, however, the French Swiss emphasize federalism and autonomy. Several French cantons (Geneva, Vaud, and Neuchatel) are among the most affluent in Switzerland, though shaken by 1990s fiscal crisis and tax incentives. "The disparities are far greater within each linguistic group than between them," Schmid notes.

The populations of the Italian-speaking cantons, being a distinct minority nationally (about 5 percent of citizens and 9 percent of the resident population), naturally view with reserve any proposal that might empower Bern, or erode local identity and autonomy. The federal government has proved a friend in some instances, however—for example, in sponsoring language programs in the Ticino and the Grisons, to preserve the Italian language and culture as well as Romansch. Though less than 1 percent of Swiss nationally speak Romansch, it is the primary language of almost one-fifth of the people in Grisons canton. Hence the Italian Swiss have some suspicion of the federal government, but also a certain affinity for it.

Yet these myriad divisions could simply balkanize the Swiss further. Furthermore, some of these same criss-crosses are present today in multilingual societies that do not enjoy Switzerland's harmony. So there must be added explanations and factors that explain why the system does not simply fly apart—some kind of binding that, while allowing freedom of movement, holds the parts together as well.

• *A history and ethic of inclusion.* Switzerland's tradition of accepting immigrants, small border states, and relying on foreign trade for much of its commerce has fostered a spirit of inclusion among the people and their institutions. The history is as old as 1291 and the effort of the Forest Cantons to form relationships with the powerful cities and peoples of Bern and Zürich, or accept Protestant and Jewish emigrés from Germany and France, and as recent as the repeated Swiss votes against efforts to set tight limits on immigration, and for promoting Romansch as an official language of Switzerland.

• *Foreign threats.* For many nations, foreign threats become a spur to ethnic rivalry—since many nations are based on, or have strong elements of ethnicity. For the Swiss, a multiethnic nation, foreign threats have generally functioned the other way around. It was ethnic or cultural nationalism and exclusionism that threatened from the outside. For the Swiss, unity against these threats meant unity, in part, in support of their own diversity.

This phenomenon has deep roots, but is also a product of recent experience. If not for the alliance with border areas, Switzerland would have been swallowed up by Austria, Italy, or Germany in the fifteenth through seventeenth centuries, or by the French in the seventeenth and eighteenth centuries—as they were, briefly, by France in the nineteenth century. In the twentieth century, of course, the threat from Germany led to a rallying against "Germanism" in Swiss culture and politics, symbolized by the building of the *Bundesbrief* Museum in 1935.

It is revealing that the one foreign invasion of Switzerland that succeeded in 1,000 years, the French occupation of the late eighteenth and early nineteenth centuries, was at the front of a powerful ideology—and a universalist, inclusionary ideology at that. By contrast, in 1914, when Swiss leaders wanted to rally the people against the Kaiser's Germany, the federal council issued a declaration rallying the people to Swiss values. Among them was "the ideal of our country as a cultural community and a political ideal above the diversity of race and language." Switzerland's French-speaking general in World War II insisted, "we are a people and culture of inclusion," in calling for a military "and philosophical" resistance to Nazism.

- *Elite leadership, and popular acceptance of it.* Swiss elites have long held a more or less self-consciously liberal view, in the European sense, on the matter of dealing with diversity. This holds on questions from trade and immigration to their own children's education. It is a common practice, for example, among German-speaking Swiss to send their children abroad for a year or two to improve their French or (popular in recent years) English. Many German-speaking Swiss attend a university, or take a first job, in the French-speaking region.

Arend Lijphart, the sociologist who first coined the term "consociational democracy," goes so far as to say that this leadership is the key to effective acceptance of diversity. This may go a bit too far. At best, it ignores the critical question of why Swiss elites have been able to achieve such a positive sum outlook, while those in many other countries seem to feel they have more to gain by engaging in divisive, winner-take-all politics. The Swiss open door, moreover, was not always laid out by elites first. During World War II, for instance, it was the Swiss people who allowed thousands of Jewish children (and in some cases their parents) over the border and into their homes. In so doing they went against government policy and, in fact, suffered occasional arrests by the border police.

Nevertheless it is true that Swiss leaders have adopted a generally liberal attitude, and have a proud record of leadership on such questions. Once again, the unusual degree of harmony between people and elites in Switzerland, the mutual respect unusual even in democratic societies, makes it very difficult to say who is leading whom.

Deliberate Policies

The most visible and most important means by which the Swiss deliberately encourage pluralistic harmony is through the schools. Instruction in a second national language is mandatory, and in a third and even fourth language is now the common practice, especially given the popularity and importance of English.

In a 1973 survey of Swiss twenty years of age or older, two-thirds had a working knowledge of at least one other official language. Sixty-five percent of German-speaking Swiss had a working knowledge of French, and 52 percent of French-speaking Swiss were capable in German. Today the figures are higher in each category, and as well, there are large numbers of Swiss who are capable in English: More than 60 percent according to official data, and more than 70 percent in my experience, which probably accepts a lower level of English as constituting some capability. Dozens of Swiss told me they were "not very good in English, but willing to use English"—and then proceeded to converse with high fluency.

This formal training is buttressed by Swiss arts, newspapers, and other teachers from the school of life and culture. Most Swiss movie theaters carry French movies with German subtitles and German movies with French subtitles. Italian films and Italian subtitling is not ubiquitous, but normally applies to 5 or 10 percent of the offerings in any major German city, and more in the French zones. The result is an easy way for students or adults to polish one language or another. Newspaper stands, television, and other mass media offer a similar range of cross-translated materials, now supplemented by the Internet. Much of this activity would take place without government assistance; some would not. The government aid, as much as adding sheer resources, gives a stamp of approval and makes a statement that this is valuable activity. The combined message of this policy and the private activities is that serious Swiss citizens should be able to communicate in two languages or more.

An important concept that contributes to Swiss harmony is the principle of territoriality. Under this principle, the language of instruction for schools, the first language of discourse for public facilities and government agencies, and so on are all set by the canton or the community. Furthermore, this language, as set, is not to be challenged. Hence if in a particular district, the number of French-speaking Swiss was to change from 47 percent to 53 percent, this would not imply a change in the official language structure. It would remain German.

This feature of medium-term immutability is not written down; it is a tacit arrangement, a *modus vivendi*. It is, however, no less powerful for being understood rather than explicit. It is, in fact, likely that if a much larger shift were to occur in the language of usage, it might, like other elements of Swiss politics, eventually be adjusted. The formula by which seats on the executive council were allocated for fifty years, for instance, appeared on the verge of change after the 1999 Swiss elections. One thing the principle would definitely rule out, however, in its subtle way, would be any sort of agitation of the question; such arrangements, once reached, tend to remain in place until circumstances have long since rendered them clearly obsolete. And by then, they are so clearly obsolete that the thing is changed with minimal fanfare or excitement.

The great Swiss jurist Walter Burckhardt describes the subtle way in which this practice can fairly be called a policy, and yet, is not a matter of statute or regulation:

> It is now a tacitly recognized principle that each locality should be able to retain its traditional language... and that linguistic boundaries once settled should not be shifted, neither to the detriment of the majority nor of minorities. It is trust in this tacit

agreement that provides a foundation for peaceful relations.... Adherence to this rule, as well as respect of each group for the individuality of the others, is an obligation of Swiss loyalty. It is no less sacred because it is not laid down in law; it is one of the foundations of the state itself.

This implicit understanding, avoiding the persistent churning and reopening of certain arrangements, is critical to making the principle of territoriality work to defuse conflicts—rather than set off new ones. If a society were to merely emulate Swiss federalism as a negative concept—letting states and localities select their own language, but allowing this to change on a regular basis—it is easy to see that the result could be the very opposite of the social peace enjoyed by the Swiss. Shifting populations would render temporary majorities tenuous, and there would be constant battles in districts with evenlybalanced minority populations. It was this dynamic, in part, that rendered the Kansas-Nebraska Act so odious to Abraham Lincoln and the American Republicans in the 1850s, as against the Missouri Compromise setting out accepted slave and free territories. Efforts at mere federalism, especially with unit rule and spoils systems, can provoke new conflicts rather than solving them.

This is an illustration of the dangers of adapting Swiss institutions or lessons piecemeal into different situations. Swiss federalism takes place in a cultural and social context. Of course, this is an argument for care in adapting them—not for ignoring these precious lessons merely because they are not an exact, test-tube match for situations elsewhere. He who ignores history, because it contains slight variations from his own situation, is condemned to repeat it, with slight variations.

The Swiss do not give minority languages, institutions, and cultures their due. They strive to give them a little more than their due. Swiss majority groups do not demand what they have coming. They demand a little less, and take comfort in their secure position as a majority.

This approach by both minority and majority groupings is another policy or tendency—or an element of many policies—that helps explain much of Switzerland's ability to thrive on diversity. The Swiss do this in both political situations such as the policies mentioned for language, and in social ones, such as the gentle race to find a person's first language and put him at ease by using it.

"No effort whatsoever is made by the Swiss Germans, who are in the overwhelming majority numerically, to assert any linguistic dominance," writes Kurt Mayer. "There are no linguistic minorities, either in a legal or in an informal sense."

Carol Schmid has an excellent term for this, suggesting that Swiss linguistic and religious majorities often "do not act like majorities." Or, one might say, they act as confident majorities—majorities that are not threatened by the rights of minorities, and gladly allow them to flourish. When asked what foreign country they would most like to live in, French-speaking Swiss, not surprisingly, named France first (45 percent), followed by Holland (22 percent), and Austria (10 percent). Interestingly, though, German-speaking Swiss also listed France first (30 percent), followed in this case by Austria (23 percent), and Holland (17 percent).

Perhaps Schmid's most interesting and certainly original evidence of this comes from her survey, mentioned previously, in which she asked members of the three major language groups to estimate what share of the Swiss population belongs to each group. For example, she asked German-speaking Swiss to estimate how many Swiss speak German as their primary language, how many speak Italian, and how many speak French. Then she repeated this procedure with speakers of French. By large majorities, both French- and German-speaking Swiss overestimated how many Swiss speak one of the minority languages (French or Italian), and members of both groups underestimated how many Swiss speak German.

In most other multilingual societies, the exact opposite phenomenon is seen. Estimates of minority population and culture tend to understate the presence of the minority, and overstate the majority. The minority groups feel aggrieved, besieged, and hence their presence as smaller than it really is. The majority feels a certain arrogance, overestimating its own strength. The Swiss have escaped both tyranny of the majority and tyranny of the minority, with both the minority and the majority acting as if they were on a rough par.

The Swiss are similarly tolerant of religion, even in their government institutions, in a way the United States, Canada, and much of Europe are not. Diversity of religion includes individual rights to worship in the church of a citizen's choice, and freedom from having religious views or practices imposed. But diversity also includes a respect for religious displays and practices by official policies. Religion and atheism, worship and nonworship, are on an equal playing field.

In their classic *History of Civilization*, Will and Ariel Durant ascribe much of the violence of the French Revolution to the preceding repression of the ancient regime. By cracking down on dissent so severely for so long, they argue, the French kings created a cauldron of deep resentments. Once it boiled over, it did so with vengeance. It may be that modern post-religious cultures are emulating the same error (though only to a slight degree, to be sure) in their treatment of the remaining religious elements of society. Clamped down on until they feel little room to breathe, regarded contemptuously by elite culture and official institutions, the religious of the United States, for example, have begun a highly politicized counter-revolution in the form of the Christian Right. This minority feels, at any right, that it must fight an aggressive war for survival and recognition.

The Swiss have avoided these errors. Thus—probably not by accident—while the Swiss have a substantial number of orthodox Catholics and socially conservative Protestants, these groups do not feel under siege the way such groups do in the United States, Canada, parts of Europe, and much of Latin America. The toleration of community standards and religious practices, while shielding the right of the individual to abstain from them, has left both the religious and nonreligious comfortable that their status is respected and secure.

The relative lack of involvement of the courts—the least democratic of institutions even in Switzerland, though not nearly so remote as in most democracies—has helped as well. Swiss religious policies, since the constitution of 1848, have for the most part been worked out through institutions such as the referendum, and to some extent the different legislatures, that are highly democratic. Thus not only the substantive solution, but the procedure, for finding workable agreements about religion, have been populist and participatory in nature.

The bottom-up nature of this elaborate patchwork of compromises, worked out over many years, makes it difficult to picture its direct transfer to other societies—perhaps even dangerous, as in the example of federalism's two-edged sword. But the basic spirit—of real tolerance (indeed, embracing) of all sorts of persons and ideas, including the politically incorrect—may hold deep lessons for other Western countries, not to mention universities, corporations, unions, churches, and other institutions.

Indirect Policies and Impacts

Tolerance, federalism, live and let live—all these concepts, while laudable, impart a negative or at best minimalist sense of how the Swiss deal with diversity. These connote a kind of grudging social armistice, in which warring factions, while they cannot agree, can at least "agree to disagree" to go their own way and leave one another alone.

In fact, the Swiss have achieved this minimalist respect for individuality and separate communities. But they have achieved more than this. The key to Swiss "tolerance" of diversity is that the Swiss, in fact, embrace diversity. More than that, they embrace (and take pride in) the ability of their democracy, and their ability as people, to have worked out such a highly functional social contract amidst such divisions.

It is not merely that the Swiss have decided to accept such cleavages. Rather, they have a real, substantive unity behind certain principles, such as civil freedom and political equality. In this sense, the Swiss appear, more than any other country, to have an actual "body politic," an organic cooperation of the social parts. It is not that the liver merely "tolerates" the heart, or the lungs "obey" the brain. The organs cooperate.

Common ideals are the most important fact in Switzerland's collaboration of the parts. None of these was invented as a conscious effort to manage diversity, nor would they work very well if they were. But whenever we tug very hard on one of the policies or principles, such as federalism, that seems a partial explanation of Swiss comity, we find these deeper dynamics of unity and idealism at work behind them.

The lesson for other societies may be that an appreciation of diversity is a thing best captured not by chasing around after it in a mad search, but instead by building unity and a shared body of principles. Happy diversity, like personal happiness, may be something that is best attained indirectly.

One of the most important factors identified by Ms. Schmid in her study of Swiss diversity is the way its highly accessible democracy encourages criss-crossing political coalitions and cooperation. Significantly, because of the number of decisions reached by direct democracy at the federal, cantonal, and community levels, much of this criss-crossing is popular in nature—people reaching agreement and working with people across different religious, linguistic, and other "divides."

"There is a recurrent tendency," as Schmid notes, "for French Switzerland to join forces with the Catholic forces of German Switzerland in opposing measures they feel to be either too centralizing or threatening to local autonomy." Swiss politics on the European Union, to take a highly current example, have brought together coalitions of greens, religious groups concerned with local autonomy, and others in opposition to early efforts at Swiss membership. The same issue has promoted combinations of business interests and blue collar workers in parts of French—and German—speaking Switzerland in favor of a more aggressive effort at integration.

Swiss voting on issues of diversity itself have produced unifying cross-alliances. When the Jura, a Catholic region of what was then Bern canton, wished to form its own separate canton, Swiss voters of all different religious and language groupings voted overwhelmingly for the constitutional amendment necessary to create the new state.

"Thus, although the referendum process is not a device for minority recognition as such," Schmid concludes, "its operation has enabled the religious and linguistic minorities to combine for structural reasons." Schmid's emphasis on direct democracy as a key sociological device is impressive because she does not appear to be seeking that conclusion. Rather one feels part of an unexpected and intriguing discovery.

The Swiss army, like the referendum, is a great civic melting pot. It brings together all male youths from the age of eighteen onward—and continues the process, for most of them, for thirty years. Included in this are the conventions by which officers address individual soldiers in their primary language, whenever practicable, and other policies directly having to do with the treatment of diversity.

In his study of America, Tocqueville was impressed by the effect that juries had as a kind of "training ground" for citizenship. Yet jury service is a rare event for Americans, something most of us will experience once or twice, for a few days, in our life. The Swiss army, as we have seen, permeates social, business, and political relationships in a populist way—not through money or interlinking interests or conflicts but through people, cooperating in a national enterprise. The importance of the Swiss army—both as a practical experience, and in the institutional message it sends to all citizens as equals and necessary contributors—cannot be overestimated.

Indeed, when we consider the activity generated by these Swiss institutions, the phrase "cross-cutting cleavages," a favorite of sociologists, emerges as too static, as insufficiently vital, to convey what is going on. An improvement on such phrases might be "cross-pollination," or "criss-crossing association-building." Swiss diversity is not sterile, but active.

Over and above these operational impacts of institutions like the referendum and the militia system is something still more profound—a real national consciousness based on shared principles.

One such concept is the principle of a nation based on principle—rather than ethnicity or language or economic interest alone—in and of itself. This is the Swiss idea of *Willensnation*. In some ways, it is difficult for other countries to even understand let alone emulate this concept. America is an exception because it, too, is a Willensnation, a nation of ideals whose ancestors, as Bill Murray once put it, "were kicked out of all the best countries in Europe." Upon reflection, however, it is not clear why the presence of a certain ethnic affinity in countries like Germany, Russia, or France, would not allow for national pride and identity based on a shared vision of good. And these are nations no longer rent by fatal internal divisions anyway. Countries such as Nigeria, South Africa, and India will have no basis in national unity unless they can forge pride in their accomplishments and principles—there is no ethnic, religious, or even linguistic unity to start from. While a Swiss- or American-style act of national and individual wills is obviously not in the prospect for them in the short term, it is what they must strive for.

Another important factor is Swiss neutrality. This includes not only neutrality as a foreign affairs policy, but as a kind of national-personal ethos of the Swiss—the act of self-abnegation and renunciation of vast schemes or imprudent efforts. What Switzerland has decided is a prudent realization of its limited influence as a nation, most Swiss have internalized as a matter of their individual philosophy. Their motto is the song of Psalm 119, "Yahweh, my heart knows no lofty ambitions; my eyes do not look too high."

Konrad Falke provided an insightful description of this national-personal philosophy in his work, *Das demokratische Ideal und unser nationale Erziehung*:

> It makes a tremendous difference whether man has been brought up to the thought: "You belong to a great power which one day must fight for world supremacy," or

whether he must always say to himself: "If it should come finally to fighting, we can hope for nothing better than to keep what we already have." This is the influence of the politics of a people upon its ethical attitude, and in the latter is influenced by the former. In this mutual action and reaction, the character of a people is formed.

It is these and other deeply shared beliefs and experiences that enable many Swiss to credibly say, as *Corriere Del Ticino* editor Giancarlo Dillena insists, "We are not a multi-cultural country. A respect for these differences, and an appreciation of a country where they can coexist—this is part of one, national Swiss culture. A pride in our democracy, our direct democracy, and a deep love for it—these are traits of nearly all Swiss."

This certainly appears to be the case on the basis of survey data and other broad surveys of national attitudes. When asked an open-ended question about their reasons for being proud to be Swiss, most named some element of the political system, such as direct democracy. This answer, provided by nearly 60 percent of Swiss, was larger than any other two answers, and almost as large as the next three most frequent answers combined. It is evidence, summarized in Figure 19.1, that the Swiss have a deeply shared ethos—and an optimism about "politics" perhaps unmatched in the world.

Yes, as Schmid concludes, "there are a number of accidental and human factors" that have enabled the Swiss to thrive on diversity. But to a large extent, "the so-called 'fortunate accidents' have often been more attributable to public policy."

Figure 19.1

Reasons for Pride in Being Swiss

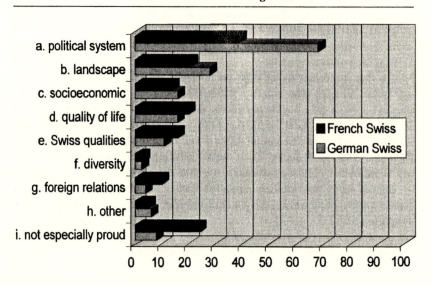

Whatever the causes, Switzerland has managed to make diversity into a strength—arguably a major source of Switzerland's greatness.

Business is only one example, but a prominent one. The Swiss facility with different languages has made them a natural power in the emerging world of global business. In an age with a premium on information, the Swiss are expert listeners. Meanwhile, as science locates new wonders, but in different languages, the Swiss are quick to assimilate its lessons—and to generate their own innovations as well. This is seen by the country's highly disproportionate share of Nobel science prizes and international patents.

Swiss investment bankers enjoy an edge not only because of the country's privacy, but because they are able to make people from many different cultures and countries feel comfortable that their needs are being heard, and will be met. Swiss manufacturers of products from chocolates to major engineering projects are able to reach markets no monolingual Frenchman, German, or American can. These countries may, indeed are likely, to eventually close the gap with the Swiss in terms of formal language instruction. But they may never be able to capture the full advantage enjoyed by a Swiss who lives his entire life, and most of every day, in a multi-lingual environment.

Ironically, perhaps—since they already have to deal with four official languages—the Swiss leaped past much of Europe in becoming a nation skilled in English, the new version of Latin as the language of international business, politics, and culture. Some years ago when a merger was announced involving Union Bank of Switzerland (which joined with Swiss Bank Corporation), many Swiss employees of the bank were informed in a press release and employee memorandum that was, revealingly, written in English. Statistics suggest perhaps 50 percent of Swiss are capable in English. In my experience, the number of Swiss that had a workable competency was somewhere closer to 70 percent—80 percent or more in the cities and in service industries there, and still between 40 percent and 60 percent even in relatively remote (and sparsely populated) areas.

As the Internet and other tools of global communication yield greater physical efficiencies, the remaining costs of dealing across languages and borders, even if declining in absolute terms, will be an even higher percentage of the remaining costs of transaction in the world. There will be even more of a premium on being able to communicate—to listen and talk, literally to "share"—over and above those remaining barriers.

Far more important than the Swiss facility with language as such, with words and symbols, is the ethic behind it. Ultimately, what the Swiss emphasis on crossing various language and other barriers teaches is a certain view of the person who is speaking the language. Swiss respect for religion is not a respect for a building, but the people inside it.

Notes

1. From Schmid's important study of Swiss social relations, *Conflict and Consensus in Switzerland*, University of California Press, 1981.
2. For instance, my Swiss friends are somewhat divided on the question of whether it is advisable for an American to address a letter to a person of some stature in business or the government in German or English. (Particularly, let us say, someone not acquainted to the American, who may speak English but may not.) The majority opinion holds for English, because any awkwardness in the German will make the exercise seem strained, and as well, as one Swiss put it, "it is insulting to the person to act as if they can't speak English." But a significant minority leans toward German, especially in light of my argument that "a Swiss would write a letter to me in English, normally, and this is merely the reciprocal or symmetrical courtesy."

Part 5

L'Idee Suisse

20

The End of History and the Next Citizen

"The people can never willfully betray their own interests; but they may possibly be betrayed by the representatives of the people."—*The Federalist*, No. 63

There is little point in studying Swiss democracy unless there is something distinctive about it—and not only distinctive, but importantly distinctive. If this is a bad assumption, then Switzerland is worth thinking about
only for the specialist. The historian interested in quaintness, in a land of
cheese and chocolates, will find it diverting but not terribly urgent. The
economist who would like to emulate the country's material economic success may find a survey of its institutions of use. What is more, as an age of
global communications and national integration sets in, we might expect
even these points of distinction to gradually decline, not sharpen, in signifi-
cance.

In that case, to paraphrase author Francis Fukiyama, then not only is the
world-historical evolution over, but it ends in Sweden or Chile. A few economic variables may alter, but the political structure and the guiding spirit of
the system are identical and unchanged. Either in the "nanny state" feared by
Alexis de Tocuqeville or the new libertarian world announced in the pompous commercials of the high-tech Internet and cellular communications companies, it is the end of history.

There is, of course, a very different possibility. It may be that Swiss democracy, while resembling European and American democracy in many features,
and most of its superficial ones, is so divergent in a few vital particulars that
it offers a meaningful alternative to the parliamentary democracies of Europe
and much of Asia, and the presidential democracies of the United States and
most of the Americas.

Certainly it tends in a different direction. This is made clear if one merely
mentions the possibility of greater use of direct democracy in the United

251

States or Europe. Immediately, from most elites anyway, one encounters a mildly hostile reaction. Interestingly, though, the reasons raised against direct democracy nearly all could be used, and in earlier times were used, to argue against the American Revolution; to argue it could not be extended elsewhere; to deny the vote to blacks, women, and other groups deemed insufficiently educated, or otherwise "not ready" as a cultural or traditional matter for democracy.

If so, it is indeed an irony that just at the moment that nearly all proclaim the historical triumph of democracy, it becomes clear that we may not even know what we mean when we say, "democracy has triumphed."[1] And it may make a difference to know which type of democracy has won. First, it may matter because the types of democracy may have important differences. Second, it may even affect the survivability of "democracy" to know which version of it will cover the globe in fifty or one-hundred years. Will it be the highly populist, accessible, citizen's democracy of the Swiss; the relatively elitist, difficult-to-access system of Britain, Japan, or Germany; or some amalgam or mix, such as the American system? The latter, by both design and accident, stands somewhat in between—closer, perhaps, in assumption and present location to the European elitist democracies, but on a gradual path of movement toward a more Swiss version over much of its history.

Is there an important difference between Swiss democracy and the others? If we consider the discussion of democracy among Western and developing-country elites, we certainly would come to this conclusion.

Among U.S. and European elites, for example, there is little interest in political reforms that would increase popular leverage over government. While many reforms are under discussion, they tend to be elitist in nature. Some favor term limits, some favor spending limits, some favor greater power to local and state governments or to private economic interests—but none places much emphasis on increasing popular access and elite accountability to the whole people. Instead, the stress is on different arrangements of power within the existing array of elite institutions. This is not to say none of those reforms would be beneficial, and surely some of them would be bad—but as a matter of fact, none of them even focuses much on popular leverage. As Tocqueville noted, many "democratic" episodes and reform periods are merely "weapons" used to defend the old regime.

When a group of elites does discuss the Swiss system of initiative and referendum, it is generally with nervous contempt—such a system would not be desirable other than under the highly specific conditions of Switzerland, and certainly, the people in the country under discussion "may not be ready for it yet." This applies even to the leadership class of such highly developed countries as the United States and Europe. Their proposals are always couched in terms of "the people," as are most appeals in a democracy, representative or direct. But any direct means of empowering the people to run the government is considered unimportant, even contemptible. The only type of popular empowerment that holds much interest is that which is achieved indirectly, by placing greater control on some other elite group. Thus a system already choking with indirection and elite maneuverings is to be reformed through indirection and maneuvering.

The thing one seldom hears Western leaders of either the right or left say, however, is that establishing a more populist or citizen's democracy would not matter. For all the proclamations that the Internet, the fax machine, or some other gizmo will change the nature of democracy, few of the evangelists ever suggest using these new devices to permit greater voter input directly on policy. When they do, there is a hopeful silence, and a preference to talk about other things.

This becomes all the more striking if we consider the popular frustration with democracy common in many of the democracies today—just as democracy seemingly is at its historical and material zenith. In the United States, Britain, and Germany, public opinion surveys show widespread dissatisfaction with the political system. In recent U.S. elections, for instance, leading members of both parties have attacked the system as corrupted by money—William Clinton in his 1992 campaign against the "greed" of the Reagan-Bush years, the Republicans in their efforts to impeach Clinton over various sexual and financial scandals, and such recent presidential candidates as John McCain and Bill Bradley in their efforts to place limits on "soft money" donations.

The votes McCain and Bradley received are dismissed by some because these challengers were not able to secure their party's nomination. But the strength of their campaigns, particularly the previously little-known Senator McCain, speaks to the powerful urge for change felt by many Americans.

In focus groups and surveys, people express a rage at the system's immobility, feelings that democracy (in America and Europe) is unresponsive to their concerns and frustrations. These findings are highly important to a discussion of representative democracy as against direct forms. They suggest an impatience with the filtering devices and indirection meant, in some sense deliberately, to temper popular opinion. Elite opinion shares some of this analysis, though leading press, business, and political figures are naturally more sanguine about a system that they have the money or clout to access. In February of 2000, *The Wall Street Journal* even ran an article extolling pork-barrel politics as a key part of the democratic system—confusing that which is necessary evil with that which is good, of course, but in a revealing way that pushes the logic of representative democracy to its logical conclusion.

In a prescient article in *The Economist* at the dawn of the new democratic discussion, Brian Beedham predicted this rise of, and rage at, the lobbyist—at least for the representative or indirect democracies. With the end of the Cold War, he wrote (1993):

The old central question that is asked at election-time—which of these two noncompatible systems of politics and economics do you prefer, and how does your preference bear upon the decisions that must now be taken?—has disappeared. What is left of the agenda of politics is, by comparison, pretty humdrum. It deals for the most part with relatively minor differences of opinion over economic management, relatively small altercations over the amount and direction of public spending, and so on.... The new politics is full of dull detail.

It is therefore ideal ground for that freebooter of the modern political world—the lobbyist. The two most dramatic things that have happened to the developed world since the end of the second world war—its huge increase in wealth. and its explosion of information technology—have had as big an effect on politics as they have had on everything else. The lobbyists, the people who want to influence governments and parliaments on behalf of special interests, now command more money than they ever did before. They also have at their disposal a new armoury of persuasion in the computer, the fax machine, and the rest of it.

In the new agenda of politics, where so much depends upon decisions of detail, the power of the lobbyist can produce striking results. It will at times be, literally, corrupting. But even when it is not as bad as that it will make representative democracy seem increasingly inadequate. The voter, already irritated at having so little control over his representatives between elections, will be even angrier when he discovers how much influence the special-interest propagandists are now able to wield over those representatives. An interloper, it will seem, has inserted himself into the democratic process. The result is not hard to guess. The voter is liable to conclude that direct democracy, in which decisions are taken by the whole people, is better than representative democracy, because the many are harder to diddle—to bribe—than the few.[2]

This is not to suggest that there is no such thing as the lobbyist, the demagogue, or the corrupt politician in Switzerland. They do appear, however, to be somewhat less of a factor, and when they are, their presence, surrounded as they are by a system of greater popular access and more popular checks, gives less offense. Most important, the shape of lobbying and electioneering takes a different tone and shape, and it focuses on different objects, than in representative democracy.

In Switzerland, by contrast, people asked an open-ended question about what makes them proud about their country were more likely to give an answer having to do with their political system than were the next several answers combined.[3] This is a rough reversal of the increasingly cynical view of politics today—and even the system—in the United States and Europe.

Comparing the salient features of the Swiss system to that of other, more indirect democracies, we see some clear differences. Indeed, Swiss democracy appears to be more different from any other democracy, than all the others differ among themselves. The distinction may be even more sharp than when Tocqueville observed the Swiss system in the 1830s and 1840s, or Bryce in the early 1920s.

If democracies were a lot of used automobiles, we would not find the Swiss model differing only in having a different color from most, or a somewhat distinctive tail-fin or external appearance. The very means of locomotion and direction—the engine and the steering apparatus, and one might even say, the animating spirit—are different.

This difference is masked by the fact that all democracies have voting, judges, some form of representation, and some degree of popular access, of course. Even so, the differences are quite stark, as becomes clear if we consider the process by which certain critical and certain typical decisions are made by the different democratic types—and whether such decisions can be made by the people, must be made by the people, or cannot be made by the people at all except through some intermediating elite.

These differences are reviewed in Table 20.1. There are, perforce, generalizations made, but in its broad strokes, the figure presents an accurate review of some of the key distinctions.

"Who commits acts of sovereignty," as Tocqueville noted in analyzing the Swiss political scene in a report to the French parliament, "is sovereign." Tocqueville based his report on two visits to Switzerland, the first in 1836, the second in 1847 and early 1848—just before the unexpectedly rapid conclusion of a federal constitution whose basic provisions have now governed the Swiss for more than 150 years.

Tocqueville was nervous about the prospects for Swiss democracy, or for a nation of Switzerland, because the national government made so few acts of sovereignty. As we have observed earlier, Switzerland had federalism, at this point in time, in great measure, but little in the way of a unifying central government. Tocqueville worried, as did many Swiss, that absent some such strong central government—which the Swiss feared—the confederation could not hold together.

Tocqueville's principle, however, applies not only to different divisions of government or different elite bodies but to the division of sovereign acts between the people and their representatives—between direct and indirect democracy. Indeed, had he lived much longer, Tocqueville would have seen both the formation of a more coherent Swiss government, and the extension of a principle that was to give the central government greater sphere for "acts of sovereignty"—national referendum and initiative. In effect, for this highly decentralized country, initiative and referendum may have been a key legitimizing device which made action by the central and even to some extent the cantonal governments a palatable thing—as any future encroachments could be checked by the people.

Applying Tocqueville's observation to this realm of popular versus elite action, of government by citizens versus government of citizens, we see that the people of Switzerland are sovereign in a way the people of France, Japan, Russia, Germany, and the United States are not. This is not to say that the ultimate answerability of elected officials to the people, in periodic elections over many issues, is not important. Nor does it mean that the people of Swit-

Table 20.1

Sovereign Acts in Direct and Representative Democracies

Act of sovereignty	Swiss "direct democracy"	U.S.-European "representative democracy"
Pass a law	People may have direct vote	People have no direct role
Challenge a law passed by parliament or congress	People can do directly (referendum)	People cannot do directly; a law can be challenged only through their representatives
Pass a treaty	Requires popular vote	No role for popular vote at all unless government desires it as a special measure
Alter the constitution	People can do directly with no elite support (initiative) and must approve for any change to be made	Some elite must initiate (Congress or convention) and a direct popular vote plays no role (ratification is by 3/4 of state legislatures)
Choose chief executive	People vote only through parliament	People vote directly (in some countries) or more directly (in the U.S.)
Send criminal to jail	People through a randomly selected jury	People through a randomly selected jury
Confer citizenship	Popular (communal or cantonal) vote	Decision of magistrate (usually unelected)
Declare federal law unconstitutional	Arguably impossible; in practice happens only when constitution is altered—which requires a popular vote	Can be done by unelected court (U.S., Germany, France, other)

zerland exercise pure democratic rule: They don't, and instead rely on a number of representative institutions to make certain decisions and carry on certain acts. But these are not the only considerations. Surely to understand a governmental system one must ask such questions as, "Who actually has the final yes or no? Who sets the initial choices that are on the agenda? Who does these things directly, by an act of their own will? And who, while they may influence the sovereign, must act indirectly, by influencing his or her superior?" It is in the way we answer these sorts of questions that Swiss democracy seems importantly different from its Western counterparts.

These distinctions become even clearer when we consider the one awful and difficult question, "Where is the bottom line? Who ultimately acts as sovereign?" This is, perforce, not a question that can be answered by recourse to mathematical formulae. Political power is often used without being visible—as when a threatened veto of a bill by the president makes it unnecessary for him to issue a veto at all; or when an idea is known to be so popular that it must be passed even if there is no direct consultation of the people on the question; or when a congressional committee kills a bill not by voting it down, but by deciding not to have a vote. Beyond the elusiveness of political acts, we have the general correspondence in form between so much of Swiss democracy and the other democracies. All vote, all have some manner of representation. All have a division of power between three or four branches of government, and all have some distinction between executive, legislative, judicial branches, as well as some sort of civil service that is not subject to change by election.

Even so, one can make the case that the fundamental, animating spirit of Swiss direct democracy is the people, the citizen—in a way that U.S. democracy, and more so European democracy, do not experience. Table 20.2 compares the character of popular consultation in direct democracy (Switzerland) with that in representative democracies (a composite sketch of the United States and major European democracies plus Japan). While one might cavil about the particulars, there is little avoiding the conclusion that Swiss democracy places greater trust in popular rule, and the other democracies, substantially less so.

The consultation with the public is more frequent in Switzerland. It is much broader as to its scope, particularly in covering policy decisions. Yet on any given item, it is likely to admit of a much more particular intervention by the people. In the communes and some of the cantons, citizens may literally vote on whether to allow a new bridge, hire this schoolteacher, outlaw (or allow) gay marriages—and so on.

When an American or European votes, he more or less accepts a train of a hundred or a thousand votes that her or his representative promises to cast—and that assumes that the promise is kept, and covers only the issues that can be known, and forced to discussion, in the election. When the Swiss votes, he

Table 20.2

How "The People" Are Heard—
Direct versus Representative Democracy

Type of popular consultation	Swiss "direct democracy"	U.S.-European "representative democracy"
Federal or state (cantonal) elections— frequency	3-4 times a year in a typical canton—and more frequent "feedback" through referenda	1 time a year or less, on average—no other formal, systematic feedback
Direct votes on policy—approve or defeat acts of elites	Frequent: 2-3 times a year for national or cantonal policies	Infrequent; less than once a year; only in certain states; and none on federal policy.
Given the above, the nature of most campaigns for office or legislation, and of campaign spending is...	An ongoing, continuous effort to persuade voters—low key, and much of it coming through the press. Nearly all focused on the public, and on the public as an end in itself. Substantial fear of lost credibility or seeming shrillness, since any temporary victory in elite institutions can be overturned, and long-term losses of credibility with the public may cause immediate losses.	Short, concentrated bursts of highly emotional attempts to get the public's attention for a key vote— electing a president or representative—the results of which will then be permanent for 2, 4, or 6 years. Much focus on elites, much on public— but that focused on the public is only a means to an end, not an end in itself. The game is to sway legislators by raising their fear of the public.
Initiate legislation	Citizen can do so directly (initiative) or through his representatives	Citizen can only do so through his elected officials
How does a citizen's vote make itself felt on the national laws?	In large clumps, by voting on representatives, but also in small, focused decisions on dozens of policy questions (through referendum)	Only in large clumps— citizen can only make his voice felt by voting for officials who have taken dozens or hundreds of positions.

Table 20.2 (cont.)

Official blocking a piece of legislation can be circumvented by...	Initiative, referendum, and the influence that the threat of these works on all elected officials.	Only by throwing the official out in a multi-issue election several years hence, or swaying a vast number of elites (such as two-thirds of the Senate) to act.
Lawmaking body or committee that can avoid a vote on a subject has killed it?	No—see above.	Yes, in the overwhelming majority of cases.
Given the above, lobbyist who spends a fortune influencing a bill through Congress and the White House, or preventing it, has won—his money is well spent.	His money may be well spent, but may not be. Especially if the measure is significantly contrary to the public interest, he now faces having all his work overturned in a referendum challenge.	The lobbyist has spent his or her money well. The new law is law (or not law), assuming it is not overturned by another elite body, such as a federal court. The public has no direct recourse—angry citizens must try to make enough noise to convince lawmakers to overturn the decision.

accepts a large degree of judgment from his representative—but he also knows that many of that representative's decisions will be referred back to him for deliberation. And that his word, unlike that given to a pollster or congressional surveyor, has the potential to become the solemn law of the country.

The Swiss citizen even knows that if his representatives and the other representatives are ignoring a particular issue that is highly important to him—campaign finance reform, education vouchers, guaranteed health insurance, and others—he can force a national vote on the issue by collecting 100,000 signatures for a national initiative.

From the nature of how the citizen is dealt with flows the very different orientation of the two systems.

In direct or populist democracy, most persuasion is directed at the people, and such persuasion is an end in itself—it goes to the bottom line sovereign of the regime. In indirect or representative democracy there is more of an emphasis on reaching elites by arguing that the people want this or that—and when there is an effort at popular persuasion, which to be sure is common, the people are an ends, not a means; they are the way you put pressure on the Congress or the president or the bureaucracy to act.[4] The maxim of indirect or representative democracy is, "Write your congressman." The maxim of direct or populist democracy is, "vote yes (or no)."

The tool with which a citizen makes his voice felt in a representative democracy are the sledge-hammer and the megaphone. Lacking the means to commit acts of sovereignty himself or herself, the U.S. or European voter needs implements that can get others who have the power to act to do so. The tools of direct democracy are more in character with a scalpel—certainly not a perfectly sharp one, nor held by a perfect surgeon, in Switzerland. But it is possible for the citizen to cut right into government and remove this, or adjust that, organ.

Representative democracy is a noisy affair, because so much of the game involves even getting the attention of some elite, or forcing that elite to take action. It is a game in which other elites (big business, lobbyists, the press) seem to wield the only clout. Direct democracy is more quiet, and more characterized by appeals to reason. Anyone who doubts this need only witness a Swiss parliamentary or federal council election, read the campaign materials and press coverage of various referenda, or even simply compare the amounts spent on campaigns and public affairs persuasion and what it is spent on.[5]

In representative democracy, there is a greater temptation to blame the government, big business, foreigners, the media, or some other group for our problems. Swiss direct democracy has some of that temptation, but it is less— because the ultimate authority of the people is less ambiguous than in indirect systems. And with authority comes responsibility.

In representative democracy, there are constant appeals for the citizen to "pitch in"—in Switzerland, citizens appeal to themselves to pitch in, because citizens by and large run the local and cantonal and even federal government.

It is difficult to improve on Beedham's analysis, which has the added value of having been an early report on the new democratic debate:

> In much of the world, democracy is still stuck at a half-way house, as it were, in which the final word is delegated to the chosen few.... It has long been pointed out that to hold an election every few years is not only a highly imprecise way of expressing the voter's wishes (because on these rare election days he has to consider a large number of issues, and his chosen "representative" will in fact not represent him on several of them) but is also notably loose-waisted (because the voter has little control over his representative between elections) The end of the battle between communism and pluralism will make representative democracy look more unsatisfactory than ever....

Deciding things by vote of the whole people is not, to be sure, a flawless process. The voter in a referendum will find some of the questions put to him dismayingly abstruse (but then so do many members of parliament). He will be rather bored by a lot of the issues of postideological politics (but then he can leave them for parliament to deal with, if he is not interested enough to call for a referendum). He will be subjected, via television, to a propaganda barrage from the rich, high- tech special-interest lobbies (but he is in one way less vulnerable to the lobbyists' pressure than members of parliament are, because lobbyists cannot bribe the whole adult population).

On the other hand, direct democracy has two great advantages.

First, it leaves no ambiguity about the answer to the question: What did the people want? The decisions of parliament are ambiguous because nobody can be sure, on any given issue, whether a parliamentary majority really does represent the wishes of a majority of the people. When the whole people does the deciding, the answer is there for all to see.

Second, direct democracy sharpens the ordinary sense of political responsibility. When one has to make up his own mind on a wide variety of specific issues—the Swiss tackled 66 federal questions by general vote in the 1980s, hundreds of cantonal ones and an unknown number (nobody added them up) of local-community matters—he learns to take politics seriously.

Since the voter is the foundation-stone of any sort of democracy, representative or direct, anything that raises his level of political efficiency is profoundly to be desired.

Other factors in the new age make the case for democracy—and therefore, for direct democracy, its more pure application—even stronger, Beedham notes. One that he does not detail is the rise of the Internet and many other improvements in telecommunications. Of course, the same observations might have been made about the rise of printed books in the fifteenth century, newspapers and journals in the eighteenth century, telegraphs in the nineteenth century, and radio and television in the twentieth. At the least, however, the growth of global telecommunications further strengthens the case that voters are equipped to take on more and more tasks. Of course, in representative democracy, the ruling class retains more means of obscuring issues, delaying votes, and producing ambiguous results than does direct democracy. That is why the hosannahs proclaimed by some are so shallow—because without systemic change, these increases in communications technology may ultimately be frustrated. There were telephones, TV sets, and fax machines in Russia too, as there are personal computers in Communist China today. The important change came when Russia's leaders allowed the system to become more tolerant of and responsive to the potential of these tools.

So too, as Beedham does note, the backgrounds of voters around the world—educational, economic, and other—are becoming more amenable to an extension of democracy. "A hundred years ago fewer than 2 percent of Americans aged between 18 and 24 went to university; now more than a quarter do. The share of the British population that stayed in education beyond the age of 15 rose sevenfold between 1921 and 1992; in western Germany, between 1955 (when the country was still recovering from Hitler's war) and today, the increase was almost double that." Rising income in the world, and especially among the voters, has made education and general knowledge outside of formal classroom still further. "We are all middle class now," Beedham quotes a Western official—"Not quite; but we are surely headed that way." Indeed, he notes ironically, "the democracies must therefore apply to themselves the argument they used to direct against the communists. As the old differences of education and social condition blur, it will be increasingly hard to go on persuading people that most of them are fit only to put a tick on a ballot paper every few years, and that the handful of men and women they thereby send to parliament must be left to make all the other decisions."

What is likely to come in the implicit competition between direct and indirect democracy over the next fifty years? And, what should we hope will come—in short, which system appears to be better?

In answering both these questions, the analyst is hampered by the fact that so far, only the Swiss, as Tocqueville put it, have taken democracy "to such an extent" of populism. Nevertheless, it is not too early—especially given 1,000 years of Swiss history, and 200 years of American evolution in the *direction* of direct democracy—to make some meaningful speculations.

Of the likely direction of political evolution, it is nearly impossible to say where the experiment is likely to begin. But we can say with high confidence that experimentation with direct democracy is extremely likely—almost certain.

There are nearly 150 democracies in the world today. The vast majority, if not all, face a curiously urgent pressure to reform either for experiential reasons (the recent democracies Russia and the Eastern Bloc, and much of Latin America), spiritual ones (America and Europe), practical political ones (Japan, Korea, Indonesia, and all the way out to China in the still-authoritarian Asian world), or material ones (Africa, India, Latin America).

We may think, in fact, in terms of those regional-political groups, as we analyze the likely course of democracy—toward elitism, populism, or a muddled middle of relatively unchanging stasis (in political terms).

Western Europe, soon to be All-of-Europe, is closest to Swiss democracy in its politics and its material conditions, not to mention geography and language and common experience. It is, therefore, an obvious candidate for evolution towards the Swiss system. Europe has the least to fear from its affluent, well-informed citizens from allowing them a greater role in political decision making, and the flimsiest excuse for not doing so. As well, it has an obvious interest in both the negative side of federalism (letting communities go their own way where possible) and the positive side (finding political instruments of unity such as European referendum and initiative—as the Swiss did in the nineteenth century).

These pressures will be focused further by the process of European integration. While the pressure from the rest of Europe on the Swiss to conform to its elitist system is obvious, indeed blatant, there is an equal and obvious pressure imposed from Switzerland on the European Union and its components. This pressure is not an instrument of Swiss policy at all; indeed, the Swiss fear to mention it. But much as Hong Kong represents an enclave within China that must either be crushed or emulated, so the Swiss populist system is within Europe. In this sense, it is remarkable how little has changed over 1,000 years.

While much discussion focuses on whether Switzerland should and will join the European Union, there is the equally important question of whether the European Union will join Switzerland. It may be that the latter will be extremely helpful to the former—even essential.

It does not follow, however, that Europe will be the easiest system to reform, or the first to do so. The very fact that Western systems are so close to a populist, democratic breakthrough in popular access sets off powerful forces of resistance among those who like democracy the way it is—comparatively inaccessible, vis-à-vis the Swiss direct method. This does not imply any kind of conspiracy. In fact, it would be impossible for the far Left, far Right, and (most important) "extreme centrist" forces to work together to resist direct democracy—they disagree about too much. Rather, as any student of history knows, it is inertia and conventional wisdom that form the most powerful cabal. Or, to paraphrase a character from one of C.S. Lewis's novels, "Sometimes the most difficult heresy to combat is one very close to the truth." Furthermore, while Europe is the closest to a populist democratic system in terms of the sophistication and development of its people, it simultaneously faces the least pressure to reform.

Seldom in human affairs are revolutions made by those who need only move a bit to reach the new revolutionary principle. They are usually made by those who feel they may be about to fall over a cliff—and will grasp at any expedient to stay in power.

Does anyone believe, for instance, that the Soviet Union was closer to democracy than China was in the late 1980s? My own analysis of this matter, in *The Democratic Imperative*, was that China was much closer to Western-style freedom up until Tienanmen Square—and, in fact, Tienanmen Square proves how close China was. Yet the country has now lapsed back into a more profound authoritarianism, while Russia, for all its economic clumsiness, has passed through many of the hard choices and difficult transitions of trusting in the people.

The greatest likelihood of some European emulation of the Swiss system is that it will come about through necessity in some Eastern Bloc country, a Russia or Poland. The next most likely dynamic would be a European Union adoption of federalism and Euro-nationalism—a European-wide referendum, limited by subject, but used as a unifying device in the formation of the new

European Nation. The Swiss themselves are often unimaginative about this matter—they see their own helplessness in material terms, but often fail to understand the power of an idea, however small its application. Thus one Swiss author, considering the evolution of Europe, writes that "in the long run, Europe and Switzerland must merge into one system." Indeed they must—or, since nothing is inevitable in human affairs, they are likely to—but on whose terms? Whether Europe joins the Swiss, or the Swiss join Europe; whether China emulates Hong Kong, or Hong Kong is swallowed by China—these are open questions. They will be settled, like all human history, by a combination of forces, brilliant personalities, and chance.

My own best guess is that there will be a European union, and it will be closer to the Swiss system in principle. If my ideas can be proven right or wrong by the record of prediction, this is one test for those ideas to stand on.

By a similar logic, the United States is even closer to Switzerland—and yet, by the same token, some greater evolutionary distance away at the same time. There are two reasons, however, to suspect that the U.S., even closer to the Swiss democracy, may yet move toward it with even greater haste.

There are many forces which argue against this. One of them is the two dominant political parties. Only occasionally does a populist Republican, a Reagan, Kemp, or Roosevelt, break through the tone-deaf ethos of GOP elitism. For the most part, this is the party of "Bush, Eisenhower, and the golf course," as one foresighted author wrote in 1989.

The Democratic Party, though still mired in the economics of class warfare, has evolved significantly, and may offer a better road to consultative democracy than the Republicans. It is perhaps significant that the first proposal to extend Internet technologies to new institutional applications—the digital democracy proposal of Congressman Jesse Jackson, Jr.—came out of the Democratic Party.

A third possible avenue for the concepts of direct democracy is for some complete outsider to work under a banner of political reform. This might be a third party, though recent U.S. third parties, while speaking in populist rhetoric, have in fact had little to say about political reform from a popular access perspective. More likely, it would come from a complete outsider—a businessman, journalist, or independent state politician who has a deep faith not in centrism, in placing himself in the middle of Left and Right elites, but in populism, the wisdom of the people.

It is hard to picture any of these three major parties making a major issue of direct democracy. But the latent interest in political reform among the American people is so strong that it would only take one leader.

Against all this, moreover, are some strong reasons to suspect that the United States will be the next great theater of advancement for direct democracy—if not the next, the next major and pivotal theater.

America enjoys a strong tradition of political entrepreneurship and experimentation. A developed, "European" society, America was nevertheless the first country to emulate the Swiss experiment with referendum—though only at the state level, a critical exception. In the late nineteenth century, America added direct election of Senators. In the twentieth century came voting rights for women and blacks. America, to a degree Europe outside of Switzerland is not, is a nation of immigrants, a cauldron of new people and new ideas. Small-business startups and entrepreneurship are traditionally higher per capita. America, to paraphrase Gertrude Stein, remains animated by the philosophy, "make it new."

Perhaps most important, in the last fifty years, is the U.S. system of presidential and party primaries. Lacking in the parliamentary systems in Europe, the U.S. enjoys an ease of access at the front end not seen in most of Europe. This access is only for persons, not for ideas, but anyway, it matters.

It is difficult to imagine people like Jesse Ventura, Pat Buchanan, Ross Perot, Jesse Jackson—and especially, a Ronald Reagan—becoming major players in the European political scene. Rob Reiner (California anti-smoking initiative), Richard Gann (Proposition 13), or Polly Williams (Milwaukee voucher policy) are possible only in America—or Switzerland. Europe is very comfortable with the idea of combining the rhetoric of popular access with an elitist system of government. America has some of that tradition, but also a vast experience at punching through to provide an even higher level of popular access.

It seems likely to me that the United States will beat Europe to the application of direct democracy at the national level, though this is only a likelihood. In some ways, Europe has already taken a first step, with the peoples of a number of European republics voting on EU membership itself. But popular consultation at the discretion of elites extends the new principle little, if at all. Hitler and Stalin, Pinochet and Marcos—all held plebiscites when it suited them. The test of a new application of direct democracy will be its automaticity, the extent to which it takes place not at the caprice of leaders, but of the people.

Developing countries—from Russia, a developed society but highly underdeveloped economy, to countries like Nigeria and Brazil and India—stand far away from Swiss development and a Swiss political economy. But might they be more willing to take a stab at implementing some of its lessons for popular government?

Some argue—perhaps wrongly—that the gulf is too great for such countries for a leap-frog to direct democracy to be either plausible or desirable.

It is true that the distance between developing-country society is great. At the same time, such societies have less to lose and more to gain by jumping beyond the tired permutations of representative democracy and engaging in the greater risks but greater possibilities of populism.

Is the fundamental difference between Indian democracy and American a difference in the quality of citizens? Perhaps. But the far greater difference seems to be in the level of institutional and systemic development than in the capacity of the people. The same is true of Bolivia, Brazil, China, Russia, Nigeria, or Uganda.

This is not to say that the evolution, if it takes place first in the less affluent countries, should or will necessarily take the same shape, or move at the same pace, as it could in the United States or Europe. The racial, ethnic, and economic divisions of developing society, for one thing, are such that a higher degree of federalism might be needed—while, of course, so is a unifying device such as the democratic quasi-sacrament of national referendum.

It might make sense for direct democracy, under such circumstances, to be adopted incrementally. Beedham, for example, recommends that some countries start with large, national matters, and small, particular ones, while leaving the bulk of questions in the middle up to more conventional, representative bodies for the time being. This is a sensible general recommendation, and may have even greater urgency for the developing world. It resembles, in fact, the road traveled by Switzerland in the second half of the nineteenth century.

Even for leaders dominated by the desire for mere material success, the logic of political experimentation is compelling. All nations are competing within the realm of "economic" policy to produce the best system—with the result that the field is crowded. Most nations are competing to produce directly the most competitive educational, corporate, and other institutions, with little chance for any country, let alone one poor in resources, to stand out.

A country that tried to develop a somewhat superior political system, by contrast, would stand out. It would find, in all probability, that with superior political decision making would come better policies for the economy, education, foreign affairs, and other matters. Is this, in fact, not the road traveled by the United States and Switzerland over the last 200 years? Did not Japan leap into the industrial age most decisively in the mid-twentieth century, when alone among the Asian despotisms it adopted a significant degree of democracy?

The developing world thus competes closely with the United States as another likely arena for experimentation. Because the risks and benefits are higher, so is the likelihood of a misstep or even a crash. Possibly the idea of direct democracy will even suffer setbacks in the developing world, by being tried in imprudent ways, or adopted half-heartedly or in the wrong fields of activity. Even so there is a compelling case for it: Developing country invention in the political sphere is a vacuum, which politics abhors.

Which system is better?

The question is difficult to answer in a present time frame, except as a matter of expressing one's arbitrary preference. We may speculate endlessly about whether the people, or a group they choose, is more trustworthy.

Yet we need not confine ourselves to the present time frame, for in discussing democracy, especially Swiss democracy, we have 700 years or more of history for material—and we can look many years ahead in making our forecast. It is sometimes easier to look across centuries, than across a generation.

Indeed, much of the discussion above has neglected what may be the most important element of discussion of all—time.

The most important impact of direct democracy in Switzerland is its influence upon the citizen. There are, as we have mentioned, other contributing causes. And there is causality in the other direction: The high quality of Swiss citizens—their interest and involvement in public affairs, their studious receptivity to information, their civic pride and community ethos—helps make populist democracy possible. This latter phenomenon, however, is well known, in Switzerland and the West. The idea of a people being "ready" for democracy, being grown up enough to stand on a par with their elites, is familiar and accepted. Even the radical antitheses have some widespread acceptance. This was captured famously by the journalist William F. Buckley, in his witty declaration that he would rather be ruled by 200 persons chosen at random from the Boston telephone directory, than by the faculty of Harvard University.

What is poorly understood—or anyway, not accepted and indeed vigorously denied by the collective subcousciousness of the Western elite—is the extent to which democratic institutions help develop the citizen. And, that the more democratic the institutions, the more rapid and complete the development of the electorate.

The most important impact of Swiss democracy among the Swiss has involved the development of the Swiss people over time. Even in the short run, Swiss have a greater incentive to follow political issues and to think seriously about them—they may well be voting on them in a few months. Over the longer run, a synergism of development sets in. The Swiss, with greater opportunity to make law, become skilled at making law much as, in the theory of representative democracy, members of Congress become skilled at legislative craftsmanship. The difference is that this phenomenon is spread over a whole society—government "by the people" in the broadest sense.

Swiss politicians, journalists, and business leaders all, in turn, adjust their behavior accordingly. More focus is placed on informing, and listening to, the people, than in any other democracy.

As a result, and following long experience with popular sovereignty, the leaders and the led, the elites and the people, have a greater mutual respect and less alienation than in any other regime.

Imagine if every American were to serve on a jury three or four times a year. Is there any doubt that the people would be closer to the legal system, and the legal system more responsive to the people, were this the case? The mere proximity, the culture of greater interaction, would produce such effects. If added to this the citizens enjoyed greater leverage over the implementation of police policies, or the development of law, the effect would be multifold.

It is no different with the frequent exercise of sovereignty by the Swiss, over hundreds of years.

Indeed, it is ironic that in an age that so exults expertise, experience, and knowledge, so little attention is paid to a people that have more years of democratic history than any other. It seems strange that amidst all the hosannahs of a "global information age," there is so little thinking about global principles, and so little information about the world's most important and revealing democratic experiment.

At the center, radical in idea yet conservative in operation, is Switzerland. It is quiet and unassuming, but highly revealing. In some ways, it is the anti-America, but in this the two are naturally complementary. America is great in space, and has extended the democratic idea, as Lincoln and Thomas Paine hoped, across the world. But Switzerland is great in time, and has extended the democratic idea internally to an extent seen nowhere else.

"Empires such as the Swiss," as the advisor to King Louis once put it with unintended irony, "extend their empire by the bad example of their liberty."

It is possible to imagine our now-democratic world, like a latter-day global Athens, lapsing into despotism. This is actually far more possible than most present-day millenarians—who only a decade ago were assuring us, "you can't change the Soviet system"—can imagine.

It is possible too to imagine an end of history, an everlasting stasis in democracy as it is without further meaningful change. It is possible even to picture an Aquarian end to political and economic problems altogether.

Yet none of these is the most likely. Instead, a long but hopefully happy struggle, striving toward ever-more-perfect freedom, if never quite arriving— in a word, history—looms. A world of ideas and facts, labor and thought, good and—yes—evil, which none of the materialists, Marxist nor Libertarian, have abolished.

It is to this, real world of mankind that Switzerland has so much to offer. In this world, it may well be, as Victor Hugo cryptically insisted: "Switzerland will have the last word in history."

Notes

1. All this is quite aside from the fact that the dialectical materialists of the Right and Left are wrong altogether. History never ends, there are no completely new ideas under the sun, and what appears at one point or another in history to be the "final verdict" on behalf of good or evil is never more than a turn of the wheel from a different order. Whether we are considering the end of war proclaimed in the late nineteenth century, the end of material want in the mid-twentieth century, or the "abolition of borders" and a "world without money" by Internet companies and technology executives in the early twenty-first century, the stubborn resiliency of

human nature remains. That history tends to favor the most just polity is clear, as the author argues in *The Democratic Imperative*, especially Chap. 3, "Ideopolitique." Between tendency and inevitability, however, is a wide and important gulf.

2. Brian Beedham, "A better way to vote: Why letting the people themselves take the decisions is the logical next step for the West," *The Economist*, 11 September 1993. Beedham is an associate editor of *The Economist* and was its foreign editor from 1964 to 1989.

3. See Carol L. Schmid's interesting survey, *Conflict and Consensus in Switzerland*, University of California Press, 1981.

4. In the paragraphs that follow we are speaking mainly about the spirit of direct democracy and of its acts insofar as they are different. Switzerland has a parliament and president too, and there is lobbying and grass-roots lobbying aimed at the parliament. But in those cases Switzerland, which itself is a mixed system, is acting as a representative democracy. Because it frequently acts as a direct democracy, however, the resulting "spirit of the laws," the animating logic of political activity, may be very different.

5. In the combined national parliamentary elections of 1999, according to an academic estimate cited by *Aargauer Zeitung* editor Peter Frey, the Swiss spent a total of 100 million Swiss francs.

Bibliography

Allen, C. J. *Switzerland's Amazing Railways*. London, 1965.

Almond, Gabriel A., and Verba, Sidney. *The Civic Culture: Political Attitudes and Democracy in Five Nations*. Newbury Park, CA: Sage, 1965.

Altermatt, Claude. Interview with the author, May 2000.

Altermatt, Urs (ed.). *Die Schweizer Bundesrate...Ein biographisches Lexicon*. Artemis & Winkler, Artemis Verlag, Zürich and München, 1991.

Amman, Hektor, and Schib, Karl. *Historischer Atlas der Schweiz*. Aarau, 1958.

Angst, Walter. *Progressive Rebels: The Founding Fathers of the Swiss Confederation*. Silver Spring, MD: Pelinicus Books, 1995.

Arnet, Morita. Interview with the author, March 1999.

Bär, Hans. "The Future of Globalization." Opening Remarks on the occasion of Goldman Sachs Discussion, New York, March 16, 1999.

_____. "The Globalization of Horace Mann." After-Dinner Remarks, 1999 Distinguished Alumnus Award Dinner, Horace Mann School, New York, March 15, 1999.

_____. Interview with the author, February 1999, and conversation, March 2000.

Bär, Matthias. Interview with the author, May 2001.

Barber, Benjamin. *The Death of Communal Liberty...A History of Freedom in a Swiss Mountain Canton*. Princeton, NJ: Princeton University Press, 1974.

_____. *Strong Democracy*. Berkeley : University of California Press, 1984.

Bärenbold, Hans. Interview with the author, May 2001.

Bell, Jeffrey. *Populism and Elitism*. Alexis de Tocqueville Institution. Washington, DC: Regnery-Gateway, 1992.

Bergier, Jean-François. *Naissance et croissance de la Suisse industrielle*. Bern, 1973.

Bergier, Jean-François, et al. Independent Commission of Experts, Switzerland, Second World War. "Switzerland and Gold Transactions in the Second World War." Independent Commission of Experts, Switzerland. Bern, July 1998.

Bierhanzel, Edward, and Dwartney, James. "Regulation, Unions, and Labor Markets," *Regulation* Vol. 21, No. 3, 1998, Florida State University.

Blocher, Christoph. Interview with the author, February 1999.

Bockli, H.R. Interviews with the author, January 2000 and June 2001.

Bodmer, Henry. Interview with the author, May 2001.

Boner, Wilhelm. Interview with the author, February 1999.

Bonjour, Edgar. *Swiss Neutrality: Its History and Meaning*. Trans. M. Hottinger. London, 1946.

Bonjour, Edgar, et al. *A Short History of Switzerland*. Oxford, 1955.

Borer, Thomas. Interview with the author, April 1999.

Boss, Walter. Correspondence with the author, September 2000.

Brooks, Robert C. *Civic Training in Switzerland: A Study of Democratic Life*. Chicago: University of Chicago Press, 1930.

Brown Boveri. *Brown Boveri 1891-1966*. (Corporate History) Baden, 1966.

Brunner, Edgar. Interview with the author, June 2001, and correspondence with the author, June-July 2001.

Bryce, James. *Modern Democracies*. The Macmillan Company, 1921.

Buhlmann, Cecile. Interview with the author, April 2000.

Buhrle, Dietrich. Interview with the author, May 2001.

Bundeskanzlei Chancellerie federal Cancelleria federale Chanzlia federala. *The Swiss Confederation...A Brief Guide 2001*. Bundeskanzlei Chancellerie federal Cancelleria federale Chanzlia federala.

Bundeskanzlei Chancellerie federal Cancelleria federale Chanzlia federala. *Der Bund kurz erklart 2001*. Bundeskanzlei Chancellerie federal Cancelleria federale Chanzlia federala.

Bundeskanzlei Chancellerie federal Cancelleria federale Chanzlia federala. *La Confederation en bref 2001*. Bundeskanzlei Chancellerie federal Cancelleria federale Chanzlia federala.

Burki, Elisabeth. Interviews with the author, December 1999 and May 2001.

Busser, E. *Swiss Churches in the Twentieth Century*. University of Zürich, 1997.

Butler, David, and Ranney, Austin (eds.). *Referendums... A Comparative Study of Practice and Theory*. Washington, DC: American Enterprise Institute, 1978.

Bütler, Hugo. Interview with the author, February 1999.

Castell, Anton. *Geschichte des Landes Schwyz*. Einsiedeln, Zürich, 1954.

Childs, Marquis. "No Peace for the Swiss." *Saturday Evening Post*, May 1, 1943.

Christen, Yves. Interview with the author, March 1999.

Codding, George. *The Federal Government of Switzerland*. Cambridge, MA: Riverside Press, 1962.

Corti, Mario. Interview with the author, March 1999.

Cotti, Flavio. Interview with the author, March 1999.

Cronin, Thomas E. *Direct Democracy...The Politics of Initiative, Referendum, and Recall*. Cambridge, MA: Harvard University Press, 1989.

Dahl, Robert. *Democracy and Its Critics*. New Haven, CT: Yale University Press, 1989.

Danzeisen, Margrit. Interview with the author, February 1999.

de Pury, David. Interview with the author, March 1999, and subsequent correspondence.

Defago, Alfred. Interviews with the author, August 1999; December 1999; May 2000; February 2001; and April 2001.

Dillena, Giancarlo. Interview with the author, June 2000.

Dulles, Allen W. *Germany's Underground*. New York: Macmillan, 1947.

Dunn, James. "Consociational Democracy and Language Conflict: A Comparison of the Belgian and Swiss Experiences." *Comparative Political Studies*, Issue 5, 1972.

Durmuller, Urs. *Changing Patterns of Multilingualism*. Pro Helvetia Documentation Information Press, 1997.

Egger, Eugene, and Blanc, Emile. *Education in Switzerland*. Geneva: Swiss Educational Development Center, 1974.

Ehrenzeller, Bernhard. Interview with the author, May 2001.

Enloe, Cynthia. *Conflict and Political Development*. Boston: Little, Brown, 1973.

Färber, Marco. Interview with the author, May 2001.

Fahrmi, Dieter. *An Outline History of Switzerland*. Zürich: Pro Helvetia Division Documentation-Information Press, 1987.

Falke, Konrad. *Das demokratische Ideal und unser nationa Erzeihung*. Zürich: Rascher, 1915.

Fasel, Hugo. Interview with the author, March 1999.

Federal Chancellery of Switzerland. *The Swiss Confederation: A Brief Guide 1998*. The Swiss Federal Chancellery, 1998.

Federal Office for Statistics, Switzerland. *Switzerland in Figures: 1996*. Federal Social Insurance Office of Switzerland Swiss Federal Statistical Office, Neuchatel, 1999.

Federal Statistics Office, Switzerland (Bundesamt fur Statistik / Office federal de la statistique). *Statistische Jahrbuch der Schweiz, 2001*. NZZ Verlag: Neue Zurcher Zeitung, 2001.

Fick, Fritz. *Gibt es eine schweizerische Nation und Kultur?* Zürich: Verlag Rascher, 1910.

Fossedal, Gregory. *The Democratic Imperative*. New York: New Republic Books, 1989.

_____. "What the tax reformers are missing." *Wall Street Journal*, November 7, 1997.

_____. "What we can do for Africa." *New York Times*, March 24, 1998.

Frey, Peter. Interview with the author, February 1999.

Fuhrer, Rita. Interview with the author, March 1999.

Furgler, Kurt. Interview with the author, February 1999.

Gagliardi, Ernst. *Geschichte der Schweiz*, 3 vols. (third edition). Zürich: Orell Fussli Verlag, 1938.

Geiger, Gérard (also Ringier AG). Baromedia 2001...Jährliches Barometer der Schweizer Medien, Ringier AG. Zurich and Lausanne, Switzerland, 2001.

Gilg, Peter. "Die Entstehung der demokratischen Bewegung und die soziale Frage." Thesis, University of Bern, 1951.

Gillett, Nicholas. *The Swiss Constitution – Can It Be Exported?* Bristol: Yes Publications, 1989.

Girsberger, Esther. Interview with the author, February 1999.

Gisler, Markus. Interview with the author, March 1999.

Glazer, Nathan, and Moynihan, Daniel P. *Beyond the Melting Pot*. Cambridge, MA: . MIT Press, 1970.

Glenn, Jacob B. "The Jews in Switzerland." Contemporary Jewish Record, American Jewish Committee, New York, 1941.

Gross, Andreas. Interviews with the author, March 1999; November 2000: and June, 2001.

Gut, Rainer E. Interview with the author, November 1999.

Gyssler, Beatrice, and colleagues (Hittnau). Interview with the author, February 1999.

Halbheer, Hans J. *Understanding Swiss Neutrality*. American-Swiss Foundation, 1993 (reprinted).

_____. "An Attempt to Explain Switzerland to a Foreigner." *The World Today*, undated, Bulletin Credit Suisse,

Halbrook, Stephen. *Target Switzerland*. Rockville Centre, NY: Sarpedon, 1998.

Hänsenberter, Irene. Interview with the author, February 1999.

Held, Thomas, and Levy, René. *Femme, famille et société, Realités Sociales*. Lausanne, Switzerland, 1984.

Honsicher, Q. Interview with the author, June 2001.

Horat, Erwin. Interview with the author, December 1998.

Huber, Hans. *How Switzerland is Governed*. Guggenbulbt & Hrber, Schweizer Spiegel Vertag, Zürich, 1968.

Hughes, Christopher. *The Federal Constitution of Switzerland*. Oxford: Clarendon Press, 1954.

_____. *The Parliament of Switzerland*. London: Trinity Press/Cassell, 1962.

_____. *Switzerland*. London: Praeger/Ernest Benn, 1975.

Hutson, James H. *The Sister Republics: Switzerland and the United States from 1776 to the Present*. Washington, DC: Library of Congress, 1991.

Isler, Fred. Interview with the author, February 1999.

Jolles, Paul L. "A Battle for Neutrality." *Newsweek*, September 1, 1997.

_____. Interview with the author, December 1998.

Julius Bär & Co. *The Euro: Europe's Single Currency*. Zürich: Bank Julius Baer & Co. Ltd, May 1998.

Jung, Joseph. Interview with the author, June 2001.

Kälin, Walter. *Verfassungsgerichtsbarkeit in der Demokratie*. Bern: Haupt, 1987.

Kappeler, Beat. Regieren Statt Revidieren: Weltwoche-ABC-Verlag, Zurich 2. Auflage Umschlaggestaltung: Heinz Unternahrer, Zurich Alle Rechte vorbehalten.

_____. Interview with the author, May 2001.

Katz, Richard (ed.). *Party Governments: European and American Experiences*. Berlin and New York: Walter de Gruyter, 1987.

Kohn, H. *Nationalism and Liberty: The Swiss Example*. London: Allen and Unwin, 1956.

Kuoni, Christian. Interview with the author, February 1999.

Lanius, Charles. "Switzerland, Axis Captive." *Saturday Evening Post*, January 23, 1943.

LeBor, Adam. *Hitler's Secret Bankers: The Myth of Swiss Neutrality During the Holocaust*. Secaucus, NJ: Birch Lane Press, 1997.

Leuenberger, Andres. Interview with the author, June 2001.

Levy, Rene. *The Social Structure of Switzerland*. Pro Helvetia Documentation Information Press, 1998.

Linder, Wolf. *Swiss Democracy... Possible Solutions to Conflict in Multicultural Societies*. The MacMillan Press Ltd, Houndmills, Basingstoke, Hampshire, 1994.

_____. *Schweizerische Demokratie*. Bern: Verlag Paul Haupt.

_____. Interview with the author, June 2001.

Lijphart, Arend. *Democracies, Patterns of Majoritarian and Consensus Government in Twenty-One Countries*. New Haven, CT, and London: Yale University Press, 1984.

Lippman, Walter. "The Faithful Witness." *New York Herald-Tribune*, January 26, 1943.

Lipset, Seymour Martin. *Political Man... The Social Bases of Politics*. Baltimore, MD: Johns Hopkins University Press, 1981 (revised from the 1960 edition).

Lipset, Seymour Martin, et al. *Party Systems and Voter Alignments: Cross-National Perspectives*. New York: Free Press, 1967.

Loeb, François. Interviews with the author, March 1999 and November 2000.

Luck, J. Murray. *Modern Switzerland*. Palo Alto, CA: The Society for the Promotion of Science and Scholarship Inc., 1978.

_____. *History of Switzerland*. Palo Alto, CA: The Society for the Promotion of Science and Scholarship, Inc., 1985.

Luthy, Herbert. "Has Switzerland a Future? The Dilemma of the Small Nation." *Encounter*, Issue 19, 1962.

_____. *Die Schweiz als Antithese*. Zürich: Verlag der Arche, 1969.

Madison, James, Hamilton, Alexander, Jay, John. *The Federalist Papers*. New York: Penguin, 1987.

Marty, Vera. Interview with the author, May 2001.

Mayer, Kurt. "Intra-European Migration During the Past Twenty Years" *International Migration Review*, Issue 9, 1975.

_____. "Migration, Cultural Tension, and Foreign Relations: Switzerland." *Journal of Conflict Resolution*, Issue 11, 1967.

_____. *The Population of Switzerland*. New York: Columbia University Press, 1952.

McPhee, John. *La Place de la Concorde Suisse*. New York: Noonday Press, 1983.

McRae, Kenneth D. *Conflict and Compromise in Multilingual Societies*, Vol. 1: *Switzerland* Wilfrid Laurier University Press, Waterloo, Ontario, Canada.

_____. *Switzerland: Example of Cultural Coexistence*. Toronto: Canadian Institute of International Affairs, 1964.

_____. (ed.). *Consociational Democracy*. Toronto: McClelland and Steward, 1974.

Meier, Werner A., and Schanne, Michael. *Media-Landscape Switzerland*. Pro Helvetia Documentation Information Press, 1995.

Meyer, Werner. *1291 L'Histoire... Les prémices de la Confédération suisse*. Zurich: Editions Silva, 1991.

Moll, Arthur. Interview with the author, June 2001.

Morikofer, Stephanie. Interview with the author, March 2000.

Muheim, Franz. Interviews with the author, December 1998 and May 2001, and correspondence.

_____. *Die Schweiz–Aufstieg oder Niedergang*. Schaffhausen: Novalis Verlag, 1998.

Narring, Françoise, Pierre-Andre Michaud, and Vinit Sharma. "Demographic and Behavioral Factors Associated with Adolescent Pregnancy in Switzerland." *Swiss Medical Journal*, Vol. 28, No. 5, September/October 1996.

Nordlinger, Eric A. "Conflict Regulation in Divided Societies." Occasional Papers in International Affairs, Harvard University, No. 29, 1972.

OECD. Organization for Economic Cooperation and Development Historical Statistics, 1960-1994. Paris: OECD, 1996.

Onken, H. Interview with the author, March 1999.

Orell Fussli Verlag (publishers). *Who's Who in Switzerland*. Zürich: Orell Fussli Publishers, 1998.

Paldiel, Mordecai, and Rozett, Robert. Nur das Gewissen: Carl Lutz und seine Budapester Aktion; Geschichte und Portrat. N.p., Switzerland, 1986, Encyclopedia of the Holocaust.

Pfinner, Albert. *Henri Nestlé...From Pharmacist's Assistant to Founder of the World's Largest Food Company, Nestlé S.A.* Vevey, Switzerland, 1995.

Pictet & Cie Banquiers. Switzerland Economic Trends: Research Department. Bernard Lambert, Jean-Pierre Beguelin, December 1998.

Pictet, Ivan. Interview with the author, February 2000.

Plotke, Herbert. Rechtsgutachten Volksinitiative in der Stadt Luzern, "Jedem Quartier sein Primarschule-Bestehende Quartierschulen erhalten," dem Stdtrat von Luzern erstattet von, October 1998.

Rabushka, Allan, and Shepsle, Kenneth. *Politics in Plural Society: A Theory of Democratic Instability*. Columbus, OH: Merrill, 1972.

Rappard, William E. *Collective Security in Swiss Experience, 1291-1948*. London: Allen & Unwin, 1948.

_____. *La facteur économique dan l'avénement de la démocratie moderne en Suisse*. George, Genéve, 1912.

Reimann, Maximilian. Interview with the author, February 2000.

Reist, Werner. *Switzerland...Life and Activity*. Mensch und Arvbeir, Publishers, Zürich No. 25.

Remak, Joachim. *A Very Civil War: The Swiss Sonderbund War of 1847*. Boulder, CO: Westview Press, 1993.

Renk, H.R. Interview with the author, March 1999.

Richardson, Donovan. "The Neutrals' Fight for Peace." *Christian Science Monitor*, August 12, 1939.

Rickover, H.G. *Swiss Schools and Ours: Why Theirs Are Better*. Boston: Little, Brown, 1962.

Rimli, E. T. (ed.). *Histoire de la Confédération*. Stauffacher, 1967.

Roduner, Ernst. Interview with the author, March 1999.

Rossier, Jacques. "Switzerland, Gold, and the Banks: Analysis of a Crisis." American Swiss Foundation Forum, Harvard Faculty Club, May 26, 1999.

Sager, Manuel. Interview with the author, February 2001, and correspondence.

Sauser-Hall, George. *The Political Institutions of Switzerland.* Zürich and New York: Swiss National Tourist Office, 1946.

Scarecrow Press, Inc. *Dictionary of American Immigration History.* Metuchen, NJ, and London: The Scarecrow Press, Inc., 1990.

Schaffner, Martin. *Die demokratische Bewegung der 1860er Jahre.* Basle and Stuttgart, 1981.

Schattschneider, E. E. *The Semisovereign People, A Realist View of Democracy in America.* Hinsdale: Dryden Press, 1960.

Schmid, Carol. *Conflict and Consensus in Switzerland.* University of California Press, Ltd., 1981.

Schmid-Sutter, Carlo. Interview with the author, February 1999 and March 1999, and subsequent correspondence.

Schramm, Patricia. Interviews with the author, November 2000 and April 2001, and related correspondence.

Selg, Casper. Interview with the author, June 2001.

Senn, Hans. *Swiss Armed Neutrality in World War II.* Lyn Shepard, Zurich.

Shirer, William. *Berlin Diary.* New York: Alfred A. Knopf, 1941.

Siegfried, André. *Switzerland: A Democratic Way of Life.* Hyperion, CT., 1980.

_____. *Le Suisse, démocratie témoin, La Baconniére.* Neuchâtel, Switzerland, 1956.

Sigg, Oswald. *Political Switzerland.* Pro Helvetia Documentation Information Press, 1997.

Soloveythik, George. *Switzerland in Perspective.* London: Oxford University Press, 1954.

Somm, Edwin. Interview with the author, February 1999.

Somm, Markus. Interviews with the author, February 1999 and June 2001, and correspondence.

_____. "Schuld und Schulden der Schweiz." *Tages-Anzeiger*, December 4, 1999.

Speer, Albert. *Inside the Third Reich.* New York: Macmillan, 1970.

Stadlin, Paul. *Die Parlamente der schweizerischen Kantone.* Kalt-Zehnder, 1990.

Stamm, Konrad. Interview with the author, February 1999.

Stanyan, Abraham. *An Account of Switzerland: Written in the Year 1714.* London, 1714 (copy on file courtesy of Credit Suisse historical archives, Zurich).

Stauch & Stauch. Switzerland's Major Goal during World War II: Task Force Switzerland-Second World War, 1998 EDA memorandum.

Steinberg, Jonathan. *Why Switzerland?* London: Cambridge University Press, 1976.

Steiner, Jurg. European Democracies. New York: Longman, 1998.

_____. *Amicable Agreement versus Majority Rule: Conflict Resolution in Switzerland.* Chapel Hill, NC: University of North Carolina Press, 1974.

Steinman, Walter. *Zwischen Markt und Staat, Verflechtungsformen von Staat und Wirtschaft in der Schweiz.* Wissit, Konstanz, 1988.

Stockli, Walter A. *Church, State, and School in Switzerland and the United States.* Bern, Switzerland: Herbert Lang.

Stussi-Lauterburg, Jurg. "The Swiss Military System and Neutrality in the Seventeenth Century as Seen by Contemporary Europe." *War & Society*, September 1984.

_____. Interview with the author, March 1999, and associated correspondence, June 2000-March 2001.

Stussi-Lauterburg, J., and Gysler-Schoni, R. *Helvetias Tochter: Frauen in der Schweizer Militargeschichte von 1291 bis 1939.*

Sutter, Kaspar. Interview with the author, June 2001.

Thurer, G. *Free and Swiss*. Trans. R. P. Heller and E. Long. London, 1970.

Time Magazine. "Switzerland: Alone, Little, & Tough." December 7, 1942.

Tocqueville, Alexis de. *Tocqueville Oeuvres*. Vols. 1-18. *Tour droits de traduction, de reproduction et d'adaptation reserves pour tous les pays*. Editions Gallimard, 1991.

———. "Tocqueville's Report to the French Parliament on the Swiss Situation in 1847." Partial translation by Gregory Fossedal, from *Oeuvres*, op cit. Alexis de Tocqueville Institution, 2000.

Togni, Alberto. Interviews with the author, March 1999 and May 2001.

Treichler, Hans, De Capitani, Francois, et al. Forum on Swiss History. Swiss National Museum, March 23, 1996.

Treschel, Alexandre, and Sciarini, Pascal. "Direct Democracy in Switzerland: Do Elites Matter?" *European Journal of Political Research* 33 (1), 1998.

Trevor-Roper, H.R. *Hitler's Secret Conversations, 1941-1944* (introduction). New York: Signet, 1976.

Trosler, Ferdinand. "Two Burning Issues in Switzerland." *Free Labour World*, Issue 295, 1975.

Tschuy, Theo. *Carl Lutz und die Juden von Budapest*. Second edition. Zurich: Verlag Neue Zurcher Zeitung, 1998.

Verfasst von Jan Vonder Muhll. Historiker. *Die Aktivitaten der schweizerischen Maschinenindustrie und ihrer Verbande ASM und VSM wahred des Xweiten Weltkrieges (1933-1945)*. Bezugsquelle Presse und Information, Zurich.

Vollmer, Peter. Interview with the author, March 1999.

Vuilleumier, Marc. *Immigrants and Refugees in Switzerland.... An Outline History*. Zurich: Pro Helvetia Documentation Information Press, 1995.

Walterskirchen, Martin von. Interview with the author, May 2001.

Ware, Alan. *Political Parties and Political Systems*. Oxford: Oxford University Press, 1996.

Wettstein, Emil. Vocational and Technical Education in Switzerland. Deutschschweizerische Berufsbildungsamter-Konferenz (DBK), 1994.

Whittlesey, Faith. "Switzerland on Trial." Address to the Council of American Ambassadors, Washington, DC, 1997.

Wicht, Bernard. *L'idee de Milice et le Modéle Suisse dans la Pensée de Machiavel*, L'Age d'Homme. Lausanne, Switzerland, 1995.

Widmer, Sigmund. Interviews with the author, February 1999 and May 2001.

Wildhaber, L. *The Swiss Judicial System*. University of Basel, 1998.

Wolf, Walter. *Faschismus in der Schweiz: Die Geschichte der Frontenbewegung in der deutschen Schweiz, 1930-1945*. Zurich, 1969.

Wyman, David S. *The Abandonment of the Jews: America and the Holocaust, 1941-45*. New York: Pantheon Books, 1984.

Ziegler, Jean. *The Swiss, the Gold, and the Dead*. London: Penguin Books, 1998 (English translation by John Brownjohn).

———. Interview with the author, June 2001.

Zisk, Betty. *Money, Media, and the Grass Roots: State Ballot Issues and the Electoral Process*. Newbury Park, CA: Sage, 1987.

Index